Other Avon Books by
Kevin D. Randle

A HISTORY OF UFO CRASHES
PROJECT MOON DUST

With Donald R. Schmitt

THE TRUTH ABOUT THE UFO CRASH AT ROSWELL
UFO CRASH AT ROSWELL

CONSPIRACY OF SILENCE

KEVIN D. RANDLE, Captain, U.S.A.F.R.

AVON BOOKS ◆ NEW YORK

AVON BOOKS, INC.
1350 Avenue of the Americas
New York, New York 10019

Visit our website at **http://www.AvonBooks.com**
Library of Congress Catalog Card Number: 96-40863
ISBN: 0-380-79918-2

Library of Congress Cataloging in Publication Data:
Randle, Kevin D., 1949–
  Conspiracy of silence / Kevin D. Randle.
    p.   cm.
Includes bibliographical references and index.
1. Unidentified flying objects.   2. Conspiracies—United States.   I. Title.
TL789.R3233—1997   96-40863
001.942—dc21   CIP

First Avon Books Mass Market Printing: July 1998
First Avon Books Trade Printing: July 1997

AVON TRADEMARK REG. U.S. PAT. OFF. AND IN OTHER COUNTRIES, MARCA REGISTRADA, HECHO EN U.S.A.

Printed in the U.S.A.

WCD   10   9   8   7   6   5   4   3   2   1

Contents

Flying Saucers:
Fact or Fiction?

I WAS A NAIVE, TENDERFOOT REPORTER WHEN I was let loose on the nation's capital in 1947. It was a congenial time when government secrecy was invested with a halo and public tolerance for dissent was at a low ebb.

The late J. Edgar Hoover ruled the FBI from a glass bubble. He compartmentalized crime, cordoned off the goats from the sheep, and postured before a friendly media. Investigative reporters of my ilk operated at particular hazard. Yet with youthful brashness, I dared to investigate a Hoover falsehood.

It was a whopper that was startling to an outlander. I found that the venerable Hoover lied unabashedly about the existence of organized crime. I tracked down evidence that disputed the great lawman. I interviewed Mafia godfathers in their lairs; I nailed down the unsavory details.

Then I wrote a series of columns that led the late Senator Estes Kefauver to conduct a Senate investigation. He issued subpoenas; he took sworn testimony; he put the crime lords under the klieg lights. There no longer was any doubt about it. Hoover had perpetrated—and tried to perpetuate—an enormous lie.

This turned out to be the crack that eventually shattered Hoover's pedestal. He was accused of conspiring and consorting with the mob. He had made a deal with the godfathers, perhaps taken a bribe, it was said.

This simply wasn't so. I know for a fact that J. Edgar Hoover was merely a confirmed bureaucrat who chose not to recognize a problem he couldn't easily solve. He could run up more impressive statistics by pursuing stolen automobiles than by tracking Mafia dons. His clean-cut, all-American FBI agents simply couldn't infiltrate the Italian crime families. As one official told me in those days, "Hoover's idea of infiltrating the underworld is to allow his agents to take off their ties."

I review this piece of history as a prelude to raising the subject of this book. Have we been visited here on Earth by aliens from faraway planets? What is the truth about flying saucers? Unlike my investigation of the Mafia, I've interviewed no extraterrestrial visitors. Nor have I uncovered secret evidence of their visits. But I know a government cover-up when I see one, and I am compelled to say that the Air Force's handling of the UFO reports has all the earmarks of a cover-up.

I'm not worried about the Air Force's dark motives. It's simply the nature of government officials to cover up what they can't explain. They hope to hide behind a curtain of secrecy not what they know but what they don't know. Otherwise, they fear they may be expected to explain mysteries that they can't understand.

The Air Force has eagerly debunked extraterrestrial sightings that could easily be debunked and discredited witnesses who could easily be discredited. It has had less to say about credible sightings by credible witnesses. It has ridiculed people who have claimed they were abducted and subjected to laboratory experiments by aliens not of this world. Yet believable persons have sworn this has happened to them, and their various accounts are tantalizingly similar.

The official history of the UFO phenomenon began in June 1947 when Kenneth Arnold reported seeing a formation of "mystery craft in fast flight." Military officers and governmental officials, as well as scientists and journalists, were confused by the sightings of "flying disks." Within two weeks, both Army and Navy officers would begin to suppress stories of flying saucers.

In late 1947, the newly created Air Force began to investigate the reports of flying saucers. Intelligence officers provided guidance to the investigators, asking them to report on "Essential Items of Intelligence." This was Project Sign.

During that investigation, the Air Force studied a number of sightings and prepared a report to be sent to the Chief of Staff that claimed flying saucers were extraterrestrial. But General Hoyt S. Vandenberg decided the conclusions weren't warranted by the evidence presented. The report was duly rewritten, concluding that flying saucers were hoaxes, illusions, and misidentifications. The Air Force also announced the end of Project Sign.

That, however, wasn't quite the truth. Project Sign continued as Project Grudge, with the attitude that there was nothing to the reports. The investigators just went through the motions. It was eventually announced that Project Grudge had been closed.

That also wasn't quite the truth. Project Grudge continued as Project Blue Book. But the investigation was revitalized with new people and new ideas. Even generals at the top were privately interested in flying saucers. The project received the assets it needed to do the job properly. For three years, Project Blue Book searched for the truth. Then came a summer filled with flying saucers.

The Air Force came under assault from the news media and the public. The result: The Robertson Panel was formed in January 1953. After five days of hearings, the panel determined that there was no scientific evidence to prove the reality of UFOs. Nevertheless, it recommended a continuation of the investigation.

Meanwhile, Project Blue Book lost much of its investigative status. The 4602d Air Intelligence Service Squadron took over. According to Air Force regulations, responsibility for investigating UFOs rested with the 4602d. Reports were transmitted electronically to ATIC (Air Technical Intelligence Center), parent of Blue Book, but the regulations didn't require the reports to be passed to Blue Book. Air Force officers and scientific consultants alike complained that "hot" cases were never received by Blue Book.

The UFO investigation stumbled along for another fifteen years. Blue Book became little more than a public relations outfit, giving the public the official line. But public pressure began to mount, and in 1966 the Air Force commissioned the University of Colorado to study UFOs. Thus was born the Condon Committee under the direction of Dr. Edward U. Condon.

After two years (and more than half a million taxpayer dollars), Condon released his report, claiming that no evidence was found that UFOs were real. Condon and the committee concluded that further study would be a waste of taxpayer money. Of course, those were the results that Air Force officers let it be known they wanted.

In December 1969, following the recommendations of the Condon Committee, the Air Force ended its twenty-two-year study of UFOs—this time for real. From that point on, the Air Force, when queried, would say its study had ended without results.

But the truth is that the 4602d, which had evolved into the 1127th Air Activities Group, was still investigating UFOs under a project code-named Moon Dust. Although Moon Dust had a mission to examine returning space debris, its mission also included UFOs. After 1969, the Air Force study continued but in a different organization and under different directives.

Air Force officers, when asked about Project Moon Dust by members of Congress, denied it had ever existed. When confronted with documentation proving that Moon Dust was real, they admitted the truth but said it had been discontinued. In 1985, however, an Air Force officer wrote that the name Moon Dust had merely been changed. Moon Dust had ended, but the mission continued. The Air Force, once again, had been less than candid.

But the Air Force brass maintained they had no interest in UFOs. Congressional queries were forwarded to the National Archives, where the Project Blue Book files were housed. Even specific questions about the topic were forwarded to the National Archives.

In 1994, however, the Air Force reinvestigated the Roswell UFO case. Researchers had been claiming for years, bolstered by the testimony of Major Jesse A. Marcel, who said he handled the debris of a flying saucer, that the Air Force had the answers and was hiding them. The growing pressure from the public sector caused the Air Force to spend more money on a phenomenon it said didn't exist.

This time the Air Force admitted it had lied about the case in 1947. It was not a weather balloon as the Air Force had claimed. It was a balloon assigned to the then top secret Project Mogul. Same balloon, same explanation, just a different name. Of course, there is no documentation to support this conclusion.

The Air Force claimed no interest in UFOs, yet in 1995 it offered a new explanation for the Lonnie Zamora sighting of April 1964. Zamora, who reported a landed craft, also claimed he saw two humanoids standing near it. Air Force records listed the case as "unidentified"—until suddenly it found a document that showed tests of the Lunar Lander on the White Sands Missile Range on the day Zamora made his sighting near Socorro. Of course, the Lunar Lander was fifty to a hundred miles from Socorro, the tests were six or seven hours earlier than Zamora's sighting, and there is no documentation to suggest it strayed off the range.

So the Air Force has claimed it has no interest in

UFOs—yet it has issued statements and reports on two separate UFO cases.

What follows is an authoritative examination of available evidence. Witnesses who have been silent for years now tell their stories. By combining the documents, some found only in the last year or so, with the eyewitness testimony, a new picture emerges. Captain Kevin D. Randle provided a hard-hitting look at the UFO phenomenon.

JACK ANDERSON
Pulitzer Prize-winning columnist

Introduction

THERE ARE THOSE IN THE UFO COMMUNITY WHO have claimed that a conspiracy of silence has existed since the first flying saucers were reported in June 1947. They have claimed that secret studies have concluded that UFOs were real, they have claimed that there was a secret investigation, and they have said that the independent studies were little more than whitewashes. Naturally, various governmental agencies and the Air Force have denied those allegations.

In the past, the UFO supporters have had few public statements to use as proof. There were suggestions, occasional misstatements, and explanations that made no logical sense. While it was clear that something was going on, the proof of it just wasn't available.

In the past, UFO investigators concentrated on sighting reports. They gathered hundreds of thousands of sightings, many of them multiple-witness with photographs or film or landing traces. Each time they found a good case, someone else was ready to show how the UFO investigators misinterpreted the evidence, how they overlooked facts, or how they manipulated the data. It caused a great deal of confusion.

The unfortunate outgrowth of this is a startling reluctance by the news media to even look at the documentation. After nearly fifty years of a governmental policy that denies the existence of UFOs, many respectable journalists and scientists refuse to entertain the idea. The safest course is to reject UFOs as extraterrestrial by asking, "Where is the evidence?"

In the past, I have seen television debates where skeptics and nonbelievers say that UFOs are not seen on radar. My response is that our stealth technology has rendered that argument obsolete. However, during July 1952, there was an incredible series of sightings over Washington, D.C. UFOs were seen on radar at three separate locations, and interceptor pilots reported seeing the objects. Their onboard radars also picked up and tracked the objects.

Others claim there are no good photographs of UFOs, yet they continue to overlook some very spectacular pictures. When scientists were unable to adequately explain the pictures of lights over Lubbock, Texas, taken in 1951, they labeled them hoaxes. They presented no viable evidence for that conclusion. They merely labeled the pictures, dismissing them in their minds.

They say there is no physical evidence, and then reject the Roswell case out of hand. Five hundred people are conspiring to create some sort of tourist Mecca in southeastern New Mexico. Air Force officers and UFO skeptics claim the Roswell case is nothing more than a commercial operation designed to line the pockets of some people. They belittle the Roswell case by simply suggesting a profit motive.

We could speculate about the motives of the Air Force and the government. We could suggest that a conspiracy of silence existed, and by examining certain cases, we could convince some that the evidence was overwhelming. We could demand independent investigation, but each time that has happened, the results were the same. Governmental agencies investigating other governmental agencies found that no secrets were being suppressed and that there was no threat to national security. That is the drum they continued to beat. No threat to national security and no evidence that UFOs were anything other than fabrications, misidentifications, and nonsense.

But then came the Freedom of Information Act. Suddenly the independent researcher had a tool that could shake the information tree. Project Blue Book files, once classified as secret, were suddenly available to UFO researchers. Governmental agencies that could once ignore requests for data from private citizens were now required, by law, to respond to those requests within a specified time limit.

The situation changed, but only a few UFO researchers realized the significance of the change. While most were still chasing lights in the night sky, a few, such as the leaders of the now-defunct Ground Saucer Watch, began to file Freedom of Information requests. A trickle of documents began to flow into the hands of researchers.

There were nuggets in those streams. Little hints that the situation was not quite what we had been led to believe. An FBI document turned up with a handwritten note by J. Edgar Hoover, who wanted access to disks recovered. No one knows exactly what Hoover meant in that cryptic note, other than to suggest that something interesting had been recovered by the Army, who refused to let anyone else examine it. Since it was on a note that referred to flying disks, it makes sense to believe that Hoover was referring to that specific phenomenon. It hints that the Roswell UFO crash is real, but only hints at it.

To counterbalance that were the studies conducted by the Air Force, the CIA, and finally the University of Colorado. Each time the results were released, those in the UFO community suggested a whitewash. Although there was some evidence supporting those allegations, there was never a smoking gun. At least not until now.

We can prove that the representatives of the government and the Air Force have lied to us about the UFO situation almost from the very beginning. In 1949, for example, the Air Force announced the end of Project Grudge. It left the impression, upon publication of a more than 600-page report, that it had finished its investigation of flying saucers. UFOs didn't exist and all sightings could be explained as natural phenomena, misidentifications of conventional aircraft and objects, or outright hoaxes. A few cases were not adequately explained, but the investigators believe that if all relevant data had been reported, then an explanation would have been found. The problem was not UFOs, but a lack of adequate information.

That announcement was designed to mislead because the investigation continued. The Air Force wanted the public to believe there was nothing to the UFO phenomenon while it actively searched for the truth. In other words, its announcement was a lie designed to keep the conspiracy of silence in effect.

In 1953, the CIA ordered research into the UFO phenomenon by the Robertson Panel, which concluded that there was nothing to it and that all files should be opened so that the public would know it. The panel also suggested that the whole UFO "myth" be debunked. There has been argument over the use of that term, but it seems they were interested in destroying interest in UFOs.

The panel, led by Dr. H. P. Robertson, was *designed* to mislead because the results of its five-day investigation were written before the first meeting. Apparently none of the recommendations made by the panel were put into effect.

Throughout the late 1950s and early 1960s, letters and memos were passed among high-level Washington officials, each of whom expressed the opinion that UFOs were not real and that the UFO project should be ended. Their concern was with what the public would think. They couldn't just end the project without building the proper foundation. They all realized they had to convince the public that UFOs were not real.

In 1969, the University of Colorado issued a report based on its eighteen-month study of UFOs. Edward U. Condon, writing the opinion, recommended that the Air Force drop its investigation. By the end of the year, the Air Force followed that recommendation and Project Blue Book was concluded. The criterion set up by the Washington officials had been met.

If the situation was as depicted on the surface, then

it could be concluded that nothing nefarious was going on in the Condon Committee study. Unfortunately for those conducting the conspiracy of silence, we can now look below the surface. In some cases there was no smoking gun, just a cold pistol on the floor. A crime had been committed. We just didn't know all the details.

Now we have them. The 1953 CIA panel had written conclusions before its first session. The panel was loaded with men who not only didn't believe in UFOs but were hostile to the *idea* of UFOs. Maybe not a smoking gun, but very close to it.

The University of Colorado study, however, provided the final evidence. The final conclusions for the Condon Committee report were written on January 16, 1967, in a letter from an Air Force lieutenant colonel to Dr. Edward U. Condon. It told him that there had been no visitations. It also complained about the cost to taxpayers of UFO investigations. Within days, Condon was telling fellow scientists that UFOs didn't exist but that he wasn't to come to that conclusion for another year and a half.

What we have now is the evidence that the UFO phenomenon has been shrouded in secrecy by the government. The government has lied to us, manipulated the situation, and then continued to lie. The smoking guns are out there in documents created by governmental officials and Air Force officers. These documents teach us that the situation is not as they would have us believe. Instead, it is one that they have tried to feed us for years.

When all else fails, they trot out experts to tell us how silly we are for believing in little green men and those crazy flying saucers. They shroud the mystery in ridicule and hope that we aren't clever enough to notice the truth. Freedom of Information and the declassification of thousands of pages of secret documents about UFOs give us the answers for which we have searched for years.

Now we must examine the UFO phenomenon from the beginning to learn what the truth is. We must see how they have altered the truth, how they have misrepresented the truth, and how they have lied when all else failed. There clearly was a directed program from inside the government whose job it was to obscure the truth. The room is littered with smoking guns. It is littered with cold pistols that provide us with additional information about UFOs. It is filled with clues—if we are smart enough to see them. And it is filled with proof—when we are smart enough to find it.

So let me present the evidence. The documents and the witness testimony are all there. Many of them require no special gifts to understand. They are explicit in what they demand of us. They tell us of a policy to bury the UFO field under a mountain of paper, written by men and women with great academic credentials, and hope that we don't see through the trick. When we do, we are labeled as flying saucer nuts.

But we have seen through it. Now we are presenting the evidence so that they know that we know. The evidence is overwhelming. The documentation is convincing. And all the thousands of witnesses can't be lying to perpetuate some sort of a massive hoax. Flying saucers are real, they are extraterrestrial, and the government, through its conspiracy of silence, has tried to keep us in the dark.

CHAPTER 1

——

The Coming of the Saucers

In June 1947, no one had ever heard the term "flying saucer." The only people who thought about life on other planets were either science fiction fans or scientists involved in the debate about canals on the planet Mars. For the vast majority of people alive then, the last thing they thought about was extraterrestrial intelligence. Life on Earth was complicated enough without worrying about visitations from other planets.

The history of the UFO phenomenon begins long before the first flying disks were reported nationally in June 1947. Ancient history is filled with stories that suggest flying saucers were seen by our ancestors. According to some UFO researchers, one of Caesar's legions refused to cross a river while two "fiery shields" hovered above it. Ancient Egyptians wrote of "flaming spears" flashing through the night sky. A medieval painting shows a spherical object in the sky with a man crouched in it as if piloting it. The suggestion by those researchers is that UFOs have been with us since the beginning of human history.

Further evidence of that comes from the late nineteenth century. In January 1878, a Texas rancher reported seeing a strange object in the sky. Ironically, he used the term "saucer" to describe the craft he saw. John Martin's was the only such sighting in that era.

The first real wave of UFO sightings, however, started in late 1896 and ended in early 1897. It became the mirror of later waves. It began with a few sightings that could not be easily explained, but quickly slipped into hoaxes, misidentifications, and outright fabrications. Newspapers of the time, as desperate for copy as those of today, printed everything they could, regardless of the facts. Pages were devoted to hoaxes that the next day were upstaged by more elaborate stories, which then faded from the scene just as quickly.

Two of those reports, now known to be hoaxes, have transcended the time. One of them, coming from Aurora, Texas, claimed that "the great airship" had hit a windmill, exploding. The badly mangled body of the pilot was recovered. Those in Aurora claimed the pilot was not from Earth, but was probably an inhabitant of Mars. They gave him a Christian burial. The story was resurrected in the 1960s, and in the 1970s it became clear that nothing happened in Aurora. It had been a story invented by a newspaper stringer for the expressed purpose of putting Aurora, his hometown, on the map.

The other report came from LeRoy, Kansas. Alexander Hamilton told of a calf stolen by the crew of the airship late one night. The following day the remains of the mutilated animal were found with no sign of footprints around the carcass. Several men who lived in LeRoy signed an affidavit attesting to the truthfulness of the event.

Jerry Clark found Hamilton's granddaughter and learned that Hamilton and the other men who signed affidavits were all members of the local liars' club. They had invented the story, just as so many others had invented theirs in later years. Yet this report is still quoted in many UFO books as fact.

After the spring of 1897, the airship was forgotten, and there were only sporadic reports of strange craft in the sky. In fact, the first flying saucer sightings in 1947 went unnoticed. The official Air Force investigation, started in the months after those early sightings, listed several from the beginning of June, one on June 2 from Rehoboth, Delaware, and one on June 10 from Hungary. All of those early cases are missing from the Project Blue Book files.

On June 24, 1947, the modern era was ushered in when Kenneth Arnold, a Boise, Idaho, businessman, saw nine objects flash across the sky. They were flying one behind the other, at about 9,500 feet, at a speed estimated to be more than 1,500 miles per hour.

When he landed his plane in Yakima, Washington, he told the assembled reporters that the objects moved with a motion like that of saucers skipping across the water. The shape, however, according to drawings that Arnold completed for the Army, showed objects that were heel-shaped. In later drawings, Arnold elaborated, showing objects that were crescent-shaped with a scalloped trailing edge.

Hearing Arnold's description of the motion of the objects, reporter Bill Bequette coined the term "flying saucer." The term, then, didn't refer to the shape of the objects, but to the style of their movement.

Arnold's sighting didn't gain front-page status immediately. Stories appeared in newspapers a day or two later. It was, at that time, the story of an oddity. Arnold claimed later that he thought he had seen some sort of the new jet aircraft.

Arnold wasn't the only person to see strange objects in the sky that day. Fred Johnson, listed as a prospector, reported watching five or six disk-shaped craft as they flew over the Cascade Mountains. He said they were round with a slight tail and were about thirty feet in diameter. They were not flying in any sort of formation, and as they banked in a turn, the sunlight flashed off them. As they approached, Johnson noticed that his compass began to spin wildly. When the objects finally vanished in the distance, the compass returned to normal.

After learning of the Arnold sighting, Johnson wrote to the Air Force on August 20, 1947, saying, "Saw in the portland [sic] paper a short time ago in regards to an article in regards to the so called flying disc having any basis in fact. I can say am a prospector and was in the Mt Adams district on June 24th the day Kenneth Arnold of Boise Idaho claims he saw a formation of flying disc [sic]. And i saw the same flying objects at about the same time. Having a telescope with me at the time I can assure you there are real and noting like them I ever saw before they did not pass verry high over where I was standing at the time. plolby 1000 ft. they were Round about 30 foot in diameter tapering sharply to a point in the head and in an oval shape. with a bright top surface. I did not hear any noise as you would from a plane. But there was an object in the tail end looked like a big hand of a clock shifting from side to side like a big magnet. There speed was far as i know seemed to be greater than anything I ever saw. Last view I got of the objects they were standing on edge Banking in a cloud." It is signed: "Yours Respectfully, Fred Johnson."[1]

The Army Air Forces had asked the FBI to interview some of those seeing flying disks. Johnson was one of those interviewed. The FBI report contained essentially the same information as the letter that Johnson had sent to the Army. The FBI report ended, saying, "Informant appeared to be a very reliable individual who advised that he had been a prospector in the states of Montana, Washington, and Oregon for the past forty years."[2]

Dr. Bruce Maccabee, a physicist with the Navy, wrote in the *International UFO Reporter* that the Johnson sighting was important, not because it took place near where Arnold saw the nine objects, but because it seemed to be an extension of the Arnold sighting. It provided independent corroboration for the Arnold sighting, strengthening that case and reducing some of the explanations that have been offered to explain it to ridiculousness.

Dr. Donald H. Menzel, a Harvard scientist, decided that Johnson was being honest in his report; that is, Johnson was not lying about it. He was merely mis-

---

[1] Johnson letter from Project Blue Book files.

[2] FBI report from Project Blue Book files, reprinted in the *International UFO Reporter*, article written by Dr. Bruce Maccabee.

taken in his analysis of the sighting. Menzel wrote that Johnson had probably seen bright reflections from patches of clouds. It didn't seem to matter to Menzel that Johnson saw the objects only about 1,000 feet over his head, watched them through a telescope, and had them in sight for almost a minute before they disappeared, turning into a cloud.

Later Air Force investigators would review the file, but they apparently didn't agree with Menzel's explanation. As Maccabee pointed out in his article, the sighting was the first to be labeled as "unidentified."

Other sightings were reported on June 25 in Kansas City, Pueblo, Colorado, and in Oklahoma City. All of these sightings involved more than one object flying in loose formations. Near Glen Falls, New York, Louis Stebbins saw a single reddish disk. None of these cases were mentioned in the Project Blue Book files.

Sighting reports continued to grow. They came from Arizona, New Mexico, Texas, and Utah. The skies over the Southwest seemed to be filled with flying disks and newspapers were beginning to report sightings on a national scale. People were learning that flying disks were not just a Western phenomenon. Local reports were made as people began scanning the skies and spotting the mystery objects.

Everyone was searching for answers, but no one seemed to have any. Various government agencies were making statements about the phenomenon, denying all knowledge of what was happening. By June 27, the situation changed as the distribution of sightings, according to the newspapers, became more widespread. Sightings were made in Canada, Australia, and New Zealand.

The *Science Survey* announced that it had made a quiet survey of the phenomenon and mentioned that ongoing research might prohibit scientists from answering all the questions about the flying saucers. It also pointed out that some of the research was still under governmental wartime regulations. The reports of the flying disks might be directly tied to some of that classified research.

Sources involved in classified aeronautical research offered three "educated" guesses about the disks. First, one scientist suggested they weren't disks at all, but hexagonal or diamond-shaped aircraft that spun at high speeds, giving the impression of a disk.[3]

Second, someone suggested that the disks were actually remote-controlled rockets and that their high speeds and their maneuvers suggested the disk shape to those observers on the ground.

Finally, because there had been reports of falling or landing disks, the theory was offered that they were controlled by some station far from the general population. The rockets, then, were research vehicles launched from a great distance, which explained why no one who saw them on the ground knew anything about them.

Others offered other suggestions. One of the wildest was that the reports were nothing more than spots before the eyes. The disks were simply afterimages caused when a person walks from a dark interior into the bright sunlight. If that was true, then

---

[3] Various newspaper articles and reports with speculation as to the origin of the "flying disks."

the images should have been black rather than silver or white, but that didn't stop some from claiming this as the solution for all the reports.

Scientists had already ruled out meteors because the disks were flying too low and too slow, and some witnesses reported that the objects climbed as they disappeared. It was also pointed out that the Earth was not moving through a swarm of meteors that could account for the sudden increase in numbers.

David Lilienthal, chairman of the Atomic Energy Commission, said that the flying disks had nothing to do with atomic experiments. *Newsweek* suggested that the "Flying Flapjack," a Naval experimental aircraft, might account for some sightings, but the Navy denied it. The "Flying Flapjack" was based in Bridgeport, Connecticut, and hadn't left that area.

By way of contrast, Captain Tom Brown, a public relations officer on the Army Air Forces staff in Washington, D.C., said that the AAF believed there was something to all the stories of flying saucers. However, like everyone else, the AAF, according to him, was mystified by the reports.

The Navy also checked, through its ordinance bureau, all its facilities to determine if they were experimenting with anything that could account for the sightings. All of the answers were negative.

The lack of answers was demonstrated from even higher-ranking authorities. Lieutenant General Nathan F. Twining, commander of the Army's Air Materiel Command (AMC) at Wright Field, Ohio, said, "Neither the AAF nor any other component of the armed forces has any plane, guided missile, or other aerial device which could possibly be mistaken for a saucer or formation of flying discs."

Twining didn't let it go there. He added, "Some of these witnesses evidently saw something, but we don't know what we are investigating." Twining, because of his position, should have been aware of almost everything being done by the Army in research and development. That was one of the major tasks of the AMC, yet Twining was denying all knowledge of the flying saucers.

A small number of scientists and reporters claimed that the flying saucers were from another planet.[4] Mars and Venus were the two favorites, though some suggested that there could be no life on either planet and believed that the saucers came from a planet outside the Solar System. With everyone denying knowledge of the flying disks and with the disks seeming to outperform the best fighters of the day, there were those who believed that only the extraterrestrial hypothesis explained what was being observed.

As the sightings continued through the end of the month, those in power became even more baffled. A few were worried that the Soviets had made some sort of breakthrough in aviation technology, but they were overruled. The last thing the Soviets would do was fly an experimental aircraft over the United States. If it crashed, then the technology would be in American hands as well and any advantage the Soviets had hoped to gain would then be lost.

Inquiries were made of various military installa-

---

[4]This was the first of the extraterrestrial explanations. The original idea was that the flying disks were from somewhere else in the Solar System. Eventually, scientists realized that the disks had to come from outside the Solar System if the extraterrestrial hypothesis is valid.

tions. In its official unit history, the Eighth Air Force headquarters in Fort Worth, Texas, reported that it had answered dozens of questions about the flying disks, but had no clue about what they were. It was just as confused as the rest of the population.

The situation didn't change as June faded into July. The reports were still being made and no one had any answers. Military pilots were seeing the disks.[5] They were giving chase, but they were having no luck catching them. And they were having no luck in identifying them.

Many of the flying saucer reports still came from the Pacific Northwest. By coincidence, the commander of the Army Air Forces, General Carl Spaatz, began a vacation there in early July. According to newspaper accounts, Spaatz was on a fishing trip in Washington State.

At the same time, the military announced that aircraft would be on alert in case the flying saucers returned. Some of the planes were on the ground, waiting for reports, while others were actively searching for some sign of the flying saucers. *The New York Times* reported that five P-51 Mustangs of the Oregon National Guard flew over the Cascade Mountains on an airborne alert, searching for the flying disks, while a sixth, in radio communication with the others, circled over Portland, Oregon. They were equipped with gun cameras to photograph the objects if they appeared.

July 4, 1947, fell on a Friday. It was the beginning

---

[5]In the beginning of the 1947 wave, many high-ranking military officers were most concerned by reports of flying saucers by military pilots. To the generals and admirals, military pilots were considered to be reliable observers.

of one of the few three-day weekends in that era. Even with that, the military had aircraft from Seattle to Los Angeles searching for flying saucers.

It was also during that weekend that one of the most spectacular of the sightings was made. Captain E. J. Smith was piloting an United Airlines plane when one of the flying saucers appeared, coming at them. The first officer, Ralph Stevens, reached down to blink the landing lights, and Smith asked Stevens what he was doing. Stevens responded that another plane was coming at them. As it closed, they realized that it wasn't another aircraft, but one of the flying disks.

They could see no real shape, but did say the craft was flat on the bottom, very thin, and seemed to be irregular on the top. The object appeared to be at the same altitude as the airplane and followed them for ten to fifteen minutes.

Moments later, four more appeared on the left of the aircraft. Smith was quoted in the newspaper, saying, "We couldn't tell what the exact shape was except to notice that they definitely were larger than our plane [a DC-4], fairly smooth on the bottom and rough on top."

On that same weekend, a Coast Guardsman, Frank Ryman, living in Seattle, Washington, took a photograph of an object over the north end of Lake Washington. A spokesman at the Acme News Pictures in New York said the photograph showed two tiny white dots, one of them a flaw in the print.

The most impressive series of sightings came from Portland, Oregon, where police officers and civilians in widely separated locations watched as a variety of disks flashed through the sky.[6] The first was reported by C. J. Bogne and a carload of witnesses north of Redmond, Oregon, who saw four disk-shaped objects flash past Mount Jefferson. The objects made no noise and performed no maneuvers.

At one o'clock, an Oaks Park employee, Don Metcalfe, saw a lone disk fly over the park. A KOIN news reporter in Portland saw twelve shiny disks as they danced in the sky high overhead.

A few minutes after 1:00 P.M., Kenneth A. McDowell, a police officer who was near the Portland police station, noticed as the pigeons began fluttering as if frightened. Overhead were three disks, one flying east and the other two south. All were moving at high speed and appeared to be oscillating.

About the same time, two other police officers, Walter A. Lissy and Robert Ellis, saw three disks overhead. They were also moving at high speed.

Just across the Columbia River, in nearby Vancover, Washington, Sergeant John Sullivan, Clarence McKay, and Fred Krives, sheriff's deputies, watched twenty to thirty disks overhead.

Not long after that, three harbor patrolmen on the river saw three to six disks traveling at high speed. According to the witnesses, the objects looked like chrome hubcaps and oscillated as they flew.

About 4:00 P.M., more civilians saw the disks. A woman called the police, telling them she watched a single object as "shiny as a new dime, flipping around." An unidentified man called to say that he'd

---

[6]Information on the Portland sightings are based on the Project Blue Book files, *The Report on Unidentified Flying Objects* by Captain Ed Ruppelt, and various newspaper articles, including those published in Portland, Oregon, and Vancover, Washington.

seen three disks, one flying to the east and the other two heading north. They were shiny, shaped like flattened saucers, and were traveling at high speed.

Finally, in Milwaukie, Oregon, not far from Portland, Sergeant Claude Cross reported three objects flying to the north. All were disk-shaped and were moving at high speed.

The question that must be asked is why none of the aircraft on alert responded to this series of sightings. It would seem logical that they would have spotted the disks at some point, but there was never any indication that such is the case. Nothing appears in the Project Blue Book files to suggest that gun camera footage was obtained by the Oregon National Guard. A few days later, it was announced that the searches would be discontinued. The lack of concrete results was the suspected reason.

Newspapers were filled with other stories. On July 7, according to the reports, Vernon Baird, while flying a P-38 above 30,000 feet, sighted a formation of disks behind him.[7] He said they were about fifteen feet in diameter and looked like yo-yos. As he watched, one of them was sucked into the prop wash of his aircraft and disintegrated. The wreckage spiraled down, crashing into the Tobacco Root Mountains of Montana, but searches failed to locate it.

A day later, Baird's boss, J. J. Archer, said the report was a joke. They had been sitting around the hangar, listening to stories of the flying saucers, and invented the tale. That seemed to end it.

The first of the occupant reports came on July 7.

[7]Information based on articles in various newspapers, including the *Los Angeles Herald-Express* and *The UFO Casebook*.

Gene Camachi and I. W. Martenson of Tacoma, Washington, said they had seen a number of the disks land on a neighbor's roof. "Little men" climbed out, but disappeared when reporters arrived.

An elderly Massachusetts woman said that she saw a moon-sized object fly by her window. Inside the craft was a slender figure dressed in what she described as a Navy uniform.

On July 8, a merchant seaman in Houston reported the landing of a silver saucer. The saucer's pilot was tiny, only two feet tall, with a round head the size of a basketball. Before the pilot climbed back into the saucer, it greeted the seaman.

The most important of the reports on July 8 came from Roswell, New Mexico. For several hours, the attention of the world was focused on the small southeastern New Mexico community. The *Roswell Daily Record* claimed that the Army, with the help of local rancher Mac Brazel, had recovered one of the flying disks. According to the newspaper, the wreckage was being shipped to a higher headquarters.

For three or four hours, the world waited. Phone lines to Roswell were jammed with reporters trying to get more information. But then Brigadier General Roger Ramey, commander of the Eighth Air Force, announced that the officers at Roswell, caught up in the flying disk hysteria, had made a mistake. What they had found was not a flying saucer but a weather balloon and a rawin radar target, a rather common weather observation device. Newspapers carried the answer the next morning.

The flying disk situation was unchanged on July 9. The Roswell saucer had been explained by the military, but the sightings by others continued, with reports coming from around the country. But that was the last day that newspapers concentrated on the topic.

The *Las Vegas Review-Journal* announced that "Reports of flying saucers whizzing through the sky fell off sharply today as the Army and Navy began a concentrated campaign to stop the rumors." That Associated Press report was carried by newspapers around the country.

Officials began to press for explanations, including the suggestion that those seeing the saucers were less than reliable. The *Chicago Sun* reported: FLYING DISKS PASS UP KANSAS! AFTER ALL, IT'S A DRY STATE. *The Arizona Republic* on July 10 claimed: "FLYING DISC" STORIES BLOW UP UNDER STUDY. It was also on July 10 that some newspapers carried Hal Boyle's Associated Press column, which reported: BOYLE SAYS HE FOUND ANSWER TO FLYING DISC MYSTERY; HE RODE ONE PILOTED BY GREEN MARTIAN.

In fact, the tone of the articles published after July 9 took a decidedly negative view. The July 13 *Dayton Daily News* reported: SAYS "DISCS" MASS HYSTERIA. Philip Wylie decided that the flying saucer reports were merely hysteria, writing, "It's even fun to be hysterical, according to some people; you check your brains for a weekend or a lifetime, and make believe something is real that isn't a vision, a threat, or the American sky suddenly filled with all sorts of discs and saucer-shaped marvels . . . I dearly enjoy to see a mass of my fellow-creatures seized with the powers of self-deception, goofing all over the place."

Walter Winchell decided that the flying disks were a secret Navy experiment, Navy denials to the contrary. Winchell wrote, ". . . despite vigorous denials by Army and Navy officials, the flying saucers are actually flying wings developed by the U.S. Navy."

Later research showed that the flying wings could not be responsible, but Winchell was satisfied and his column appeared in newspapers around the country.

In the days after July 9, few straight reports about the flying saucers appeared. In one of the wildest, a radio commentator, Carl George, created a whirlwind of controversy with his tale of seeing a flying disk and its flight crew. It was admitted to be a hoax after the station's phone lines were flooded with telephone calls. This too was reported around the country.

The real change in the coverage can be dated from July 9. Prior to that, the stories seemed to hint there was a mystery that everyone wanted to solve. After July 9, the stories hinted that the mystery had been solved and that solution was that there was nothing to the phenomenon. It was the result of hysteria, misidentification, experimental aircraft or missiles, and drunks who no longer saw pink elephants but silver saucers.

Ed Ruppelt, who would revitalize the Air Force's Project Blue Book in 1952, confirmed this change of attitude in the middle of July and offered an explanation. "By the end of July 1947, the security lid was down tight. The few members of the press who did inquire about what the Air Force was doing got the same treatment that you would get today if you inquired about the number of thermonuclear weapons stockpiled in the U.S.'s atomic arsenal. No one, outside of a few high-ranking officers in the Pentagon, knew what the people in the barbed-wire-enclosed Quonset huts that housed the Air Technical Intelligence Center were thinking or doing."[8]

---

[8]Ed Ruppelt, *The Report on Unidentified Flying Objects* (New York: Ace Books, 1956).

Ruppelt had access to all of the old memos, correspondence, and records that had been created in 1947. When he took over as head of Project Blue Book, he had the opportunity to review all of those records and reports. He learned that officials in July 1947 took the situation seriously. He also noted that there was a period of confusion at the top. No one in the government, the Army Air Forces, or at ATIC knew what to do about the phenomenon. By the middle of July, the officials and officers had learned one thing. Too much had been published about the flying saucers. Something had to be done to eliminate that, and they began their campaign. The curtain of silence was being lowered.

The change came right after the July 4 weekend. That is easily demonstrated by a close reading of the newspapers. The question that begs to be asked is what happened over that weekend that caused the sudden change. Why did they want that curtain to be lowered?

The key to the change might be the story that surfaced briefly on July 8 and 9. Roswell, New Mexico, might hold the answers as to why the government suddenly cared about the flying saucer reports. The case from Roswell was more than just a balloon.

CHAPTER 2

━━

The Roswell Perspective

THE STORY OF A UFO CRASH AT ROSWELL HAS become quite complex over the last several years. The problem stems from a multitude of investigators, each with his own agenda, a variety of witnesses, all clamoring for the spotlight, an Air Force investigation that reaffirmed its own earlier conclusion (after dressing it up with a new name), and a cottage industry that has grown up in the town. Throw in a large helping of news media, from the legitimate to the tabloid, reporters all searching for an angle that hasn't been explored, and it becomes difficult, if not impossible, to sort the fact from the fiction.

For more than six years, I have studied this case, trying to sort it out. I have talked to witnesses who claim to have been on the inside and would share only a little of what they knew. I have talked to witnesses who claimed to have seen it all, but remembered little because of advanced age. And I have talked to people who claimed to have been witnesses and who have significantly altered their stories over the years.

However, my personal investigations into this case and the fact that I have talked to witnesses, interviewing many on audio or videotape so that there is a documented record, have given me a unique perspective into the report. I can determine where fact ends and fiction begins. And by ignoring the witnesses whose testimony is wrapped in controversy, whether that controversy is the invention of debunkers or the private agendas of UFO believers, I can draw a new, important picture of Roswell.

To do this, I have selected only the testimony that seems to be universally accepted as accurate or that has not been challenged as inaccurate. In this case, the rejection of or the failure to use specific testimonies, such as that by Frank Kaufmann, is no commentary by me on the reliability of those testimonies. Those points will be addressed later. Instead, this is an attempt to straighten out the twisted and convoluted case that now marks the Roswell investigation.

The best evidence available suggests that the crash took place late on the evening of July 4, about 11:17 P.M.[1] Witnesses at widely scattered locations, such as William Woody, saw a bright light in the sky. Woody, who lived east of the Roswell base, told Dr. Mark Rodeghier that the light first appeared west-northwest, apparently moving northward. It was in sight for ten or eleven seconds as it fell. The object was white and left a white trail with red streaks through it. Woody was sure that it wasn't a meteor

---

[1] Time and date are based on firsthand testimony of multiple witnesses and a written record kept by Catholic nuns in Roswell.

because he'd seen a number of them while working around the ranch. He thought it fell thirty to forty miles away, but couldn't be sure.

Closer to Roswell, assigned to one of the small outlying bases attached to the 509th Bomb Group, was Corporal E. L. Pyles. While walking across the parade ground on the main base, he looked up in time to see what he thought was a shooting star. It was larger and brighter than any he had seen in the past. It moved across the sky and then arced downward, disappearing in seconds. There seemed to be an orange glow around it and a halo near the front.

Pyles could not remember the date of the incident. He knew it was 1947 and thought it was July, but just didn't know. He did say, however, that when he read that a balloon was responsible for the flying disk sightings a couple of days later, he knew that answer was wrong. The newspaper was dated July 8, which puts the date of his sighting in the first part of that month. The July 4 date offered by others fits into the time frame recalled by Pyles when he was interviewed more than forty-five years later.

Dr. W. Curry Holden, professor of history and anthropology at Texas Tech in Lubbock, came across the wreckage on the morning of July 5, 1947. Because of the long weekend, he had taken a group of students into eastern New Mexico on an archaeological expedition. Just after sunrise, Holden and the students found what they first thought were the remains of a crashed airplane. Holden sent one of the students toward the highway to look for a telephone so they could alert the authorities. Holden stayed on the scene with the rest of the students.

In the only interview conducted with Holden in the

weeks just prior to his death, Holden told me that he had been in the field, north of Roswell, and seen both the craft and the bodies. He also mentioned that it was so long ago that he had forgotten many of the details. At the time of the interview, Holden was ninety-six. Although he was frail, his mind was sound and his grasp of reality was complete. As I asked the questions, often putting a negative spin on them so there could be no accusation of leading the witness, Holden confirmed that he had been on the scene. The craft was impacted into the cliff, there were small bodies near it, and it looked like nothing he had ever seen.

As I left their home, Mrs. Holden cautioned me that her husband's memory wasn't as sharp as it once had been. He sometimes restructured his life's events, moving them in time so that they were subtly changed. She didn't suggest that he was making them up or that his memories were delusions but that he didn't always have the timing right.

Both Mrs. Holden and their adult daughter, Dr. Jane Holden Kelly, said that Holden had never mentioned the event to them. Of course, if the military had cautioned him about it, suggesting professional ruin to those who told of the classified event without permission, that makes sense. Why would he burden his family with something like that? Many others kept their involvement in these events from friends and family.[2]

And there was independent corroboration of Holden's report. Dr. C. Bertrand Schultz, a paleontologist

---

[2]Extensive searches of Holden's personal papers at the Southwestern Collections at Texas Tech have failed to produce any corroboration for his activities on the critical weekend. By the same token, there was nothing in the records to refute the idea.

from the University of Nebraska, told both Tom Carey and me that Holden was involved. Holden and Schultz were friends and when I asked Holden about it, he told me that Schultz had visited them in Lubbock a number of times.

Not only did Schultz confirm the story as told by Holden to me but said he had heard the story a number of times in the past himself. Schultz, driving north from Roswell in July 1947, saw the military cordon erected by officers of the Roswell Army Air Field.[3]

Major Edwin Easley, provost marshal at the Roswell base, was in charge of security on what has become known as the impact site. When Easley and the rest of the military contingent arrived, they moved Holden and the civilians back, away from the craft. It was Easley's MPs who guarded the civilians, later escorting them to the base for a "debriefing."

I interviewed Easley a number of times before he fell ill with terminal cancer. During the first interview, conducted on January 11, 1990, Easley confirmed that he had been stationed at Roswell, had been the provost marshal, and had commanded both the MP company and the security squadron. When I asked about the "flying saucer crash," Easley said, "I can't talk about it."

Several times during the conversation, Easley answered questions by telling me that he couldn't talk about it. Finally he said, "I can't talk about it. I was sworn to secrecy. I told you that."

During other conversations with Easley, including

---

[3]Schultz's papers provide no corroboration for his location on the critical weekend. However, both Schultz's daughters confirm that he has told them the story of the crashed saucer and the military cordon for many years, beginning in the early 1950s.

one on February 2, 1990, another on June 23, 1990, and still others held later in the year, he revealed what information he could. The sense I got from him was that he wanted to help, he believed that withholding the information was wrong, yet he had promised that he wouldn't talk about it. He would answer all questions that didn't violate his oath quickly and directly, and he would suggest alternative ways of finding the truth when they did. He provided the names of a number of others who might be helpful, mentioning specifically James R. Breece.[4] Unfortunately, Breece died ten years before I ever thought about investigating the Roswell case.

On February 2, 1990, I asked Easley if I was following the right path. He asked what I meant, and I told him that I believed the craft had been of extraterrestrial manufacture. He was quiet for a moment and then said, "That's the right path. You're not following the wrong one."

It was also during that conversation that Easley told me that Mac Brazel, the rancher from the Corona area, had been held at the guest house on base. This would be important corroboration to part of the story. And, since this was not part of the recovery operation or descriptions of the craft and bodies, Easley didn't believe that he was violating his oath by telling me that detail.

Easley became ill later in that year and was finally hospitalized. During his last days, one of his granddaughters asked him about the events outside of Roswell. According to one of his daughters and to his

---

[4] Other names provided by Easley included Virgil Cloyd, deceased, and Captain Beverly Tripp.

doctor, Harold Granik, Easley responded, "Oh, the creatures." He also told them that he had promised the President, Truman, that he would not talk about it.

It was never made clear if Easley spoke to the President personally or if he made the promise to a presidential representative, but it amounts to the same thing. Easley believed that he had made a promise to the President, and he wasn't going to break the promise. The information he provided to family members and to me was the little he felt he could say without violating his word.

When all he told me is examined carefully, Easley confirmed the events outside of Roswell involved an extraterrestrial craft, that they were highly classified even after more than forty years, and that the President had been involved, if only as the Commander-in-Chief of the Army.

By Sunday, July 6, according to all accounts, the majority of the recovery had been completed on the impact site just north of town. The craft had been removed and the bodies were at the main base. If any evidence remained, it was tiny and inconclusive. The operation was suspended.

It was also on Sunday that Mac Brazel appeared at the office of the Chaves County sheriff, George Wilcox. He brought a box of metallic debris that he had found scattered on his ranch about seventy-five miles northwest of Roswell. Brazel died before any UFO researchers had an opportunity to speak to him. His story is recreated through the newspaper interviews published in 1947, those who knew him at the time, and members of the Brazel family, including his son, William Brazel, Jr. Much of the information

I have about Mac came during several interviews with his son and family friends.

Brazel had picked up some of the smaller pieces a day earlier and then headed off to see his nearest neighbors, Floyd and Loretta Proctor. Neither of the Proctors could tell him what he had found. Loretta said that Floyd tried to whittle on a small fragment that Brazel showed him, but couldn't make a scratch on it. When Brazel held a match to it, the debris wouldn't heat or burn and wouldn't blacken.[5]

The next day, Sunday, Brazel made the drive from his ranch house to Roswell. There he spoke to Sheriff Wilcox in person and to radio announcer-newscaster Frank Joyce on the telephone. Someone suggested that Brazel should also speak to the officers at the air base. Major Jesse A. Marcel, the air intelligence officer of the 509th, took the call at the Officers' Club, where he was eating lunch.

After lunch Marcel drove to the sheriff's office, spoke to Brazel, and realized that he would have to make a trip to the ranch for a personal examination of the debris field. The descriptions provided by Brazel suggested that something very unusual had crashed out there. Marcel wanted some help and Colonel William Blanchard, commanding officer of the 509th, reminded him that he had the assistance of a number of people, including a counterintelligence corps agent later identified by Marcel as Captain Sheridan Cavitt. (Cavitt has repeatedly denied his involvement in the events at Roswell, though he was clearly the man in charge of the counterintelligence office in July 1947 and the descriptions offered by

---

[5]Loretta Proctor, recorded interview, March 1989.

others fit him perfectly. And in an interview conducted by Colonel Richard Weaver, Cavitt admitted that he had collected debris which he identified as that of a balloon.[6] See Chapter 12 for more details.)

Brazel ran a few errands in town and Marcel reported back to the base. Late in the afternoon, Brazel in his truck, Marcel in his car, and Cavitt in a jeep carryall began the long drive back to the ranch. They arrived too late for anything to be accomplished that night. Instead, they waited for morning in a small cabin, eating cold beans and crackers for supper.

During the evening, according to UFO researcher Len Stringfield, Marcel took a Geiger counter to a livestock shed where Brazel had stored a large piece of the debris. He found no sign of radiation.

At first light on July 7, Brazel saddled two horses. Marcel didn't ride, but Cavitt was a West Texas boy who could. Marcel said he would follow in the jeep. They then rode and drove to the field full of the metallic debris that Brazel had told them about.

Years later, Marcel would tell various researchers and reporters, including Bob Pratt,[7] that the debris was scattered "as far as you could see . . . three quarters of a mile long and two to three hundred feet wide." Marcel couldn't identify the debris, saying, "I don't know what we were picking up. I still don't know. As of this day [1979], I still don't know what it was."

As the intelligence officer, Marcel was acquainted with foreign aircraft, rockets, missiles, and balloons.

---

[6]Both before and after Weaver's interview, Cavitt told me that he wasn't involved and had not been out to the Brazel ranch. He couldn't explain why both Marcel and Lewis Rickett, Cavitt's NCOIC, reported that he was on the field with them.

[7]Pratt interview conducted with Marcel in December 1979.

He said that it couldn't be part of an experimental aircraft or experimental balloon. He did say, "For one thing, if it had been a balloon, like the parts we picked up, it would not have been porous. It was porous." It should also be noted that Marcel had participated in Operation Crossroads, where rawin targets and balloons had been used. This was the type of balloon later identified by the skeptics as the culprit in the Roswell case.

Even had it been some type of secret project to which Marcel was not privy, he certainly should have recognized the material. It wasn't required that he recognize the debris as being from a specific project, only that he identify it as being of terrestrial manufacture. Pieces of a new kind of airplane, debris from a rocket, or fragments of a balloon would have all been identifiable as being made on Earth. Marcel was convinced that the metal had not been manufactured on Earth. He would later say, "I still believe it was nothing that came from Earth. It came to Earth but wasn't from Earth."

Marcel and Cavitt spent the day on the debris field first walking around it, surveying it, and then trying to gather the material. They moved the big pieces from the edges of the field toward the center and then loaded the jeep. Later in the afternoon, with the jeep crammed with debris, Marcel sent Cavitt back to the base. Marcel wanted to load his car before he began the long drive into Roswell.

At dusk he headed back to town with his car filled with the mysterious metal. On the way to the base, Marcel stopped at his house, wanting to show his wife, Viaud, and son, Jesse Marcel, Jr., the material. He knew he had found something extraordinary.

Jesse Jr. said that his father woke him and showed

him the metallic debris spread out on the kitchen floor. Jesse Jr. said that they saw symbols on some of the small I-beams. The symbols were a bright purple and looked like geometric designs along the side of the beams. These, according to Jesse Jr., appeared to have been embossed on the metal rather than stamped into it or painted on it. He didn't recognize any of the symbols, other than by shape such as circles or squares.

Jesse Jr., interviewed years later, made it clear that his father told him the pieces were from a flying saucer. Although only eleven years old, he said that he had never seen anything like the debris. The metal was extremely lightweight, strong, and slightly cool to the touch.

Walt Whitmore, Sr., majority owner of KGFL radio in Roswell, was intrigued by the story reported by Frank Joyce on Sunday. He questioned Joyce about it and then decided that he wanted more information. According to Joyce, Whitmore was concerned about the station's credibility.[8] It seems now that sometime on July 7 (probably late in the day), Whitmore drove to the Corona area with another employee of the radio station in search of Mac Brazel. They returned with Brazel that evening, keeping him at Whitmore's house overnight, making a wire recording of an interview with Brazel for broadcast.

It was next day, on July 8, that the curtain of silence began to descend permanently. Blanchard, after hearing from Marcel and Cavitt, ordered First Lieutenant Walter Haut, the base public relations officer, to issue a press release explaining that they were in possession of a flying saucer. Many researchers have suggested that this press release was the only mistake made by the

---

[8]Based on information supplied by Walt Whitmore, Jr., and Frank Joyce.

military, and had it not been for that single document, no one would be discussing the Roswell case today.

According to Walter Haut, it was midmorning when Blanchard called, ordering him to issue the press release about the flying saucer. Haut, interviewed later, said that all the information in his release was provided by Blanchard. Haut wrote his release and then carried it into town, giving copies to both newspapers, the *Roswell Daily Record* and the *Roswell Morning Dispatch,* and both radio stations, KGFL and KSWS. Art McQuiddy, editor of the *Morning Dispatch,* later complained because he was last on the list of media outlets to receive a copy of the press release. By the time Haut reached him, the story was already out on the AP radio wire.

But by examining that report, released to the Roswell media just after noon, New Mexico time, it becomes clear that the purpose was to mislead rather than inform. First, it says that the saucer had been recovered, yet at the time the release was written, debris was still scattered over the field found by Brazel. Second, it mentioned that the debris was found seventy-five miles northwest of Roswell, so that if anyone was inclined to search, they would be miles from the impact site where the craft and bodies had been located. And finally they suggested that everything was on its way to Fort Worth, so that anyone wanting additional information was now directed to Eighth Air Force headquarters in Fort Worth, Texas, instead of the base in Roswell.

The emphasis also shifted. Marcel was ordered by Blanchard to take the debris to Wright Field in Ohio with a stop in Fort Worth. But in Fort Worth, Brigadier General Roger Ramey, commanding officer of the

Eighth Air Force, had other ideas. Almost from the moment that Marcel arrived, Ramey claimed it was all part of a weather balloon. Marcel was to travel no farther and was ordered to return to Roswell.

At KGFL radio in Roswell, George "Jud" Roberts received a number of telephone calls from Washington, D.C., on July 8. Roberts remembered that the calls came from the New Mexico congressional delegation, possibly Senators Carl Hatch or Dennis Chavez. Roberts was told that KGFL should not broadcast the Brazel recording. If the station did play it, the employees could start looking for new jobs. Roberts didn't know how those in Washington knew about the Brazel interview, though KGFL had promoted it on the air several times that morning. He only knew that they were ordering him not to broadcast it.

In Fort Worth, J. Bond Johnson,[9] a reporter-photographer for the *Fort Worth Star-Telegram* in July 1947, was told by his editor, Cullen Green, that something from Roswell was on its way to the base. Johnson later said that he didn't believe that it was a flying saucer that he was going to see, but that he had been prepared to witness something unusual. What did surprise him was that he was to go to Ramey's office rather than the Public Information Office as was the normal routine.

When he entered, he saw metallic debris spread out on the floor of Ramey's office. It was a pile of rubble that, according to Johnson, gave off an offensive odor. There was nothing spectacular about the debris and he later said, "I posed General Ramey

---

[9]Johnson, interviewed by others, has altered his story, but my taped interviews of February 27, 1989, March 24, 1989, and May 28, 1990, and the article he wrote for the *Fort Worth Star-Telegram* provide a good basis for understanding his role in the case.

with this debris. At that time I was briefed on the idea that it was not a flying disk as first reported, but in fact was a weather balloon that had crashed."

Johnson took four photographs while in the office. Two showed Ramey crouched near the debris. The other two had Ramey and his chief of staff, Colonel Thomas J. DuBose, looking at the debris.

When he left, Johnson was sure that all he had seen was some kind of balloon. He wrote a story for the newspaper that evening claiming that the saucer found at Roswell was nothing more than a weather observation balloon.

At 5:30 P.M. on that same day, a reporter with the *Dallas Morning News* interviewed Major Edwin Kirton of the Eighth Air Force intelligence office, who said that a weather balloon was responsible for all the fuss. That was duly reported in the next edition of the newspaper.

At 6:17 P.M., the FBI in Dallas, quoting the same Major Kirton (though they misspelled his name as Curtan), sent a telex to the FBI in Washington, D.C., repeating the balloon story. The telex also suggested that the balloon theory had not been borne out by the telephone inquiry with Wright Field outside Dayton, Ohio. The material was being forwarded to Wright Field for analysis by the laboratories there.

Later that evening, Ramey held a press conference. Colonel Thomas J. DuBose was there. Interviewed later, DuBose said that the conference was attended by three or four reporters; Major Marcel; Captain Roy Showalter, Ramey's aide; and the public information officer, Major Charles A. Cashon. Warrant Officer Irving Newton, one of the Eighth Air Force weather officers, was called after the beginning of the press conference and told to report to Ramey immediately.

Newton, interviewed by telephone years later, said repeatedly that he had been working in the weather office when one of Ramey's staff officers called, requesting that Newton rush over. Newton said that he was alone in the office and couldn't leave. General Ramey then called, demanding that Newton report immediately and to steal the first car he came to if he didn't have one of his own.

When Newton arrived at Ramey's office, he saw the remains of a neoprene balloon and rawin target device torn up on the floor. He said that the moment he saw it, he knew what it was. He'd launched hundreds of them himself during the invasion of Okinawa.

According to Newton, the reporters didn't ask questions, but the major there kept pointing to parts of the balloon, asking if that piece would be on a normal balloon. Newton said that they were and wondered if the major wasn't trying to save face. The major seemed confused. Newton thought the major was Marcel, but Newton didn't know either Marcel or Cashon. It is his assumption that it was Marcel talking, though Marcel had been ordered by Ramey not to say a word and, according to Marcel, he didn't talk during the press conference. It seems more likely it was Cashon, the public information officer, making sure that the reporters understood that the object on the floor was nothing unusual or spectacular.

As soon as Newton identified the debris as a common weather balloon for the press, Ramey turned to his aide, Showalter, and ordered, "Cancel the special flight."

At 10:00 P.M., ABC News *Headline Edition* reported

the find but suggested that it was nothing more than a balloon. They mentioned that officials at Wright Field expected it to arrive there soon but that it hadn't yet made it. They reported that Ramey had said the device was of flimsy construction, had no obvious power source, and didn't look as if it could carry a man aloft.

Ramey was telling anyone who would listen to him that the officers at Roswell had been caught up in the hysteria of the flying disk reports. They had made a mistake because what they had found was nothing more extraordinary than a balloon. No one asked why no one in Roswell could recognize the balloon as such. Everyone who had seen the debris in New Mexico, including the rancher, the sheriff, his deputies, and various officers and enlisted men from the base, failed to identify it.

This is in stark contrast to a similar event in Circleville, Ohio, that took place just days before the Roswell events broke in the newspaper. Sherman Campbell, a farmer, found the remains of a rawin target and neoprene balloon and then, because of the shining foil used in its construction, suspected it might explain some of the flying disk reports. Campbell took it to the sheriff, who recognized it as a balloon, and then on to the local newspaper, where the reporters recognized it as a balloon. They didn't know the proper name, but they did identify it as a balloon and balloon-borne device.

The local military was alerted but expressed no interest in the balloon. It was displayed at the Circleville newspaper office and then returned to Campbell, who put it in his barn, where it sat for a number of years. No one wondered why everyone in Ohio could identify the balloon, while the trained officers and men in New Mexico could not. In fact, the military flew the balloon to Texas before anyone allegedly identified it.

Confirmation of the extraterrestrial nature of the Roswell events has been difficult to find. Edwin Easley was among the first of the retired military officers who added to the growing body of testimony. His cryptic "Oh, the creatures," said to his doctor and family, provided a link to the alien bodies. It suggested that Marcel hadn't been fooled by a balloon that had been identified by civilians elsewhere. And when Easley told me that the craft was extraterrestrial, it added a new, important dimension to the investigation.

Easley's statements were subtle confirmations. He said nothing startling but danced around the questions, saying what he could. Learning from him was difficult but not impossible. He was a kind man who recognized his duty, but who also wanted to help.

Another retired officer, Brigadier General Arthur Exon,[10] whose credentials, like those of Easley and others, can be and have been checked, was at Wright Field in July 1947 when the various aircraft from Roswell, carrying everything from metallic debris to the dead bodies of the alien flight crew, arrived. Although he didn't see the bodies unloaded, he did hear tales about them. And while he didn't participate in the analysis of the metal recovered outside of Roswell, he did talk to friends of his who did the actual work.

Because Exon is a retired general, his words carry more authority than those of privates and corporals

---

[10]For the shifting nature of Exon's tales about what he meant, see Chapter 10.

who spent three or four years in the Army. And because he is a retired general, he would have access to information that was not available to those same privates and corporals.

Exon's information about the retrieval and the arrival of the various materials at Wright Field is interesting. And even if he didn't see the materials himself, his friends did. There is no question that the debris and bodies arrived at Wright Field for analysis. There is no question that it was something extraordinary and not common or mundane.

But Exon's contribution to the Roswell case comes from his firsthand observations of the impact site and the debris field. Sometime after the events of July 1947, Exon flew over the sites. He said, "[It was] probably part of the same accident but two distinct sites. One, assuming that the thing, as I understand it, as I remember flying the area later, that the damage to the vehicle seemed to be coming from the southeast and northwest but it could have been going in the opposite direction but it doesn't seem likely. So that farther northwest pieces found on the ranch, those pieces were mostly metal . . ."

What Exon did, in that one small quote, was corroborate the data that had been uncovered over a period of two years. His offhand comment confirmed that there were two sites, one northwest of the other, and that the one to the northwest contained just metallic debris. It is a precise and accurate description of the situation as it existed in 1947.

Exon, in a letter to me dated November 24, 1991, went even farther, telling me that there were obvious gouges in the terrain and tire tracks over both sites. William Brazel, Jr., had told me in February 1989 that there had been a gouge through the center of the debris field. Exon confirmed the existence of that gouge, based on his firsthand eyewitness testimony.

Bill Brazel's testimony, again, almost universally unchallenged, provides a long and detailed description of the site and the metallic debris. When he showed the pieces of debris to his father, he was told, "That looks like some of the contraption I found."

Although the debris found by Bill Brazel resembled conventional items in a gross sense, they were not conventional. He said, "Actually, this was before monofilament fishing line was a popular item and that's the nearest I could compare it to . . . And there were some pieces of wood. I had several of those."

Asked if it was real wood or like wood, Bill Brazel said, "No, they were like wood. They were like balsa wood . . . The longest piece I found, about six inches, would flex a little. I couldn't break it and I couldn't whittle it with my pocketknife."

Bill Brazel also described the site. He said, "Well, naturally, I was curious. This thing made quite a track down through there. It took a year or two for it to grass back over and heal up."

Marcel never said a word about a gouge in the terrain, and no one ever asked him about it. Bill Brazel did mention it, and that was corroborated by General Exon.

On July 9, newspapers across the country carried what they believed to be the end of the Roswell story. They also announced that the Roswell saucer was nothing more than a fairly common weather balloon. Even those newspapers that hadn't carried the original announcement printed the ultimate solution.

Of course, the balloon solution, as offered at the time,

had flaws. For example, a balloon wouldn't have created a gouge in the terrain, especially as dramatic as the one described by Bill Brazel. Balloon structures are lightweight and flimsy, yet Bill Brazel couldn't break the "wood" or cut it with his knife.[11] Reporters and the public might have been satisfied with the balloon explanation, but it was clearly inadequate.

Many of those same newspapers also carried an announcement that the Army and the Navy were beginning a concentrated effort to suppress the stories of "flying saucers whizzing through the atmosphere." From that point on, the number of flying saucers reported in the media dropped off dramatically until they faded completely from the press by the end of July.

With that, the Roswell case and the flying disks in general slipped from the 1947 newspapers. Although discussion of the flying saucers would continue, many believed them to be a summer fad that would not return. The Roswell case, if mentioned at all, was generally believed to have been a hoax or the result of mistaken identity. It wouldn't be seriously discussed again for more than thirty years.

It wasn't until 1978 that the key was found by Stanton Friedman and Len Stringfield. Both interviewed Jesse Marcel in February and March of that year. Marcel provided them with the clues that led to Roswell in 1947.

An outgrowth of all this is the large number of people telling stories that seem to relate to the case. All of these stories, many of them unsubstantiated

---

[11]The point must be stressed because of the arguments that what fell on the Brazel ranch was a balloon and array train from Project Mogul. Bill Brazel said it looked like wood, but it wasn't wood. It was much stronger.

and uncorroborated, have been reported and investigated. Some are accepted as authentic, even when there are serious questions that have arisen. Unless these stories are examined carefully, they begin to undermine the credibility of the entire Roswell case.

One of those who came forward after seeing the Roswell segment broadcast on NBC's *Unsolved Mysteries* was Gerald Anderson.[12] Although Anderson was one of the first people I spoke to who claimed to have seen the bodies of the alien flight crew, I was suspicious of him.

Anderson spun a marvelous tale of seeing the crashed saucer, the dead aliens, and of communication, mentally, with the survivor. He told of being chased from the scene by nasty military officers and told of being threatened by those men. He told stories of huge military operations, aircraft landing on the highway, and archaeologists stealing and hiding samples of the strange metallic debris.

Under questioning and investigation, Anderson's tale unraveled. No corroboration was found, and Anderson was caught in lies and document forgery. A diary, offered as evidence, turned out to have been written, probably by Anderson himself, no earlier than 1974 and probably in 1990 or 1991. As the controversy surrounding his claim continued, he was exposed as having manufactured documents on his home computer.

Anderson's story was discarded by almost every UFO researcher. It was obvious to them that Anderson had invented the tale under the unconscious

---

[12]For the whole story of Gerald Anderson and his false representations, see Kevin D. Randle, *A History of UFO Crashes* (New York: Avon Books, 1995).

coaching of his proponents and the various magazine articles and television programs in the public arena.

Others who told stories about the case were believed but had no corroboration for their tales. Glenn Dennis, an embalmer who worked at the Ballard Funeral Home in July 1947, told of seeing strange metallic debris and hearing about the alien bodies from a nurse. Unlike Anderson's tale, proof that Dennis was in Roswell in 1947 as an embalmer and that he had told his tale long before 1978 was found. At least that much of Dennis's talk could be corroborated.

Unfortunately, much of what Dennis knew came from the nurse, who had been stationed briefly at the Roswell Army Air Field, and cannot be corroborated. According to Dennis, the nurse had seen the bodies, and she had been transferred from the base shortly after the event. Dennis had seen a drawing of the alien beings that she had made.

According to Dennis, she had been killed in an aircraft accident, along with four or five other Army nurses, shortly after the events in Roswell. A letter that he had sent to her came back to him marked DECEASED. Another nurse at the base told him about the plane wreck.

I searched *The New York Times Index* for the years 1947 to 1955 but found no story relating to the deaths of five Army nurses. Don Berliner, an aviation writer, searched the *Stars and Stripes*, a military newspaper published for the soldiers and sailors overseas, and found it contained no story of the aircraft accident. Army and Air Force records reveal no trace of a crash that killed five nurses. In other words, the story didn't check out. Dennis's nurse was not killed in an aircraft accident.

To make matters worse, there is absolutely no record that she ever existed. Dennis believed that he knew where she was from, but searches of state archives failed to produce a birth certificate, high school diploma, or any evidence that she had graduated from nursing school. Extensive searches of military files, morning reports, unit histories, and other assorted documentation failed to produce any results. If she ever existed, no documented evidence was found.

Few of the people assigned to the medical unit at the Roswell base in 1947 survive today. One of the men went on to become a dentist, but he did not remember Dennis's nurse. Of course, he worked in the dental clinic in 1947, and if she was only there a short time, he might not have gotten to know her well, if at all.

Only a few of the nurses assigned to the base in 1947 are still alive. Contrary to what has been reported by some, the records are easily available at the Army Record Center in St. Louis. Rosemary Brown (Rosemary McManus in 1947) said that she didn't remember a nurse by the name that Glenn Dennis supplied to researchers.

The lone exception to this is David Wagnon, whose record shows he was assigned to the base at Roswell but was not physically present in July 1947. He says that he remembers a nurse by the name given by Dennis, and his description of her seems to match that provided by Dennis. This is a bit of corroboration but of little use in the face of the lack of solid documentation.

Glenn Dennis tells a marvelous story and he appears to be sincere. Former Roswell Chief of Police L. M. Hall said that he remembered Glenn telling him about the visits by Sheriff George Wilcox and the threats by military officers. So another small piece of corroboration is added to the pile, which is outweighed by all the uncorroborated areas of the tale.

And that's where we are. These events took place fifty years ago. Many of the primary participants are dead. Apparently none of them left a written record. A few of them have left an oral tradition in the form of audio and videotapes.

The Roswell case is still wrapped in controversy—and, given the nature of the topic, that's not surprising. After all, we are talking about the crash of an alien spacecraft. Documentation is limited but does exist. What's more important, at the moment, is the eyewitness testimony. Naturally, that is wrapped in controversy as well.

When I reexamine the Roswell case, I often think of the leads that have disintegrated, the tall tales told by would-be eyewitnesses, and the misdirection of the so-called investigators. But in the end, I'm left with a number of disturbing questions. The answers don't lead to the mundane but to the extraterrestrial.

For example, I look at the newspaper articles published in late June and early July 1947 and see that all the experts are confused. Speculation about the nature of the flying disks runs from extraterrestrial craft to spots before the eyes of the witnesses. Governmental, military, and scientific spokesmen provided a wide range of excuses, explanations, and wild guesses about the flying saucers. It is clear from the newspapers that these experts are as bewildered as the rest of us.

Then, suddenly, on July 9, the military begins a campaign to "suppress" the idea that flying saucers "are whizzing through the atmosphere." Why do they care about the reports on July 9 when, prior to that, they had no clue? In fact, we can ask that question again today. Why does the government care what we believe if there is nothing to the stories of flying saucers?

As some of the disturbing evidence comes to light, as we learn more about those reporting their involvement in the Roswell case, I worry about the discrepancies. When dealing with testimony, it is only as reliable as those who give it. When their reputations are not as sterling as they were thought to be, or when their backgrounds fail to check out, or when the information they offer seems to have no basis in fact, it is very disturbing. It requires us to rethink our positions and look for additional flaws in the case. It suggests that we might be led down the garden path for some unknown reason.

And then I come back to Edwin Easley. He was who he said he was. He retired as a colonel. He tried to live up to the oath he took while helping me understand the events outside of Roswell. When I asked if the extraterrestrial path was the correct one, he told me it was. That is the one thing that I can't get past. For me, it is the one bit of evidence that I need because it is what he told me. Others might need more, but for me it says it all. Roswell was the result of an extraterrestrial craft coming to Earth.

CHAPTER 3

Project Sign, Project Saucer, Project Grudge, and the Early Days of the Investigation

THE CONSPIRACY OF SILENCE MIGHT HAVE BEEN born, not of an organized attempt to confound and obscure, but because of the confusion inside the military establishment in the beginning. It is clear from the documentation that has since been declassified and reviewed that military officers, scientists, and governmental officials had no clue about the nature of the flying saucers in 1947. Reporters asking for statements from highly placed sources were receiving a wide variety of speculations but no definitive answers.

Within days of the Kenneth Arnold sighting, those at the top of the military establishment were very interested in the flying disks. The real problem is that the whole question fell into a void that was created by the Army Air Forces splitting from the Army and by President Truman's consolidation of the various intelligence functions that had grown out of the Second World War.

The reorganization of the civilian departments of the military establishment was under way. The Department of War, which controlled the Army, and the Department of the Navy, responsible for the Navy and the Marine Corps, were combined into the Department of Defense. The Secretary of War became the Secretary of the Army and ranked under the Secretary of Defense. In 1947, James Forrestal was the Secretary of the Navy. He was replaced in that capacity so that he could assume the position of the first Secretary of Defense.

In 1947, the Under Secretary of War for Air ranked as the first civilian over the Army Air Forces. When the Air Force became a separate branch in September 1947, he became the Secretary of the Air Force in a Defense Department position equal in rank to his counterparts in civilian command of the other services.

On July 26, 1947, the National Security Act dismantled the old National Intelligence Authority, which had replaced the wartime Office of Strategic Services. Created were the National Security Council and the Central Intelligence Agency. The state of flux in the civilian intelligence community had been going on since the end of the Second World War. It seems, according to the documentation now available, that the communication among the various intelligence functions was no better in 1947 than it had been before passage of the act. In other words, as the flying saucers began to appear, the intelligence network needed was not available to process the information.

Rear Admiral Sidney Souers was appointed as the Director of Central Intelligence, replaced by Lieutenant General Hoyt S. Vandenberg in June 1946, who was replaced by Rear Admiral Roscoe Hillenkoetter in the spring of 1947. The succession of military directors in the head chair of the civilian intelligence community left it in a state of confusion as well.

This was the situation in June 1947 when Kenneth Arnold reported the bright objects flashing through the air "like saucers skipping across the pond."[1] The intelligence community, as well as the military services, took little notice of the sighting by a civilian pilot. Newspapers of the day gave it some play, but many of the stories were buried on inside pages days after Arnold's report.

But within days of Arnold's report, newspapers were filled with stories of the mysterious flying saucers. Every newspaper in the country was printing stories about national sightings, as well as those with a local flavor. Police officers and military pilots were also reporting flying disks. By the first of July, several impressive cases had been reported to military intelligence, including multiple-witness sightings that involved Army Air Forces pilots and civilian experts on guided missiles.

As the excitement grew and interest increased, it's clear that no one had any answers. Spokesmen began to make public statements. On July 3, an Army Air Forces spokesman said, "If some foreign power is

---

[1] This gave rise to the term "flying saucer." It didn't originally suggest a shape of the craft, but the motion of it.

sending flying disks over the United States, it is our responsibility to know about it and take proper action."[2]

A few days later, Captain Tom Brown told Donald Keyhoe, a retired Marine Corps major who would later become one of the key figures in UFO research, that "we can't ignore it. There are too many reliable pilots telling us the same story—flat, round objects able to outmaneuver ordinary planes, and faster than anything we have." Brown also told Keyhoe that some bases had been placed on alert to investigate appearances of the flying saucers. Someone told Keyhoe that orders had been issued to shoot down one of the flying disks if possible.

While the orders to shoot down a flying saucer have not been substantiated, there is no question that fighters were on alert all along the Pacific coast. Aircraft in Washington and Oregon were flying searches for the disks, some of them with loaded gun cameras. These aircraft were airborne on the long July 4 weekend.

At the same time, early July 1947, the commander of the Army Air Forces, General Carl Spaatz, was on vacation in the Pacific Northwest, where the first and the majority of the sightings had been made. It might have been a coincidence, but it is an amazing one. More likely, his fishing trip was a cover story for his examination of the situation there.

Equally interesting, the alerts and the airborne searches were publicly called off as of July 9. The newspapers reported that the "reports of flying saucers whizzing through the sky fell off today as the

[2]The statement was reported in various newspapers.

Army and the Navy began a concentrated campaign to stop the rumors."[3] After that point, interest in the phenomenon waned in the public sector.

But not so at the Pentagon. Ed Ruppelt, onetime head of Project Blue Book, the name of the Air Force UFO investigation for the majority of its life, wrote, "By the end of July 1947, the security lid was down tight. The few members of the press who did inquire about what the Air Force was doing got the same treatment that you would get today if you inquired about the number of thermonuclear weapons stockpiled in the U.S.'s atomic arsenal. No one, outside of a few high-ranking officers in the Pentagon, knew what the people in the barbed-wire-enclosed Quonset huts that housed the Air Technical Intelligence Center were thinking or doing."[4]

Public perception, then, was that the flying saucer craze of the summer had ended in July. If sightings were being made by anyone, they weren't even of local importance. A survey of the newspapers shows that reports by the public peaked around July 9 or 10 and then dropped off sharply. There was no indication that anyone in the government, either civilian or military, was still interested in flying saucers.

That, however, wasn't the case. Even as the number of sighting reports was reaching a peak, the government was attempting to learn more. An FBI document from the time states, "In passing, General Schulgen [Brigadier General George F. Schulgen,

---

[3]FLYING DISK REPORTS DROP OFF SHARPLY, the *Las Vegas Review-Journal*, July 9, 1947.

[4]Ed Ruppelt, *The Report on Unidentified Flying Objects* (New York: Ace Books, 1956).

chief of the Requirements Intelligence Branch of Army Air Force Intelligence] stated that an Air Force pilot who believed that he saw one of these objects was thoroughly interrogated by General Schulgen and scientists, as well as a psychologist, and the pilot was adamant in his claim that he saw a flying disk."

On July 9, the day the Army and Navy began a "campaign to stop the rumors," General Schulgen requested that FBI special agent S. W. Reynolds ask for FBI assistance in solving the problem of flying disks.[5] Colonel L. R. Forney, of what would later become the Defense Intelligence Agency, told Reynolds that the disks were not Army or Navy vehicles.

Confusion inside the military continued. Panic, according to Ruppelt, had swept through the halls of the Pentagon and the buildings at Wright Field. The theory that the flying disks might be some sort of new Soviet weapon, developed from captured German documents by captured German scientists and engineers, dominated the thinking.

It also became clear to those investigating flying saucers in late July that there was a strange silence from the men at the top. At the beginning of July, according to Ruppelt and others, there was a state of near panic. But, by the end of the month, there was nothing from the topside. Those inside the intelligence community not privy to all the information circulating at the highest levels could draw but a single conclusion. If those at the top were no longer interested in the flying disks, then they must know all about them. Further investigation would be a waste of time.

---

[5]The idea was that the FBI would investigate the backgrounds of those who reported flying saucers.

Dr. Michael Swords noted in "The Summer of 1947: UFOs and the U.S. Government at the Beginning"[6] that "the evidence for this can be found in documents released through Freedom of Information Act (FOIA) requests to the FBI. In a page probably attached to, and certainly related to, an FBI copy of an Air Force document dated July 30, 1947, a ranking USAF intelligence officer states unambiguously: 'Lack of topside inquiries, when compared to the prompt and demanding inquiries that have originated topside upon former events [such as the Swedish ghost rockets of 1946], give more than ordinary weight to the possibility that this is a domestic project, about which the President, etc., know.' "

At the same time, General Schulgen, trying to find out what was happening, was unhappy with the lack of information in his office. He decided to make a direct request to the Air Materiel Command, where the labs and resources to identify the saucers were housed. Accompanying the request was the first "Estimate of the Situation."[7] Although the study contained the specifics of sixteen cases, the body of the report mentioned eighteen. These were the best sightings reported as early as May 17, 1947, and as late as July 12. Five of the cases involved military pilots, including a Maxwell Field sighting by four pilots on June 28. Six of them involved civilian pilots, including the July 4 sighting near Emmett, Idaho, made by a United Airlines crew and most of the passengers.

---

[6]George Eberhart (ed.), *The Roswell Report* (Chicago: CUFOS, 1991).

[7]This should not be confused with a later "Estimate of the Situation" that was written in 1948 and was eventually sent to the Chief of Staff of the Air Force, General Hoyt S. Vandenberg.

The estimate contained the conclusions based on the information used to prepare it. It seemed that the officers did not think the flying saucers were much of a mystery. They believed they were mechanical aerial objects. They just didn't know whose, but based on the apparent lack of concern from the top, they believed that the disks had to be a highly classified U.S. project. No other conclusion made sense to them.

The response from Twining's AMC staff probably surprised those at the lower levels. Those below believed that the AMC would know all about the flying disks, yet in his response Twining was telling them that the phenomenon was something real and not visionary or fictitious. Not only that, Twining was telling them that his command didn't know what the flying disks were and that they should be investigated.

That had to be confusing. If the flying disks were a U.S. project, then the last thing anyone would have wanted would be an official investigation into them. Any investigation would be a threat to the security of the project. To end such an investigation, one of those on the inside of the secret would have to drop a hint to someone on the outside. If, for example, it was such a secret project that General Twining and the AMC were outside the loop, then another general, on the inside, could call Twining to tell him to drop the investigation. He wouldn't have to spill any details of the project, only tell Twining that it was something he didn't need to worry about. Twining would then end his inquiries, secure in the knowledge that the solution to the mystery was already known.

That, however, didn't happen. Instead, Twining suggested that a priority project, with a rating of 2A, be created to investigate the flying saucers. He wanted information found and reported to his office. The priority level of the new project also suggested that Twining wanted his answers quickly.

At that point, it seems that the gathering of intelligence data by the Army Air Forces as conducted by the military in 1947 was disorganized, inefficient, and confused. A review of the documents showed that interviews conducted with key witnesses, such as Kenneth Arnold, were not completed until weeks after their sightings, and then not all the questions were asked. To make it worse, the critical corroboration of the Arnold sighting by Fred Johnson was overlooked. In the "Estimate" sent up by General Schulgen, the dates of some reports are wrong, suggesting that only a superficial investigation had been conducted. It was clear that a coordinated effort to gather data had not been attempted, and the "not stated" entries in many of the cases showed that no one cared enough to reinterview witnesses to get proper answers.

Swords, commenting on this first "Estimate," wrote, "What explains this confident display of mediocrity? Although we are apparently not dealing with genius here, neither should we assume complete stupidity. This report was not put together with any greater intensity because the authors did not feel that it was necessary. They did not think that UFOs were any great mystery. It was obvious to them that UFOs were mechanical, aerial devices. Whose devices was still up in the air (so to speak), but the indications were fairly clear: despite assurances to the contrary, *they must be our own.* 'Lack of topside inquiries' made this the only reasonable conclusion in their eyes."

These men, who hadn't exactly shined during their investigation, had no burning passion to find the answers because they were convinced the answers already existed at the very top. Their estimate, according to Swords, was little more than a plea, asking, "Can we please quit this nonsense?"

Swords said that he believed the report was not forwarded to Twining until late August or early September of that year. Twining's response came on September 24, 1947. According to the documentation reviewed by Swords, the people at Wright Field and the Aircraft Laboratory Engineering Division (Wright Field's secret aeronautical engineering facility) added nothing to the discussion "except a sales pitch for a new project." That is a key point. They merely reviewed what Schulgen had sent to them and nothing more.

The original study had concluded that the UFOs were probably our own and we should quit chasing them. Logic dictated that Twining and the others would say exactly that. Quit chasing them. Instead, they were told that the UFOs weren't ours and not only to keep the investigation going, but there would be a new project under a new banner with a high priority attached to it. That was not an expected result.

This, then, was the beginning of Project Sign. According to Ed Ruppelt, the 2A priority was the second-highest priority possible. Only the top people at ATIC were assigned to the new project. This was a serious project designed to obtain specific answers to specific questions.

The mission of Project Sign, then, was to determine the nature of the flying saucers. According to Ruppelt, there were two schools of thought. One believed that the Soviets, using their captured German scientists, had developed the flying disks. ATIC technical analysts searched for data on the German projects in captured documents in the United States, and intelligence officers in Germany were doing the same there.

It became clear, however, that the second school of thought—that is, that the UFOs were not manufactured on Earth—began to take hold. No evidence was found that the Soviets had made some sort of technological breakthrough. Even if they had, it seemed unlikely that they would be flying their new craft over the United States. If one crashed, they would have just handed the breakthrough to our government.

The initial panic that had bubbled through the Pentagon during the summer of 1947 began to subside. Twining's suggestion for a project was accepted and implemented. That proved that the objects, whatever they were, did not belong to the United States. According to Ruppelt, by the end of 1947, the situation at ATIC had slipped back into routine.

There were, however, some interesting documents prepared. In a "Draft of Collection Memorandum,"[8] General Schulgen outlined what those working on Project Sign would be doing. It was a listing of intelligence data that would be valuable not only in determining what the flying disks were, but also in

---

[8]In military circles, a "Collection Memorandum" is a document that tells intelligence officers the specific types of information sought in an investigation. It is, in essence, a series of guidelines for the men and women doing the work.

discovering how they operated. The "Collection Memorandum" outlined the "essential elements of intelligence," or "the current intelligence requirements in the field of flying saucer type aircraft." That is, it was telling the field offices what information was desired by those at the top. It was a way of coordinating the collection of information to ensure that everyone was operating in the same fashion.

Project Sign was beginning to work in a coordinated fashion, collecting information to be forwarded to ATIC. The era of panic and confusion was ending by the late summer of 1947. The reason for that is probably no more complex than the passing of time. The pressure from the top for immediate answers had passed. The generals and the top civilians still needed the answers, but as the days mounted, it became clear that nothing new was going to happen. They could relax slightly.

Ruppelt wrote, "As 1947 drew to a close, the Air Force's Project Sign had outgrown its initial panic and had settled down to a routine operation. Every intelligence report dealing with the Germans' World War II aeronautical research had been studied to find out if the Russians could have developed any of the late German designs into flying saucers."[9] The conclusion was no. The flying saucers were not an extrapolation of German designs.

If they weren't Soviet, and there was no evidence they were, and if they weren't American, and all aspects of the U.S. government from the Department of Defense to the Department of States were denying they were secret U.S. projects, then what were they?

---

[9] Ruppelt, *The Report on Unidentified Flying Objects.*

If the flying saucers were real and if they weren't based on terrestrial technology, a new answer began to push to the front. The disks were obviously extra-terrestrial in origin.

The Air Force continued to investigate flying saucer sightings, assembling as much data as possible. In early January 1948, a National Guard pilot was killed chasing an object over Kentucky. Captain Thomas Mantell, after being alerted that something strange was hovering over the Godman Army Air Field, tried to catch it.

Mantell, flying an F-51, climbed toward the large object. According to the official accident investigation records, he climbed too high without proper oxygen equipment on his aircraft. Mantell apparently blacked out and his aircraft rolled over, entering a power dive. There was no evidence that Mantell ever regained consciousness. He was killed when his plane slammed into the ground on a farm in Kentucky.[10]

The Air Force would offer a series of conflicting explanations for the accident that made no sense at the time. While it is clear that Mantell was killed not by hostile action, but in an aircraft accident, the skyhook balloon he was chasing when he died would not be found for a number of years. That sort of secrecy, on the part of the Air Force, just added to the notion that something was being hidden. The conspiracy of silence kept the answer out of the hands of those outside the government.

In September 1948, ATIC produced another "Esti-

[10]Information on the Mantell case comes from the Project Blue Book files and a variety of other sources.

mate of the Situation," this one sent to the Pentagon. This was the "Estimate" that has become part of UFO folklore. Although originally classified top secret according to everyone, including Ruppelt, and eventually destroyed, the contents have leaked into the public arena. The conclusion of this "Estimate" was that flying saucers were of extraterrestrial origin.

Ruppelt again was the source of so much written about the "Estimate." CUFOS, with the help of FUFOR, obtained Ruppelt's personal files in 1994. Contained in them were earlier drafts of Ruppelt's book, *The Report on Unidentified Flying Objects*. Examination of those drafts provides some interesting insights into Project Sign and the now-infamous "Estimate."

Swords, writing in the *International UFO Reporter*, provided much of that information. To illustrate what had been left out of the book as published, he used italics to show the deleted material. That text as published was printed in a normal typeface.

In intelligence, if you have something to say about some vital problem you write a report that is known as an "Estimate of the Situation." A few days after the DC-3 was buzzed, the people at ATIC decided that the time had arrived to make an "Estimate of the Situation." The situation was UFO's; the estimate was that they were interplanetary!

It was a rather thick document with a black cover and it was printed on legal-sized paper. Stamped across the front were the words TOP SECRET.

It contained the Air Force's analysis of many of the incidents I have told you about plus many similar ones. All of them had come from scientists, pilots, and other equally credible observers, and each one was an unknown.

It concluded that UFO's were interplanetary. As documented proof, many unexplained sightings were quoted. The original UFO sighting by Kenneth Arnold; the series of sightings from the secret Air Force Test Center, MUROC AFB; the F-51 pilot's observation of a formation of spheres near Lake Mead; the report of an F-80 pilot who saw two round objects diving toward the ground near the Grand Canyon; and a report by the pilot of an Idaho National Guard T-6 trainer who saw a violently maneuvering black object.

As further documentation, the report quoted an interview with an Air Force major from Rapid City AFB (now Ellsworth AFB) who saw twelve UFO's flying a tight diamond formation. When he first saw them they were high but soon they went into a fantastically high-speed dive, leveled out, made a perfect formation turn, and climbed at a 30 to 40 degree angle, accelerating all the time. The UFO's were oval-shaped and brilliant yellowish-white.

Also included was one of the reports from the AEC's Los Alamos Laboratory. The incident occurred at 9:40 A.M. on September 23, 1948. A group of people were waiting for an airplane at the landing strip in Los Alamos when one of them noticed something glint in the sun. It was a flat, circular object, high in the northern sky. The appearance and relative size was the same as a dime held edgewise and slightly tipped, about fifty feet away.

The document pointed out that the reports hadn't actually started with the Arnold Incident. Belated reports from a weather observer in Richmond, Virginia, who observed a "silver disk" through his theodolite telescope; an F-47 pilot and three pilots in his formation who saw a "silvery flying wing"; and the English "ghost airplanes" that had been picked up on radar early in 1947 proved the point. Although reports on them were not received until after the Arnold sighting, these incidents had all taken place earlier.

When the estimate was completed, typed, and approved, it started up through channels to higher-command echelons. It drew considerable comment but no one stopped it on its way up.

General Vandenberg at the Pentagon eventually received the "Estimate" but was apparently less than impressed. At that point, according to Ruppelt, "it was batted back down. The general wouldn't buy interplanetary vehicles. The report lacked proof."

A group of military officers and civilian technical intelligence engineers was then called to the Pentagon to defend the "Estimate." According to the work done by Michael Swords, these were probably Lawrence H. Truettner, A. B. Deyarmond, and Alfred Loedding. Swords noted, parenthetically, that "Truettner and Deyarmond were the authors of the Project Sign report that contained many of these same cases and sympathies; Loedding was a frequent Pentagon liaison in 1947 and considered himself the 'civilian project leader' of Sign."

The military participants were probably the official project officer, Captain Robert Sneider, as well as Colonels Howard McCoy or William Clingerman, who would have had to sign off on the "Estimate."

Swords noted that the defense was unsuccessful, but not long after the visit to the Pentagon, everyone named was reassigned. Swords writes, "So great was the carnage that only the lowest grades in the project, civilian George Towles and Lieutenant H. W. Smith, were left to write the 1949 Project Grudge document about the same cases."

Swords pointed out that Donald Keyhoe had mentioned the existence of the "Estimate" a number of times and was told that it was a myth. According to Swords, "The famous *Armstrong Circle Theater* fiasco of 1958, where Keyhoe was cut off in midsentence, was partly due to the fact that he was about to mention this document."

After Vandenberg "batted" the report back down, after the staff was reduced, and after the fire went out of the investigation, Project Sign limped along. It was clear to everyone inside the military, particularly those who worked around ATIC, that Vandenberg was not a proponent of the extraterrestrial hypothesis. Those who supported the idea risked the wrath of the number-one man in the Air Force. They had just had a practical demonstration of that. If an officer was not smart enough to pick up the clues from what had just happened, then that officer's career could be severely limited.

Project Blue Book files show this to be the case. When Sign evolved into Project Grudge and then into Blue Book, a final report about Sign was written. Those inside Sign originally believed that UFOs were extraterrestrial until Vandenberg said he didn't find their reasoning adequate. Then those inside Sign—those who were left—decided that other answers must be the correct ones. UFOs, flying saucers, were not extraterrestrial.

A report, entitled "The Findings of Project Sign,"

was eventually written.[11] It outlined the motivation behind Project Sign, who the players were, and the results of their research. In the summary, it was noted that the data in the report were "derived from reports of 243 domestic and thirty (30) foreign incidents. Data from these incidents is being summarized, reproduced, and distributed to agencies and individuals cooperating in the analysis and evaluation . . . The data obtained in reports received are studied in relation to many factors, such as guided missile research research activity, weather and other atmospheric sounding balloon launchings, commercial and military aircraft flights, flights of migratory birds, and other considerations, to determine possible explanations for sightings."

The authors of the report wanted to make the situation clear. They wrote, "Based on the possibility that the objects are really unidentified and unconventional types of aircraft, a technical analysis is made of some of the reports to determine the aerodynamic, propulsion, and control features that would be required for the objects to perform as described in the reports. The objects sighted have been grouped into four classifications according to configuration:

"1. Flying disks, i.e., very low aspect ration aircraft.

"2. Torpedo or cigar-shaped bodies with no wings or fins visible in flight.

"3. Spherical or balloon-shaped objects.

"4. Balls of light."

The authors reported that "Approximately twenty percent of the incidents have been identified as con-

---

[11]The report was put together at the end of Project Sign.

ventional aerial objects to the satisfaction of personnel assigned to Project 'Sign' in this Command. It is expected that a study of the incidents in relation to weather and other atmospheric sounding balloons will provide solutions for an equivalent number . . . Elimination of incidents with reasonably satisfactory explanations will clarify the problem presented by a project of this nature.

"The possibility that some of the incidents may represent technical developments far in advance of knowledge available to engineers and scientists of this country has been considered. No facts are available to personnel at this Command that will permit an objective assessment of this possibility. All information so far presented on the possible existence of space ships from another planet or of aircraft propelled by an advanced type of atomic power plant have been largely conjecture."

They provided a number of recommendations, writing, "Future activity on this project should be carried on at the minimum level necessary to record, summarize, and evaluate the data received on future reports and to complete the specialized investigations now in progress." They then added a phrase that too many UFO researchers had overlooked in the past. They wrote, "When and if a sufficient number of incidents are solved to indicate that these sightings do not represent a threat to the security of the nation, the assignment of special project status to the activity could be terminated."

This is a theme that would be repeated in one official UFO investigation after another. The investigators would mention this aspect again and again. Each of the investigations, from Sign forward, had national security as its main concern. If national security wasn't threatened, then the question of the reality of the sightings became unimportant. And as time passed, it became more likely to all of those military investigators that no threat to the nation was posed.

The authors also wrote, "Reporting agencies should be impressed with the necessity for getting more factual evidence on sightings, such as photographs, physical evidence, radar sightings, and data on size and shape."

The conclusions of the report are interesting. "No definite and conclusive evidence is yet available that would prove or disprove the existence of these unidentified objects as real aircraft of unknown and unconventional configuration. It is unlikely that positive proof of their existence will be obtained without examination of the remains of crashed objects. Proof of the nonexistence is equally impossible to obtain unless a reasonable and convincing explanation is determined for each incident."

They then wrote, "Many sightings by qualified and apparently reliable witnesses have been reported. However, each incident has unsatisfactory features, such as shortness of time under observation, distance from observer, vagueness of description or photographs, inconsistencies between individual observers, and lack of descriptive data, that prevents conclusions being drawn."

This one paragraph would also become important to understanding the UFO investigations of the future. Time and again those in the government would suggest that there were no good photographs, that eyewitness testimony was unreliable, and that the sightings were of nothing more spectacular than a fuzzy object in the distance. Those arguing against the reality of the phenomenon would often make these same claims.

The reason for the recommendation for a continuation of the project had nothing to do with research into the phenomenon. The authors wrote, "Evaluation of reports of unidentified objects is a necessary activity of military intelligence agencies. Such sightings are inevitable, and under wartime conditions rapid and convincing solutions of such occurrences are necessary to maintain morale of military and civilian personnel. In this respect, it is considered that the establishment of procedures and training of personnel is in itself worth the effort expended on this project."

About a year earlier, the personnel assigned to Sign had concluded that flying saucers were extraterrestrial. Now, using the same cases and the same evidence, those who survived at ATIC were claiming that there was nothing to the UFO phenomenon. More importantly, they were saying there was no threat to national security, but that the project should be continued for training proposes.

Attached to "The Findings of Project Sign" as Appendix D was a report that seemed to have been inspired by Brigadier General Putt. In a letter (which is basically Appendix D), Dr. James E. Lipp, an aeronautical engineer and a division head at the Rand Corporation, speculated about the extraterrestrial hypothesis.

It's clear from his letter that he believed that the craft would be coming from inside the Solar System. He pointed specifically to Mars, ignoring Venus. The state of astronomical thought at that time—that is,

1947—was that both planets might support intelligent life, though most believed Mars the more likely candidate.

Looking at that from today's perspective, with probes having landed on both planets, we now realize that neither supports any type of intelligent life. If flying saucers are real, then they come from outside the Solar System.

In the text of his letter, however, Lipp made a point that has been noted since by various members of the UFO community. Lipp wrote, "One other hypothesis needs to be discussed. It is that the Martians have kept a long-term routine watch on Earth and have been alarmed by the sight of our A-bomb shots as evidence that we are warlike and on the threshold of space travel. (Venus is eliminated here because her cloudy atmosphere would make such a survey impractical.) The first flying objects were sighted in the spring of 1947 after a total of five atomic bomb explosions, i.e., Alamogordo, Hiroshima, Nagasaki, Crossroads A, and Crossroads B. Of these, the first two were in positions to be seen from Mars, the third was very doubtful (at the edge of the Earth's disc in daylight), and the last two were on the wrong side of Earth."

Lipp then explained why he didn't believe this to be significant, suggesting that it would mean a long-term surveillance of the Earth. While our astronomers studied Mars, it was not with the intensity suggested if they had seen the atomic blasts and then began a close survey. He wrote, "The weakest point in the hypothesis is that a continual, defensive watch of Earth for long periods of time (possibly thousands of years) would be dull sport . . ."

Lipp's suggestion that our atomic research some-how caused the flying saucers to appear is interesting but probably wrong. Once the planets in the Solar System are eliminated as the home worlds of the space travelers, then we must postulate a source out-side of the Solar System. The distances are just too vast. Light travels only so fast, and even if the beings in another solar system could detect the atomic deto-nations on our planet, it would take more than four years for the light to reach them. That is, if they happen to live on a planet orbiting the closest star.

No, it is an interesting idea but one that seems to have no merit. Unless those beings on those planets in those other systems have been watching us for years. Then it would seem the survey craft would be closer and their response quicker than two years. The detonations of the atomic bombs probably had no causal relationship with the flying saucers.

Lipp concluded, "Although visits from outer space are believed to be possible, they are believed to be very improbable. In particular, the actions attributed to the 'flying objects' reported during 1947 and 1948 seem inconsistent with the requirements for space travel."

Lipp's letter only tells us that the extraterrestrial hypothesis was being considered by some inside Project Sign, ATIC, and the Air Force. However, it also tells us how opinions had changed after the "Es-timate of the Situation" had been "batted" back down. Find out what is going on, sort of, and let us know.

Many conclusions can be drawn from this. It can be suggested that the military had begun an active campaign to suppress information about the flying saucers. It can be said that a conspiracy of silence developed in those first days of July 1947. The newspaper reports that the Army and Navy had begun a campaign to suppress the stories certainly leads to that conclusion.

Ruppelt reinforced the idea to a limited extent in his book. He wrote, "Officially the military uses the term 'flying saucer' on only two occasions. First in an explanatory sense, as when briefing people who are unacquainted with the term 'UFO': 'UFO—you know—flying saucers.' And second in a derogatory sense, for purposes of ridicule, as when it is observed, 'He says he saw a flying saucer.' "

But as we examine the documentation from Project Sign, it seems that no actual conspiracy existed after someone decided that flying saucers posed no threat to the security of the United States. Once they were satisfied that there was no threat to the United States, interest waned. And once Vandenberg had swatted those who had the audacity to suggest that flying saucers were extraterrestrial, then the last of the fire went out of the investigation, at least at the lower levels.

It could be suggested, then, that those at the top, those who everyone suspected of having the answers to the nature of the flying saucers, did, in fact, have those answers. And they wanted no one else to find them. A vital, energized investigation might stumble across the truth. If they were looking in the right area—that is, the extraterrestrial hypothesis—then they might find the truth. Stop the search and the truth could be protected.

The documentation suggests that the failure to find the truth was just a case of incompetence and bungling, but we must look beyond it. The clue is in the "Estimate of the Situation." If the document was so poorly drawn, if the conclusions didn't hold up, why order it destroyed? There is nothing of value in it. And why deny its existence at all?

No, what the facts show, what the documents show, and what the actions of the men at the top show is that the conspiracy of silence was born in the summer of 1947, and it was operated from the very top. Threats to the silence were eliminated ruthlessly. Those who didn't want to see their careers ended had to pick up the clues. When the Chief of Staff of the Air Force suggests that your report is in error, you had better listen. And when those summoned to Washington to defend that report find themselves looking for new jobs, the message is unmistakable. No one is to talk about flying saucers in a positive light. Those who see flying saucers are drunk or crazy and those who believe in them are uneducated and quickly out of a job.

That was the attitude that existed when the code name of the UFO project was compromised and the name was changed to Grudge. It might have been a coincidence. But that seems unlikely. The Air Force had been trying to keep the lid down since the summer of 1947.

Proof of this is seen in some of the earliest of the magazines and books about flying saucers. All talked of the military's Project Saucer. This was the public name for Project Sign. Everyone seemed to know that an investigation existed, but they didn't know the proper name, nor could they track the extent of that investigation.

After the true name leaked into the press, apparently sometime in 1949, the name was changed to Grudge, but the project still had a 2A priority. That is interesting because, after Vandenberg had "batted back" the 1948 "Estimate," everyone was recommending that the project be reduced in scope and importance.

In a Project Sign report prepared in February 1949, it was recommended that "Future activity on this project should be carried on at the minimum level necessary to record, summarize, and evaluate the data received on future reports and to complete the specialized investigations now in progress. When and if sufficient number of incidents are solved to indicate that these sightings do not represent a threat to the security of the nation, the assignment of special project status to the activity could be terminated. Future investigations of reports would then be handled on a routine basis like any other intelligence work."

It was also recommended that "Reporting agencies should be impressed with the necessity for getting more factual evidence on sightings . . . Personnel sighting such objects should engage the assistance of others, when possible, to get more definite data . . ."

The report concluded "No definite and conclusive evidence is yet available that would prove or disprove the existence of these unidentified objects as real aircraft of unknown and unconventional configuration. It is unlikely that positive proof of their existence will be obtained without examination of the remains of crashed objects . . ."

That would seem to suggest that Roswell did not represent the crash of an extraterrestrial craft. Who would be more likely to know about such an event than those involved in the investigation of the flying saucers? What it actually demonstrates is the extent of the conspiracy of silence. Those in the trenches, conducting the investigations, were not privy to all the data held at the top. Military security regulations demanded that the Roswell crash information be compartmentalized so that the men working on Project Sign were unaware of its existence.

How else to explain the appalling lack of any information about Roswell in the Project Blue Book files? The only reference to Roswell in the Project Blue Book files is a single mention in a short clipping[12] contained in a file that has nothing to do with the Roswell events. It is clear that the military investigators in that time frame were collecting data from the newspapers. Since the military was heavily involved in the Roswell case, and the sources of the information were military officers, there should have been a file. There is not.

And even when it seems that everyone in the Air Force, from the top on down, believed that the flying saucer project should be reduced in scope, if not eliminated altogether, it continued at a high priority. In the Sign report of February 1949, there is a page that notes the title of the project is now Grudge, the authority for it is "Hq, USAF, Deputy Chief of Staff, Materiel, Washington 25, D.C., dated 30 Dec. 1947." The project retained its 2A priority, and the purpose was "To collect, collate, evaluate, and interpret data obtained relative to the sighting of unidentified flying objects in the atmosphere which may have importance on the national security, and to control and effect distribution of all objective information as re-

---

[12]The clipping was in a file that related to a case in Boise, Idaho, on July 10, 1947, and had no relation to the Roswell case.

quested to interested governmental agencies and contractors."

That sounded good, but it wasn't the case. According to Ruppelt, "Everything was being evaluated on the premise that UFO's couldn't exist. No matter what you hear, don't believe it."

In August 1949, another report was issued and again recommended "That the investigation and study of reports of unidentified flying objects be reduced in scope." Interestingly, the authors of the report suggested "That psychological Warfare Division and other governmental agencies interested in psychological warfare be informed of the results of this study."

Just a few months later, on December 27, 1949, it was announced that Project Grudge had been closed. The final report would be available to the press. It was a large document, hundreds of pages long and filled with the type of jargon that identified it as a military report.

The "Grudge Report," as it became known, studied 237 of the best sighting reports. J. Allen Hynek and his staff were able to explain some of them as astronomical phenomena. The Air Force Air Weather Service and the Cambridge Research laboratory had been able to reduce the number of unexplained sightings. Weather balloons and huge Skyhook research balloons accounted for some sightings, including that of Thomas Mantell.

Captain A. C. Trakowski[13] from the Cambridge facility also reviewed the records of then-classified Project Mogul. Reviewing the data provided in the

---

[13]This is the same Captain A. C. Trakowski who was part of the research team in New Mexico that made up the military end of Project Mogul.

sighting reports, Trakowski found none that could be explained by the project.

When all the sightings had been carefully studied, the "Grudge Report" explained all but 23 percent. In 23 percent of the sightings, no explanation was found. The Psychology Branch of the Air Force's Aeromedical Laboratory took the final shot at eliminating that 23 percent.

The psychologists wrote, "There are sufficient psychological explanations for the reports of unidentified objects to provide plausible explanations for reports not otherwise explainable . . . [some witnesses] have spots before their eyes."

Ruppelt elaborated in his book, writing, "They pointed out that some people are just plain nuts."

Ruppelt noted that the media grabbed the appendix labeled "Summary of the Evaluation of Remaining Reports." After reading it and finding it impossible to believe, the media didn't report on the findings of Grudge. Ruppelt elaborated by interviewing a longtime Washington correspondent, writing, "He said the report had been quite impressive, but only in its ambiguousness, illogical reasoning, and very apparent effort to write off all UFO reports at any cost. He, personally, thought it was a poor attempt to put out a 'fake' report, full of misleading information, to cover up the real story. Others, he told me, just plainly and simply didn't know what to think—they were confused."

The final conclusions of Grudge were:

1. Evaluation of reports of unidentified flying objects constitute no direct threat to the national security of the United States.

2. Reports of unidentified flying objects are the result of:
   a. A mild form of mass hysteria, or "war nerves."
   b. Individuals who fabricate such reports to perpetuate a hoax or seek publicity.
   c. Psychological persons.
   d. Misidentification of various conventional objects.

Ruppelt seemed puzzled by this situation. After all, he had, on orders from the highest levels of the Air Force, reevaluated the UFO project. He knew that there was no break in the investigation of the objects, yet here was this confusing report. Why would the Air Force issue such a report, unless it was just another example of the conspiracy of silence at work?

In September 1951, after the announced closing of Grudge and claims that no UFO investigation was in progress, Major General C. B. Cabell asked Lieutenant Jerry Cummings what was happening with the "flying saucers." Told "Not much," he ordered an overhaul of the system.

Cabell's question was prompted by the investigation of the series of sightings that came from Lubbock, Texas. In August 1951, professors at Texas Tech saw strange lights in the night sky. Over the next several weeks, dozens would see the lights as they flew over not only Lubbock but a number of West Texas towns. With that, the UFO project would be back on track.

CHAPTER 4

Anatomy of an Investigation: The Lubbock Lights

ALTHOUGH THE CASE BECAME IDENTIFIED WITH Lubbock, Texas, the first sighting was made in Albuquerque, New Mexico, in the early evening of August 25, 1951. A man and his wife (unidentified in the Project Blue Book files) watched a huge "wing-shaped" UFO with blue lights on the trailing edge as it passed over the outskirts of the city. Because the craft was only at 800 to 1,000 feet, the man, an employee of the Atomic Energy Commission, got a very good look at it. He saw the "wing" was sharply swept back, about one and a half times the size of the B-36 (the largest American bomber), with dark bands running from the front to the back and softly glowing blue-green lights. The object disappeared in seconds.

Air Force officers at Kirtland Air Force Base in Albuquerque investigated. They found that a commercial airliner and an Air Force B-25 were in the area but not in a position to be seen by the witnesses. Besides, the witnesses' description didn't fit either of those aircraft. The Air Force investigators were concerned because the man held a very high-level security clearance that made it "highly unlikely" he would be participating in any sort of a hoax.

Not long after the Albuquerque sighting, several college professors, while sitting on a porch in Lubbock,[1] saw a formation of lights sweep overhead. The lights were in sight for only three or four seconds and none of the men managed to get a very clear look at them. Air Force investigators would later say that sightings of a short duration are virtually useless because everything happens too fast. The human eye and brain do not have time to record the event.

The professors, W. L. Ducker, A. G. Oberg, and W. I. Robinson, were upset that they had not seen more. They discussed what to do if the lights should reappear. Before the night was over, they had their chance and made a series of quick and well-coordinated observations.

The lights were softly glowing bluish objects in a loose formation. The first group, they believed, had been in a more rigid and more structured formation than later groups.

Jay Harris, the managing editor of the *Lubbock Avalanche*, first learned of the lights when Ducker called the news desk to tell of the sighting. Harris wasn't interested at first, but Ducker convinced him that it was important. Ducker wanted a story written so that others who might have seen the lights could be

-----
[1] Information came from the Project Blue Book files, various other published sources, and personal interviews conducted with the main participants.

found and comparisons with their information could be made. Harris finally agreed, but only if the newspaper could print Ducker's name. Ducker didn't like that condition and refused.

But a few minutes later, Ducker called back and said that Harris could print his name and the names of Oberg and Robinson. The only condition was that Harris would have to get permission from the Texas Tech public relations department first.

There were at least four others who saw the lights on that first night. Mrs. Earl Mediock, Mrs. F. A. Rogers, Mrs. R. A. Rogers,[2] and Professor Carl Henninger all reported seeing the lights at 9:10 P.M. That was the first flight described by the professors.

Joe Bryant of Brownsfield, Texas, said that he also saw the lights on the night of August 25. According to him, he was sitting in his backyard when a group of the lights flew overhead. He said there was "kind of a glow, a little bigger than a star." A short time later, a second group of lights appeared. Neither group was in any kind of regular formation.

Bryant saw a third flight, but instead of flying over the house, this time the lights dropped down and circled the building. Now he could see the object quite clearly. They were birds. One of them chirped and Bryant recognized them as "plover." The next day, as he read the account of the lights in the newspaper, Bryant realized that if he hadn't identified the lights as birds, he would have been as fooled as the professors.

Over the next two weeks, the professors saw the

---

[2] All the women were identified using their married names, a convention of the times.

lights on several occasions but were unable to obtain any useful data. Joined by Grayson Meade, E. R. Hienaman, and J. P. Brand, they equipped two teams with two-way radios, measured a baseline from the location of the original sightings, and sent the teams out to watch. They hoped that sightings along the baseline would provide them with enough information to allow triangulation. They hoped to determine the size of the lights, altitude, and speed.

They did manage to make a few observations. The lights traveled through about 90 degrees of sky in a matter of seconds. They normally appeared 45 degrees above the horizon and disappeared about 45 degrees above the opposite horizon. During the first observation, the lights had been in a roughly semicircular formation. In subsequent sightings, no regular pattern was noticed.

None of the teams ever made a sighting, though on one or two occasions, the wives of the men said they had seen the lights while the men were at the baseline. That would suggest that the lights were much lower than the professors had originally thought.

On August 31, the case took a radical turn. A nineteen-year-old amateur photographer, Carl Hart, Jr., managed to take five pictures of the lights as they flew over his house. Because it was hot that night, he had pushed his bed close to the window and was looking out and up. He said, "I liked to sleep with the windows open with my head stuck out the window—and there they were." Knowing that they had returned on several occasions from having read the articles in the newspaper, Hart grabbed his 35mm camera, set the shutter at f-3.5, and went outside.

A few minutes later, the lights flew over a second time and Hart took two photographs of them. Not long after that, another group of lights appeared, and Hart took three additional pictures.

Jay Harris, the newspaper editor who had spoken to Ducker on the first night, learned of the pictures when a photographer who worked for the newspaper called to tell him that Hart had just been to his studio to develop the film. Harris, reluctant as ever, suggested that Hart should bring the pictures to the newspaper office.

Harris and the newspaper's head photographer, William Hams, feared a hoax. Harris, after seeing the photos, called Hart a number of times and bluntly asked the young man if he had faked them.

Hart replied that he hadn't faked anything, that he had photographed something as it flew over his house. Hart didn't really care what Harris thought. He didn't care about payment of the pictures either, though he eventually received about ten dollars for them from the newspaper. Later the pictures were printed in dozens of magazines and books, but Hart rarely received any payment for them. He had failed to have any of the pictures copyrighted.

"Advice from a friend and professional journalist at the time was that if [I] copyright them, somebody's going to think [I] faked them and [was] trying to make money out of them," Hart told me. "I was interested in that part of it [proving the pictures authentic] and didn't do it [copyright them]."

Harris later decided to put the photos on the news wire, but before he did, he called Hart one more time. This time Harris warned Hart that if he found out the pictures were faked, there would be grave consequences. Once the photographs went out on the wire, nationwide, Hart's problems would be far worse if he was lying about them. Hart insisted the pictures were authentic. There was no fraud.

Hams, however, decided that he was going to try to duplicate Hart's pictures. By doing that, Hams believed he might be able to figure out exactly what they showed or, at the very least, how Hart had gotten them. He took a Speed Graphic camera loaded with a tungsten ASA 80 film and a GE #22 flashbulb in a concentrating reflector to the roof of the *Avalanche* building. It was the same equipment that he used to photograph night football games at the local high schools and college.

Hams waited but saw nothing other than a flight of migratory birds. They were visible in the glow of the sodium vapor lights on the street five or six floors below him. They flew in a ragged V-formation, and he could see them dimly outlined against the deeper black of the night sky. He was surprised because they were so quiet. Ducks and geese, as they flew, could be heard squawking.

When Hams developed the film, he found an image that was so weak that he couldn't print it. He repeated the experiment on another occasion and failed again. From his own experience, he was convinced that Hart could not have photographed birds under any circumstances.

This became one of the most important aspects of the Lubbock case. Here was physical evidence that could be seen and tested. Measurements and studies of the photos could be made, and professionals could attempt to duplicate them. Hams and the photography staff at the newspaper could find no evidence of a hoax. They believed that if Hart faked the pictures, he was wasting his time in college. Clearly, he was the best photographer in the area.

Hart continued to insist that he had not faked them. In fact, he told me, "I heard some unofficial things that came out later . . . about [how] they thought I had faked them somehow or another."

In September 1951, the Air Force began the official investigation of the Lubbock Lights. The Albuquerque sighting was checked by the intelligence officer from Kirtland AFB. The intelligence officer made several visits to the house of the witnesses and asked hundreds of questions during his interrogation. The witness gave him a drawing of the object, which was forwarded to Wright-Patterson AFB. After several weeks and partly because of the reliability of the witness, the sighting was listed as "unidentified." That is the way it was carried until the end of the official Air Force investigation in 1969.

In Lubbock, quite a bit of time was spent on the photographs taken by Hart. Although the official file contains the results of other aspects of the investigation, the majority of the paperwork covers the photographs. Officers, including Lieutenant John Farley and Special Agent Howard N. Bossert from Reese AFB, just outside of Lubbock, were dispatched a number of times with questions for Hart. Lieutenant (later Captain) Ed Ruppelt even made a trip into Lubbock to conduct his own investigation into the lights and to interview Hart himself. The negatives were examined by a variety of military and civilian experts at photo labs at Wright-Patterson.

On September 20, 1951, Bossert and Farley interviewed Hart at his home and asked for the negatives.

Hart could only find four of the five. He turned these over to the military for analysis. Bossert's initial report, dated October 8, 1951, was sent to OSI headquarters in Washington, D.C. Copies were also sent to the commanding general of the Air Material Command and to the commanding officer at Reese AFB.

Between November 6 and November 9, another investigation of the Lubbock Lights was conducted. Ruppelt and Bossert again interviewed Hart at his home and were told the same story that Hart had told the others. "Hart's story could not be 'picked apart' because it was entirely logical," the official report states. "He [Hart] was questioned on why he did certain things and his answers were all logical, concise, and without hesitation."

Ruppelt also interviewed the college professors. They provided signed statements about what they had seen and done. In addition to recounting several flights, they mentioned an unusual event on September 2. While the flight passed directly overhead, as had the others, and was made up of fifteen to thirty lights, one professor noticed an irregularly shaped yellow light at the rear of the formation.

A technical report, "WCEFP-2-4, Physics Branch Sensitometry Unit," dated 29 November 1951, revealed nothing about the sightings other than that the lights photographed by Hart were individual lights and not part of a larger dark object. The lights moved in relation to one another in the formation. The Air Force physicists did estimate that if the lights had been attached to an object one mile from the camera [or at 5,280 feet of altitude], it would have been 310 feet in diameter. If closer, it would be smaller, and if farther away, it would be larger.

Hart had shown military investigators his camera and the report said that the type of lens used was a 50mm f/3.5 Anastor Kodak lens. The film was Plus X and "was exposed for 1/10 sec with lens aperture wide open . . . the film was processed in Panthermic 777 developer for 15 min."

The report concluded, "There is relative movement within the formation of spots, so that there are not lights on a fixed object." The important statement, however, came from the final conclusion. "The pattern of spot brightness is such as to prove conclusively that all 3 frames [negatives]—5, 7, and 8—were exposed to the same object pattern of spots."

An examination of the photographs and the negatives turned up no evidence that Hart was lying. The sequence of shots, as he described them, was corroborated by the negatives. Hart's story was hanging together.

Ruppelt's interview in November was not the last conducted. On December 2, Hart was questioned yet again. This time, according to the documentation, Hart was given his rights. These were explained to him as "The rights of a private citizen under the Fifth Amendment of the Constitution of the United States . . . he acknowledged his understanding of such rights."[3]

According to the OSI report, Hart was interviewed in private and was asked for a written statement. The statement said, "On August 50, 1951 [typographical error in letter of transmittal and not original statement] at about 11:30 P.M. took pictures of strange

---

[3]This was the 1951 equivalent of reading Hart his Miranda rights. It was a ploy to intimidate him.

objects passing overhead from north to south. I saw three separate groups of objects. Two pictures are of the second group. Three are of the third group. The last negative was not found and is not in my possession."

(I had hoped that a search of the newspaper office file on the Lubbock Light case might produce a print of the missing picture. Unfortunately, some so-called UFO researcher beat me to Lubbock and stole the whole file. I failed to locate it.)

Evidently the military hoped they could break Hart's story, which was a continuing obstacle to the bird explanation. If a professional photographer could not get a picture of birds at night, how had a teenaged amateur done it? The obvious answer was that Hart had not photographed birds. If so, that meant the objects he had photographed were unidentified.

Documentation in the files reveals that an extraordinary effort went into investigating the Lubbock case. Murray S. Sturgis, the air adjutant at Carswell AFB [Fort Worth, Texas] wrote, "Reference OSI Letter 24-0 dated 7 September 1951 to OSI, Hq USAF, concerning unidentified aircraft at Lubbock, Texas. Request A-2 [air intelligence officer] forward by air mail as expeditiously as possible form 112 on subjects Carl Hart, Jr., Mrs. Tom Tilson, Mrs. M. G. Bethard; if possible forward by air mail original negatives of photographs Carl Hart, Jr., is stated to have taken . . ."

The "Report of Investigation" was written by Howard N. Bossart. He said that he, along with Lieutenant John Farley, interviewed Hart at his home. Bossart reported that he found Hart to be "a very intelligent young man, very interested in photography, which is a hobby. He seemed sincere in his efforts to relate all incidents to the best of his ability."

Bossert learned that Hart had also seen the lights on September 1, but he hadn't photographed them. Although they looked the same, he thought they were at a greater altitude and were in a single line. They flew from the northwest to the southeast.

Bossert's report also covered a sighting in Matador, Texas, by Mrs. Tom Tilson on August 31. The pear-shaped object sighted was aluminum or silver in color and had a port or door at the point where the object began to taper toward the smaller end. There was only the single object, moving through the sky without sound, exhaust, or smoke. The object tilted, climbed rapidly, and disappeared in a matter of seconds.

Tilson's daughter, Mrs. Berthard (the only name provided in the Project Blue Book file), stopped the car and got out. She thought the object was about forty-five feet in diameter and said that it wasn't a balloon, jet, or any other conventional object.

The sighting, although grouped with the Lubbock Lights, seems to be related to the Lubbock case only by timing and location. Matador, Texas, is not far from Lubbock. The Matador sighting is still carried in the Blue Book files as "unidentified."

By the end of the year, the Air Force investigation began to wind down. Investigators had spoken to all the witnesses several times, concentrating on Hart. After they interviewed Bryant, the man who had seen the "plover," and another West Texan, T. E. Snider, who reported he had seen the lights but identified them as ducks, the official answer became birds.

In still another, later report, investigators wrote, "It was concluded that birds, with streetlights reflecting from them, were the probable cause of these sightings. The angular velocity was less. In all instances the witnesses were located in an area where their eyes were dark-adapted, thus making the objects appear brighter."

Of course, that conclusion overlooked the fact that there are no migratory birds in the Lubbock area at that time of year. Loren Smith at Texas Tech told me that there are ducks that fly in V-formations in the area in late August. They just aren't migratory.

The Glossy Iris,[4] for example, inhabits West Texas and does fly in the proper formation. The problem, however, is that the species is reddish-maroon and has no white to reflect the streetlights. The Glossy Iris is not a satisfactory explanation. In fact, there are no birds in West Texas that are satisfactory as an explanation for all the sightings.

The report continued, "Mr. Hart, when taking his pictures, had to do so by 'panning' his camera. Panning is quite difficult, and the relative high degree of success of this photographer is further indication that the angular velocity of the objects was not as high as estimated."

The report concluded, "The kind of birds responsible for this sighting is not known, but it is highly probable that they were ducks or plover. Since plover

---

[4]This is the only species that flies in the proper formations in West Texas at the time the photographs were taken, according to the wildlife specialists at Texas Tech.

CONSPIRACY OF SILENCE — 93

do not usually fly in formations of more than six or seven, ducks become the more probable . . ."

Such a solution might be the proper explanation for some of the sightings, especially those by Bryant and Snider. There might be other reports from the Lubbock area that are explained by the birds, but certainly not all of them. Each sighting should be investigated as a separate event because each was a separate event. Their relation to one another is simply the timing and the location. A solution for one set of sightings does not translate into a solution for the others.

The photographs taken by Hart show this. Clearly, the pictures taken by him do not show birds. Experimentation by professionals was unable to duplicate the photos taken by Hart. Project Blue Book records, however, list the case as solved—as birds.

But that wasn't the last of it. In June 1952, Dr. Donald H. Menzel, a Harvard astronomer, published an article in *Look* claiming that the Lubbock Lights are not birds but reflections of the city's lights . . . "mirages caused by atmospheric conditions known as 'temperature inversion.' "

Menzel, using chemicals, was able to reproduce what he claimed were the Lubbock Lights in his laboratory. His pictures, taken of stationary objects in his lab, showed lights in a similar formation, but the lights were more diffused than those taken by Hart.

Dr. E. F. George, one of the scientists who had seen the lights, disagreed with Menzel. He said, "I don't believe what I saw was a reflection from streetlights."

Ducker, who was involved in the original sightings, said that he and the others had never tried to say what it was they had seen, but only that they had seen something. He pointed out that a reproduction in the laboratory would not mean that the original sightings were "trickery."

Ruppelt examined the whole of the Lubbock Lights case from a unique perspective in his book. As one of the Air Force officers involved in the investigation, he spoke to the individuals within weeks of the events. He was on the scene.

Of the photographs by Hart, Ruppelt wrote, ". . . the investigation ended at a blank wall. My official conclusion, which was later given to the press, was that, 'The photos were never proven to be a hoax but neither were they proven to be genuine.' There is no definite answer."

Of the other sightings, Ruppelt wrote, "Personally I thought that the professor's lights might have been some kind of bird reflecting from mercury-vapor streetlights, but I was wrong. They weren't birds, they weren't refracted light, but they weren't spaceships. The lights that the professors saw—the backbone of the Lubbock Light series—have been positively identified as a very commonplace and easily explainable natural phenomena."

Ruppelt then explained that he couldn't offer the final answer because it came from a professor who would be easily identified if the solution was published. Ruppelt said that it made perfect sense to him, but he was going to honor his promise to the scientist.

In the years before his death, Ruppelt received letters from UFO investigators who wanted to know the final answer. Ruppelt always answered the same way. He would not violate the confidence. But Ruppelt left notes, and in those notes and documents, now housed at the J. Allen Hynek Center for UFO Studies, is Ruppelt's answer. The professors saw fireflies.

Ruppelt's explanation is as ridiculous as the "birds" explanation. It does not explain the situation, nor does it explain the photographs. And it doesn't explain why the professors only saw the fireflies at the end of August and the beginning of September 1951. Did the conditions around Lubbock change to produce an abundance of fireflies that year and then return to the original conditions so that they didn't fly over in later years?

In 1977, Donald Menzel offered the "temperature inversion" explanation in his book coauthored with Ernest H. Taves, *The UFO Enigma.* He devoted less than a paragraph to the Lubbock Lights, dismissing Hart's photographs by saying, ". . . we believe that some of the Lubbock photographs may have been hoaxes." He further wrote that this was in no way inconsistent with the conclusion reached by some of the Lubbock viewers themselves, that flying flocks of birds illuminated by city lights produced the apparitions.

Not a single shred of evidence has ever been presented to suggest that the photographs taken by Hart are hoaxes. No one in the Lubbock area was able to reproduce them under the same conditions that faced Hart. The various investigators were not able to break his story and, in fact, threatened him from the very beginning. First, Harris, of the *Lubbock Avalanche,* told Hart of the consequences of perpetrating a fraud. Later, Air Force officers told him of his rights under the Fifth Amendment to the Constitution. In all those cases, Hart maintained that his story was true and that he had not faked anything. No one has ever offered any proof that he faked them. Just allegations.

The Lubbock Lights case is a textbook example of the conspiracy of silence. It began as a mysterious case with highly qualified witnesses. The college professors, given the diversity of their disciplines that provided them with a unique background, were considered experts. They were familiar with the sky and the atmosphere around them. Yet they were unable to identify the lights.

Others, in widely scattered locations, saw the lights on the first night and on subsequent nights. Some of them identified the lights they saw as birds. There is no question that some of the reports were of birds, identified as such by the witnesses.

Armed with that information, the investigators made a tremendous leap of logic. If some of the identified sightings were of birds, then all of them were of birds. There is no reason to make that assumption, especially when considering the Hart photographs. Those pictures prove that birds are not responsible for all the sightings in the area.

When confronted with evidence that is difficult to explain, the philosophy inside the conspiracy of silence seems to be to offer many explanations. Publish those explanations as if there is no question that they are accurate, even when they are not. Public perception, then, is that the case has been solved, even when it has not. It doesn't matter if part of the public believes it was birds, or temperature inversions, or even a hoax. An answer has been offered and some of the people believe it.

Menzel was very good at this. He wrote many articles about UFOs. He explained UFOs in all of his articles and books, but paid no attention to the facts. His dismissal of the Lubbock case demonstrates his lack of scientific analysis. When he failed to explain a case with atmospheric phenomena, or birds, he resorted to labeling it as a hoax with absolutely no evidence of a hoax.

Oftentimes, long after the event, a man who was responsible for a hoax will confess it. Those who have faked photographs as teenagers have come forward as adults to explain the situation. But Carl Hart is not among that rather large number. Interviewed again in 1993, Hart told me that he had no explanation for the pictures. I asked if he believed in flying saucers. Hart said, "I don't particularly disbelieve." When asked if he knew what the lights were, he told me, "I really don't."

CHAPTER 5

▬

The Washington Nationals

To those studying the Project Grudge reports, it is clear that an unbiased analysis of the information concerning the UFO phenomenon was not being made. Ed Ruppelt, the head of Project Blue Book, wrote, ". . . it doesn't take a great deal of study of the old UFO files to see that standard intelligence procedures were no longer being used by Project Grudge. Everything was being evaluated on the premise that UFO's couldn't exist."[1]

The group of sightings that became known as the Washington Nationals demonstrates that this attitude of explaining all the sightings, regardless of facts, continued through the end of Blue Book and continues until today. Although Ruppelt, by July 1952, had revitalized the UFO project at the lower levels, those at the highest, in Washington political circles and at

---

[1]Ed Ruppelt, *The Report on Unidentified Flying Objects* (New York: Ace Books, 1956).

the Pentagon, were not interested in the truth, they were interested in answers. While it can be suggested that much of the conspiracy of silence in this case was the result of bungling and incompetence, there is evidence to suggest that someone was pulling strings at the very top to ensure that solid information did not leak into the public arena.

Ruppelt, in his book, said that the Washington Nationals had been predicted by a scientist, who told him, "Within the next few days, they're [the flying saucers] going to blow up and you're going to have the granddaddy of all UFO sightings. The sighting will occur in Washington or New York, probably Washington."

A few days later, the Washington Nationals began when, according to the CAA's (forerunner of the Federal Aeronautics Administration) logbook, two radars at the Air Routing and Traffic Control Center (ARTC) picked up eight unidentified targets near Andrews Air Force Base at 11:40 P.M. on the evening of July 19. These were not airplanes because they were traveling too fast. First they moved along at only 100 miles per hour, then suddenly would accelerate to fantastic speeds. One of the objects was tracked, according to the calculations made at the center, at 7,000 miles per hour.

About twenty minutes later, or just after midnight on July 20, the tower at Washington's National Airport had five targets on their radarscopes.[2] This made it three radars at three separate sites that had solid targets that were not already identified as aircraft.

---

[2]Because the center of the radar sightings was Washington's National Airport, the sightings have become known as the Washington Nationals.

One of the controllers at the ARTC called for a senior controller, Harry C. Barnes, who in turn called the National Airport control tower. The controllers at National had unidentified targets on their scopes, as did the controllers at Andrews Air Force Base. They had already eliminated a mechanical malfunction as the cause, but with the objects on other scopes in other locations, there was no longer any question of their reality. The performance of the blips ruled out airplanes. All of the men, including Barnes, were sure they were looking at solid objects based on their years of experience with radar. Weather-related phenomena wouldn't produce the same effect on all the radars at the widely scattered locations. In fact, if weather was the explanation, the targets would have varied from scope to scope.

Just after midnight, Airman Second Class Bill Goodman called the Andrews control tower to tell the controllers he was watching a bright orange light about the size of a softball that was gaining and losing altitude as it zipped through the sky.

During this time, Goodman talked to Airman First Class William B. Brady, who was in the tower. Goodman told Brady that the object was to the immediate south. Brady saw a ball of orange fire. There were discrepancies between the physical descriptions given by Goodman and Brady, but the problems were relatively small. It can be argued that the discrepancies are the result of the points of view of the two observers.

Joseph DeBoves, who was also on the scene as a civilian control tower operator at Andrews, said that Brady became excited during one of his telephone conversations, yelling, "There one goes!" DeBoves believed that Brady was watching nothing more interesting than a meteor.

At about 2:00 A.M. on July 20, the radar officer at Andrews Approach Control, Captain Harold C. Way, learned that the ARTC had a target east of Andrews. He went outside and saw a strange light which he didn't believe to be a star. Later, however, Way went back outside, and this time decided that he was looking at a star.

Bolling Air Force Base became involved briefly about the time Way went outside. The tower operator there said that he saw a "roundish" object drifting low in the sky to the southeast of Bolling. There were no radar confirmations of the sighting, and that was the last of the reports from that base.

The ARTC controllers again told controllers at Andrews that they still had the targets on their scopes. There is conflicting data because some of the reports suggest that the Andrews radar showed nothing, while other reports claim they did. DeBoves and two others in the tower, Monte Banning and John P. Izzo, Jr., swept the sky with binoculars, but could see no lights other than the stars.

The sightings lasted through the night. During that time, the crews of several airliners saw the lights right where the radars showed them to be. Tower operators also saw them, and jet fighters were brought in for attempted intercepts. Associated Press stories written hours after the sightings claimed that no intercepts had been attempted that night, but those stories were inaccurate. Documents in the Project Blue Book files, as well as eyewitnesses, confirm the attempted intercepts.

Typical of the sightings were those made by Captain Casey Pierman on Capital Airlines Flight 807. The flight was between Washington and Martinsburg, West Virginia, 1:15 A.M. on July 20 when Pierman and the rest of the crew saw seven objects flash across the sky. Pierman said, "They were like falling stars without trails."

Capital Airlines officials said that National Airport radar picked up the objects and asked Pierman to keep an eye on them. Shortly after takeoff, Pierman radioed that he had the objects in sight. He was flying between 180 and 200 miles per hour and reported that the objects were traveling at a tremendous speed. Official Air Force records confirm this.

Another Capital Airlines pilot, Captain Howard Dermott on Capital Flight 610, reported that a single light followed the flight from Herndon, Virginia, to within four miles of National Airport. Both the ARTC and the National tower confirmed that an unidentified target followed the aircraft to within four miles of landing. At about the same time, an Air Force radar at Andrews AFB was tracking eight additional unknown objects as they flew over the Washington area.

One of the most persuasive sightings came early in the morning when one of the ARTC controllers called the Andrews Air Force Base control tower to tell the controllers that there was a target south of the tower, over the Andrews radio range station. The tower operators looked to the south, where a "huge fiery-orange sphere" was hovering. This was also later explained by the Air Force as a star.

Just before daylight, at about 4:00 A.M., after repeated requests from the ARTC, an F-94 interceptor arrived on the scene, but it was too little too late. All the targets were gone. Although the flight crew made a short search of the local area, they found nothing unusual and returned to their base quickly.

During the night, the three radar facilities only once reported a target that was seen by all three facilities. There were, however, a number of times when the ARTC radar and the Washington National tower radars had simultaneous contacts. It also seems that the radars were displaying the same targets that were seen by the crews of the Capital Airlines flights. What it boils down to is that multiple radars and multiple eyewitnesses were showing and seeing objects in the sky over Washington.

Air Force intelligence, including ATIC and the officers assigned to the UFO project, had no idea that these sightings had taken place. They learned of the Saturday night to Sunday morning UFO show when the information was published in several newspapers on Monday. Ruppelt, on business in Washington and unaware of the sightings, reported, ''I got off an airliner from Dayton and I bought a newspaper in the lobby of Washington National Airport Terminal Building. I called Major Dewey Fournet, but all he knew was what he read in the papers.''[3]

During the day, Ruppelt was briefed on the various episodes of the Saturday night aerial display. He knew what had to be done, what questions should be asked, and where to go to get the statements and evidence he needed for a complete investigation. Bureaucracy, however, was no more interested in flying saucers than the Pentagon seemed to be.

Ruppelt wrote, ''Feeling like a national martyr be-

---

[3]Ruppelt, *The Report on Unidentified Flying Objects.*

cause I planned to work all night if necessary, I laid the course of my investigation."

His orders had called for him to return to Dayton after his scheduled meetings at the Pentagon. He tried to arrange a staff car, but in brass-heavy Washington, only very senior colonels and generals could get staff cars on short notice. Ruppelt called the men he knew at the Pentagon, but none of them were available, so no staff car could be had.

He could have rented a car, but he wouldn't have been able to charge it as a travel expense because city buses were available, according to the bureaucrats. He could have taken a cab, but that wasn't a legitimate expense because city buses were available. Riding a bus was not the best way to conduct an important intelligence investigation, according to Ruppelt.

Ruppelt was also told that his orders didn't cover an overnight stay in Washington. If he didn't return to Dayton that day and get his orders amended, he wouldn't be able to collect his expense money (per diem) and would be, technically at least, AWOL. And he couldn't talk to the finance officer because the finance officer was already gone for the day, even though it was before four-thirty in the afternoon.

Ruppelt then called Colonel Donald Bower, told him of the experience, and said that he would have to return to Dayton. Bower agreed that there was no other solution available to them. Bureaucracy had won over investigation.

These events became important when we examine the Air Force files on the case. Ruppelt wanted to stay, tried to work his way through the bureaucracy to stay, but was stymied at every turn. In the official records, a slightly different spin is put on it. In a "Memorandum for the Record," dated 23 July 1952 with a subject of "ATIC Participation in the Investigation of the Washington Incident of 20 July 1952," another version of this event appears. According to the document, "3. Before the afternoon was over it appeared that this was going to be a 'hot' incident. Capt. Ruppelt called Col. Bower in Lt. Col. Teaburg's office and offered to stay over in Washington to get the investigation started but was advised that this should not be done."

The question to be asked is if the bureaucratic nightmare that Ruppelt encountered was just one subtle aspect of the conspiracy of silence, or was it just everyone trying to get out of the extra paperwork that Ruppelt's proposed overnight stay would have generated? At best, it can be described as another aspect of the incompetency that plagued the UFO investigation from the very beginning. At worst, it was designed to keep Ruppelt away from any meaningful study of the sightings because of their very nature. After all, those who claim UFOs are nothing more extraordinary than hoaxes and misidentifications had always claimed that UFOs were not seen on radar. Now there were dozens of witnesses to objects in the sky and blips on the radars and all were competent observers. Many were charged with the safety of millions of air travelers.

But that wasn't the end of the Washington Nationals. There were other sightings, including a good one from New Jersey and one from Massachusetts in which F-94s tried, unsuccessfully, to intercept unidentified lights. According to Project Blue Book files, in both cases the pilots reported radar locks on the objects, but within seconds those locks were broken by the evasion maneuvers of the UFOs.

Ruppelt wrote in his book that during the week following the first round of sightings at Washington National Airport, he spoke to Captain Roy James, a radar expert based at Wright-Patterson. James suggested that the sightings sounded as if the radar targets had been caused by weather. Later, Ruppelt wrote, "But Captain James has a powerful dislike for UFO's—especially on Saturday night."

The Saturday night on which James professed his dislike was the second time, a week later and almost to the hour, that the UFOs visited Washington National Airport. At about 10:30 P.M., the same radar operators who had been on duty the week before again spotted several slow-moving targets. This time the controllers carefully marked each of the "unidentifieds." When they were all marked, they called the Andrews AFB radar facility. The unidentified targets were on the Andrews scope too.

An hour later, with targets being tracked continually, the controllers called for interceptors. Al Chop, the Pentagon spokesman for the UFO project, told me that he was in communication with the main basement command post at the Pentagon. He requested that interceptors be sent. As a civilian, he could only make the request and then wait for the flag officer (general or admiral) in command at the Pentagon to make the official decision.

As happened the week before, there was a delay, but by midnight, two F-94s were on station over Washington. At that point, the reporters who had assembled to observe the situation were asked, by Chop, to leave the radar room at National Airport because classified radio and intercept procedures would be in operation.

Although that fact was well reported, Ruppelt wrote, "I knew this was absurd because any radio ham worth his salt could build equipment and listen in on any intercept. The real reason for the press dismissal, I learned, was that not a few people in the radar room were positive that this night would be the big night in UFO history—the night when a pilot would close in on and get a good look at a UFO—and they didn't want the press to be in on it."

We can argue about the reality of a conspiracy of silence, but here is the truth. Military representatives forced reporters from the radar rooms because they didn't want the reporters to learn what was happening. They wanted to maintain the silence in case something extraordinary happened. All of this in the face of repeated Air Force and Pentagon spokesmen claiming there was nothing to UFOs and the sightings were the result of weather.

There may have been a second consideration. Major Dewey Fournet, the Pentagon liaison between the UFO project in Dayton and the intelligence community in Washington, was at National Airport. Also there were Al Chop, a public information officer, and Naval Lieutenant Holcomb, an electronics specialist assigned to the Air Force Directorate of Intelligence.

With those men watching, as well as the controllers at various facilities using various radars, the F-94s arrived. And the UFOs vanished from the scopes immediately. The jets were vectored to the last known position of the UFOs, but even though visibility was unrestricted in the area, the pilots could see nothing. The fighters made a systematic search of the area, but since they could find nothing, they returned to their base.

Chop told me, "The minute the first two interceptors appeared on our scope, all our unknowns disappeared. It was likely they just wiped them all off. All our other flights—all the known flights—were still on the scope . . . We watched these two planes leave. When they were out of our range, immediately we got our UFOs back."

Later, Air Force officers would learn that as the fighters appeared over Washington, people in the area of Langley Air Force Base, Virginia, spotted weird lights in the sky. An F-94 in the area on a routine mission was diverted to search for the light. The pilot saw it and turned toward it, but it disappeared "like somebody turning off a lightbulb."

The pilot continued the intercept and did get a radar lock on the target, which was now unlighted and unseen. The radar lock, however, was broken by the object as it sped away. The fighter continued the pursuit, obtaining two more radar locks on the object, but each time the locks were broken.

The scene then shifted back to Washington National. Again the Air Defense Command was alerted and again fighters were sent. This time the pilots were able to see the objects, vectored toward them by the air traffic controllers. But the fighters couldn't close on the lights. The pilots saw no external details other than lights where the radar suggested that something should be seen.

After several minutes of failure to close on a target, one of them was spotted loping along. A fighter piloted by Lieutenant William Patterson turned, kicked in the afterburner, and tried to catch the object. It disappeared before Patterson could see much of anything.

Interviewed the next day, Patterson said, "I tried to make contact with the bogies below one thousand feet, but they [the controllers] vectored us around. I saw several bright lights. I was at my maximum speed, but even then I had no closing speed. I ceased chasing them because I saw no chance of overtaking them. I was vectored into new objects. Later I chased a single bright light, which I estimated about ten miles away. I lost visual contact with it . . ."[4]

Al Chop remembered this intercept, as did Dewey Fournet. Chop said, "The flight controllers had directed him to them [the unknowns]. We had a little cluster of them. Five or six of them and he suddenly reports that he sees some lights . . . He said they are very brilliant blue-white lights. He was going to try to close in to get a better look . . . he flew into the area where they were clustered and he reported they were all around him."

Chop said that he, along with the others in the radar room, watched the intercept on the radarscope. What the pilot was telling them, they could see on the radar.

Patterson had to break off the intercept, though there were still lights in the sky and objects on the scope. According to Chop, the pilot radioed that he was running low on fuel. He turned so that he could head back to his base.

Chop said that the last of the objects disappeared from the scope about the time the sun came up. Ruppelt later quizzed Fournet about the activities that

---

[4]Patterson's statements are from the Project Blue Book files.

night. According to Ruppelt, Fournet and Holcomb, the radar expert, were convinced the targets were solid metallic objects. Fournet told Ruppelt that there were weather-related targets on the scopes, but the controllers were ignoring them. Everyone was convinced that the targets were real.

The situation was a repeat of the week before. Headlines around the world on Tuesday, July 29, told the whole story. In a banner headline that could have come from a science fiction movie, the *Cedar Rapids Gazette* reported, SAUCERS SWARM OVER CAPITAL.

At 4:00 P.M. in Washington, D.C., Major General John A. Samford, Chief of Air Intelligence, held a press conference. Of that conference, Ruppelt wrote, "General Samford made an honest attempt to straighten out the Washington National sightings, but the cards were stacked against him. He had to hedge on many answers to questions from the press because he didn't know the answers. This hedging gave the impression that he was trying to cover up something more than just the fact his people fouled up in not fully investigating the sightings. Then he brought in Captain Roy James from ATIC to handle all the queries about radar. James didn't do any better because he'd just arrived in Washington that morning and didn't know very much more about the sightings than he'd read in the papers. Major Dewey Fournet and Lieutenant Holcomb, who had been at the airport during the sightings, were extremely conspicuous by their absence . . ."[5] As was the Pentagon spokesman on UFOs, Al Chop.

Ruppelt noted that the press decided that Sam-

---

[5]Ruppelt, *The Report on Unidentified Flying Objects.*

ford's suggestion of a weather-related explanation for the sightings was the final solution. Ruppelt reported in 1956 that the sightings were still carried as unknowns in the Project Blue Book files.

But that wasn't the end of it. Other investigations were made of all the "unidentifieds" in the Project Blue Book files. The purpose was to determine if solutions for those "unidentifieds" could be found. Labels and conclusions were changed. Documentation available through the Project Blue Book files provides the evidence of this. For example, in a letter written by Colonel Edward H. Wynn, Deputy for Science and Components, in April 1960, he suggested that "Probable causes for sightings based on limited information should be accepted." The explanation of the Washington Nationals shifted slowly from unknowns to temperature inversions.

Ruppelt, however, didn't see it that way. He wrote, "Some people said, 'Weather targets,' but the chances of a weather target's making a 180-degree turn just as an airplane turns into it, giving a radar lock-on, then changing speed to stay just out of the range of the airplane's radar, and then slowing down when the airplane leaves is as close to nil as you can get."

Others argued that the situation was created out of the hysteria in the ARTC, at Washington National, and at Andrews Air Force Base. Many times, according to some experts, when there is a visual sighting, there are "uncollorated" targets on the radarscope. It was suggested that the excitement of the night, coupled with that fact, produced the frightening results reported by the men at the various radar locations. In other words, with the weather the way it was, pilots seeing lights in the sky would have those sightings confirmed by radar if they had initiated them. Of course, in this case, it was the radar operators who started it by asking pilots to search the sky for those "uncollorated" targets.

There were reports that tower operators at Andrews Air Force Base, who said they had seen a "fiery-orange sphere" over the radio range when told by National Airport radar controllers that an object was there, weren't quite as sure of their facts later. They completely changed their story, according to some later investigators, saying they had seen nothing more spectacular than a bright star. They said that they had been excited by all of the reports of flying saucers that were being called to them by the radar operators at other facilities.

Ruppelt reported that no exceptionally bright stars were in the sky in a position to be seen over the radio range. He then wrote, "And I heard from a good source that the tower men had been 'persuaded' a bit." Persuaded by their superiors to suggest that they might have been looking at a nonexistent bright star.

A series of sightings, over two separate nights, over the national capital, had to be explained by the military. To leave them labeled as unknowns was to admit that something was going on. It was to admit that the Air Force couldn't do its job properly. After all, if flying saucers can flash through the sky at will, what good is an Air Force charged with keeping our skies free of the "enemy." So the answer began to evolve from "It sounds like a temperature inversion" to "It definitely was some kind of temperature inversion."

When the University of Colorado[6] assumed the task of investigating UFO sightings under a grant from the Air Force, the Washington Nationals were one of the few "classic" sighting reports that demanded further attention. According to the final report by the Condon Committee, "One of the earliest of our field trips (December 1966) was made to Washington, D.C., to interview separately two air traffic control operators who had been involved in the great UFO flap there in the summer of 1952. Fourteen years later, these two men were still quite annoyed at the newspaper publicity they had received, because it had tended to ridicule their reports. Our conclusion from this trip was that these men were telling stories in 1966 that were thoroughly consistent with the main points of their stories in 1952."[7]

The investigation, reported by the University of Colorado scientists, suggested a situation that was different than that reported by Ruppelt and others. The scientists wrote, "There are a tremendous number of reports of UFOs observed on these two nights. In most of the instances visual observers, especially in scrambled aircraft, *were unable to see targets indicated on ground radar, or to make airborne radar contact* [Emphasis added]."

This is a strange thing to say, because Michael Wertheimer, who made the preliminary investigation in over a day and half in December 1966 for the Condon Committee, learned the truth. He spoke to

[6]The Air Force provided a grant to the University of Colorado to study UFOs. The study was headed by Dr. Edward U. Condon. The University of Colorado study is the same as the Condon Committee.

[7]Daniel S. Gillmor (ed.), *Final Report of the Scientific Study of Unidentified Flying Objects* (New York: Bantam Books, 1968).

Harry Barnes, Andrews AFB tower operator Monte Banning, as well as other personnel at both National Airport and Andrews. Writing of the sightings on July 20, Tad Foster of the Condon Committee noted, "Thus, Pierman, Dermott, and Patterson [airline pilots and the interceptor pilot] each observed a visible light, and verbally described its position and/or motion which in turn correlated with the blip on the radar screen."[8]

Joe Zacko, who had been in the tower, also confirmed that he had seen the lights in the sky. As had some of the Air Force personnel, who later changed their stories. In other words, it is clear that there is a body of testimony from a number of different witnesses in different locations who saw lights where the radars showed objects were located.

The official Condon Committee report also seems to be at odds with what Ruppelt and others reported, including those who were on the scene in July 1952. Interceptor pilots did see the lights and onboard radars did lock onto solid objects. In one case, the ARTC radar returns vanished as the interceptors arrived on the scene, and once the fighters left, the objects returned. According to Ruppelt, the objects seemed to respond to the interceptor aircraft. Al Chop reported this to me during the interview I conducted. Weather-related phenomena would not be adversely affected by the appearance of the fighters.

The University of Colorado report includes a number of eyewitness statements, including one from "A USAF Captain [undoubtedly Captain Harold C. Way]

---

[8]Quote is from the unpublished casebook that was to be part of the University of Colorado study.

at Andrews AFB radar center." The unidentified captain reported, "At about 0200 EST Washington Center advised that their radar had a target five miles east of Andrews Field. Andrews tower reported seeing a light, which changed color, and said it was moving towards Andrews. I went outside as no target appeared on Andrews radar and saw a light as reported by the tower. It was between 10 degrees and 15 degrees above the horizon and seemed to change color, from red to orange to green and red again. It seemed to float, but at times to dip suddenly and appear to lose altitude. It did not have the appearance of any star I have ever observed before. At the time of the observation there was a star due east of my position. Its brilliance was approximately the same as the object and it appeared at about the same angle, 10 degrees to 15 degrees about the horizon. The star did not change color or have any apparent movement. I estimated the object to be between three and four miles east of Andrews Field at approximately 2,000 ft. During the next hour very few reports were received from Washington Center. (According to Washington Center's account, however, the 0200 EST object was seen on radar to pass over Andrews and fade out to the southwest of Andrews—G.D.T. [parenthetical statement in original]). At approximately 0300 EST I again went outside to look at the object. At this time both the star and the object had increased elevation by about 10 degrees. (The azimuth would have also increased about 10 degrees, so that the observed change was apparently equal to the sidereal rate, 15 degrees of right ascension per hour—G.D.T. [parenthetical statement in original]). The object had ceased to have any apparent movement, but still appeared to be changing color. On the basis of the second observation, I believe the unidentified object was a star."

Of course, we must remember that Ruppelt had said that the Andrews personnel had been pressured into altering their reports. The "unidentifieds," on second thought, became stars.

The University of Colorado study concluded, "The atmospheric conditions during the period . . . in the Washington, D.C., area, was conducive to anomalous propagation of radar signals . . . The unidentified radar returns obtained during the incidents were most likely the result of anomalous propagation (AP) . . . The visual objects were, with one or two possible exceptions, identifiable most probably as meteors and scintilling stars."

In Appendix L to the final (Condon) report, Loren W. Crow, a certified consulting meteorologist, wrote, "It is the author's opinion that hot, humid air prevailed on both nights in both Washington and Norfolk. The general weather would have been considered fair weather by the trained observers at the various airports and they may not have reported all the scattered clouds which actually existed. It would have been considered an 'easy shift.' Visibilities remained above six miles at all times. The horizontal movement of scattered clouds, plus formation and dissipation of some few low clouds, both could have been seen at various times by ground observers whose eyes were well adjusted to the darkened sky. Anomalous propagation could have been observed on weather radar units during both nights at both locations. The echoes due to anomalous propagation would have had horizontal motion similar to clouds." Of course, we do have one report of a cloud traveling at 7,000 miles per hour and we have other reports of clouds outrunning the interceptors.

Interestingly, the two Pentagon personnel I interviewed, Major Dewey Fournet and Al Chop, disagreed with the weather-related explanation. Both were sure, based on their observations in the radar room, that the returns showed solid objects. Both were listening to Holcomb, the acknowledged expert in radar. In fact, Chop said that he was unimpressed with the analysis made by a man from over 1,000 miles away and fifteen years after the fact.

In 1952, the sightings over Washington National were "unidentified."[9] Those in the various radar rooms reported the objects they saw were solid and metallic, not the sort of returns caused by temperature inversions. Pilots ordered to intercept spotted objects where they were reported to be and obtained radar locks, only to have them broken. Airline pilots saw the lights and reported them to the radar facilities.

Seventeen years later, as the University of Colorado report was put together, the situation seems to have changed. Now we have only a few radar sightings that have visual counterparts. And we're told that "in most instances visual observers, especially in scrambled aircraft, were unable to see targets indicated on ground radar, or to make airborne radar contact." That isn't the situation reported by Dewey Fournet, who was there. It is not the situation re-

---

[9]By the time the Condon Committee was commissioned, the explanation for the Washington Nationals had been changed to "identified." It was, according to the files, weather-related phenomena that had caused the sightings.

ported by Al Chop, who was there. And it is not the situation as indicated in the UFO project's files.

What we see by studying the Washington Nationals is the shift in official policy. In 1952, Ruppelt and those in the UFO investigation wanted to discover what happened over Washington, D.C. The policy shift began about six months after the sightings at Washington National. This was called the Robertson Panel.

CHAPTER 6

The Whole Story of the Robertson Panel

IT WAS AN OUTGROWTH OF THE SUMMER OF 1952 when flying saucers filled the skies around the country and targeted Washington, D.C., on two memorable nights. Prior to 1952, the UFO investigations of the Air Force had limped along, as few sighting reports were made and even fewer withstood the biased investigations of military officers. But in the summer of 1952, all that changed. Thousands of reports were made, and by the end of the year more than 300 would be listed as "unidentified." People at the Pentagon, in Congress, in the military, and in the civilian population were as puzzled as ever.

In fact, before the wave of sightings began to taper, the CIA, aware of a potential intelligence problem involved with the UFO sightings, began a series of informal discussions about them. These meetings, held by the CIA, were chaired by H. Marshall Chadwell, Assistant Director of Scientific Intelligence. Chadwell, in fact, apparently traveled with Frederick Durant to Wright-Patterson for a series of briefings about UFOs from the officers of Project Blue Book.

In late September 1952, Chadwell sent a memo to General Walter Bedell Smith, the Director of Central Intelligence (DCI). Chadwell wrote, "Recently an inquiry was conducted by the Office of Scientific Intelligence to determine whether there are national security implications in the problem of 'unidentified flying objects,' i.e., flying saucers; whether adequate study and research is currently being directed to this problem in its relation to such national security implications; and what further investigation and research should be instituted, by whom, and under what aegis."

Chadwell further wrote, "It was found that the only unit of government currently studying the problem is the Directorate of Intelligence, USAF, which has charged the Air Technical Intelligence Center (ATIC) with the responsibility for investigating the reports of sightings . . . and major Air Force bases have been ordered to make interceptions of unidentified flying objects . . ."

Chadwell then made the claims that so many others have echoed. ". . . [P]ublic concern with the phenomena indicates that a fair proportion of our population is mentally conditioned to the acceptance of the incredible. In this fact lies the potential for the touching-off of mass hysteria . . . In order to minimize risk of panic, a national policy should be established as to what should be told to the public regarding the phenomena."

The letter, dated September 24, 1952, and from the CIA, had suggested part of the conclusions that would be reached by the Robertson Panel some five months later.[1] Chadwell was wondering what the public should be told and was suggesting that the information be managed by responsible agencies inside the federal government.

These meetings and discussions carried into the late fall of 1952, when Major Dewey Fournet, who had been present during one night of sightings over Washington National Airport, received a call from Frederick Durant. According to Fournet, "[He] asked me to make a presentation to the CIA which I did. I gave them a few of my own opinions based on what I had observed . . . from that the idea of the Robertson Panel spawned. And Fred, through his superiors, convened it."

It can be argued that the idea had already spawned by the time Fournet made his presentation to the CIA. In December of 1952, just weeks before the group actually met, Chadwell decided to form the scientific advisory panel. Dr. Michael Swords, who reviewed the history carefully, said that H. P. Robertson, who would eventually chair the panel, had apparently accompanied Chadwell and Durant to Wright-Patterson. According to Swords, Robertson accepted the assignment against his will, but Chadwell insisted. Robertson then had to "strong-arm" four others to join him in their scientific evaluation.

Swords, reconstructing the history, said, "The first guy he gets to do this is Thorton Page because Page is handy. Page turns out to be a junior member on the committee . . . but he doesn't know anything about UFOs. Robertson sends him an article to read . . ."

---

[1] Although the conclusions weren't precisely laid out, the letter certainly suggests them to Robertson.

Swords said, "I think Alverez [Dr. Luis Alverez] is the guy he gets next talked into it and Alverez comes into it hostile . . . Then he tries John Wheeler . . . Wheeler told Robertson he wasn't coming so then Robertson has to get two more people. I think Goudsmit [Dr. Samuel Goudsmit] is the guy he probably gets last and I'm not sure when they talk Lloyd Berkner into [it] . . . Goudsmit is just incredibly hostile."

Swords, having interviewed Dr. J. Allen Hynek,[2] a participant in part of the panel's discussions, said, "As far as Allen Hynek is concerned [these guys] have an immediate aura about the committee room that this thing is going to be debunked from the absolute beginning . . . Alverez and Goudsmit are saying nothing but hostile things and Goudsmit is also saying wiseass things . . . Page is more open minded. Berkner is not there . . ." Hynek had the feeling that the panel members had already studied the cases that were going to be presented to them, or they simply had their minds made up before they sat down for the first meeting.

In his book, Ed Ruppelt wrote, "When this high court convened . . . one of three verdicts would be acceptable. 1. All UFO reports are explainable as known objects or natural phenomena; therefore the investigation should be permanently discontinued. 2. The UFO reports do not contain enough data upon which to base a final conclusion. Project Blue Book should be continued in hopes of obtaining better data. 3. The UFO's

[2]Swords knew Hynek for a number of years and engaged him in many conversations about the UFO phenomenon. He also has a tape on which Hynek relates some of the information that was important to Swords and his understanding of the Robertson Panel.

are interplanetary spacecraft." The written verdict would be passed on to the National Security Council.

Even with that, and with more than forty years having passed before I interviewed him, Fournet was convinced that the Robertson Panel was a sincere effort by a few scientists to understand the situation as it existed in early 1953. According to Fournet, "It was legitimate."

Swords, reviewing the history of the UFO phenomenon, had a slightly different opinion. According to him, the panel was "another of these things that is a *fait accompli* before the panel actually meets. But it's not a *fait accompli* for all the guys who are meeting on the panel."

So, under the auspices of the CIA and headed by Dr. H. P. Robertson, the panel convened on January 14, 1953. According to Ruppelt, the first two days were made up of his review,[3] for the scientists, of the findings of Projects Sign, Grudge, and Blue Book and the situation at ATIC. The team had analyzed 1,593 reports and found explanations for all but 429. Confidence in the explanations ranged from known to possible, meaning that Ruppelt and his staff sometimes felt they had an answer but weren't positive about it.

Swords provided additional details about the chronology of the proceedings. During the first half-day, no one was allowed into the meeting room except the panel members and a couple of CIA men, including Chadwell and Philip G. Strong. Hynek and Ruppelt were kept outside, cooling their heels.

Records suggest that Chadwell and Strong had

---

[3]Ruppelt's writings don't agree, exactly, with the scenario developed by Dr. Swords. The disagreement between the two, however, is of little real consequence.

prepared a briefing for the panel. They had been to Wright-Patterson and Ruppelt supposedly briefed them on the findings of Project Blue Book. The briefing to the panel included the intelligence security concerns and a brief history of the UFO project, though it would seem that Ruppelt could have provided a more comprehensive analysis of the situation at Wright-Patterson.

Once those concerns had been discussed, Ruppelt, Hynek, and other observers were allowed into the meeting room on Wednesday, all day Thursday, and Friday.

Ruppelt made it clear during his presentation that much of the data was observed. That is, the reports relied on the abilities of the witness to accurately estimate the size and speed of the object. Ruppelt wrote, "We could say only that some of the UFO's had been traveling pretty fast."

Objective data, such as that from radar sites, was available, but again, it was open to the interpretation of the radar operators. Ruppelt mentioned that the best cases from the files were those in which radar had tracked the objects at 700 to 800 miles per hour. In his book, he said nothing about the radar sightings over Washington, D.C., in which the speed of one object was estimated at 7,000 miles per hour.[4]

Ruppelt also mentioned that they had no persuasive physical evidence. Dewey Fournet told me that he didn't remember reading anything about the Ros-

---

[4]The 7,000 miles per hour figure is based on the radar operator's calculation and the time of the sweep of the radar. Some have disputed the figure, suggesting that a slower speed can be calculated using the same data. However, the man on the scene, who was in the radar room that night, insisted that 7,000 was the proper number.

well case in the Blue Book files, which would, of course, be the ultimate physical evidence case. In fact, he thought that he heard nothing about Roswell until long after he had left the military service.

Ruppelt also discussed the photographs, suggesting that many were fakes, some so crude that the hubcap thrown into the air was easily recognizable. Others were sophisticated. Some photos were of natural phenomena. Still pictures didn't prove the case.

The difference was the two UFO movies taken in 1950 and 1952. To fake a convincing film took an expert with elaborate equipment. If the Air Force had seen an original film, then there was little chance that the photographer had faked it. The explanation had to lie elsewhere.

Swords has said that these UFO movies was one reason why the panel was formed. The scientists were all very interested in the movies and wanted to see them. Swords said, "As soon as they get finished with all the preliminary briefings, that's the only thing they want to do is look at the films."

In 1952, the Air Force possessed two good—although short—movies that showed UFOs. They also had two other films that had been taken at White Sands Proving Ground (later White Sands Missile Range) in 1950.[5] But the Montana movie, taken in August 1950, and the Tremonton, Utah, movie, taken by a Navy warrant officer in July 1952, were considered the best. The Tremonton film and the Montana movie were subjected to thousands of hours of research that concluded little of importance.

----

[5]Neither of the other films showed anything spectacular. Both showed white objects against a blue background.

On July 2, 1952, Navy Warrant Officer Delbert C. Newhouse was driving toward a new duty station with his wife and two children. Just after eleven in the morning, his wife noticed a group of bright objects that she couldn't easily identify. Newhouse, a trained Navy photographer, stopped the car to retrieve his 16mm camera from the trunk.

By the time he got the camera out, the objects had moved away from the car. Newhouse said later than when one object broke from the formation, he tracked it so that analysts would have something to work with. He let it fly across the field of view. He did that two or three times. When he turned back, the whole formation was gone.

The details of the story vary, depending on the source. Air Force files, based on the information supplied by others, show that Newhouse and his wife saw the objects at close range. By the time he got the car stopped and the camera out of the trunk, the objects had moved to a long range. In an interview I conducted in 1976, Newhouse confirmed he had seen the objects at close range. He said they were large, disk-shaped, and brightly lighted. Dewey Fournet told me that Newhouse had said the same thing to him.

After filming the objects, Newhouse stored his camera, got back into the car, and drove on to his new duty station. Once there, he had the film processed and sent a copy to the Air Force, suggesting the Air Force might find it interesting.

The Air Force investigation lasted for months, including analysis of the film. The Air Force tried everything to identify the objects but failed. When coupled to the report and the reliability of the photographer, the Air Force was stuck. The Air Force investigators had no explanation.

When the Air Force finished, the Navy asked for it. The Navy investigators made a frame-by-frame analysis that took more than a thousand man-hours. They studied the motion of the objects, their relation to one another in the formation, the lighting of the objects, and every other piece of data they could find on the film. In the end, like their Air Force counterparts, they were left with no explanations.

But, unlike their Air Force counterparts, the Navy experts were not restricted in their praise of the film. Their report said that the objects were internally lighted spheres that were not reflecting sunlight. They also estimated the speed of 3,780 miles an hour if the spheres were five miles away. At twice the distance, they would have been moving twice as fast. At half the distance, half the speed. If the objects were just under a mile distant, they were traveling at 472 miles an hour.

When the Robertson Panel reviewed the film, Dr. Alverez said that they might be birds. Fournet told me, "Dr. Alverez suggested that as a possible solution to that Tremonton movie . . ."

The next morning, after the scientists on the panel had seen the Tremonton film, according to Swords, ". . . the Air Force, the CIA, has mysteriously produced this film of seagulls to show them and you just wonder: Wasn't that convenient? They just happened to have that seagull film handy in the stacks somewhere."

In the years that followed, the Tremonton movie's suggested explanation of seagulls became the solid explanation. Donald H. Menzel and L. G. Boyd, in their book,[6] wrote of the Tremonton film, "The pictures are of such poor quality and show so little that even the most enthusiastic home-movie fan today would hesitate to show them to his friends. Only a stimulated imagination could suggest that the moving objects are anything but very badly photographed birds."

The Condon Committee investigator on the Tremonton film, William K. Hartmann,[7] reexamined the case years after the Robertson Panel. After reviewing the evidence, Hartmann concluded, "These observations give *strong evidence that the Tremonton films do show birds* [emphasis in original], as hypothesized above, and I now regard the objects as so indentified [sic]."

So a possible answer suggested by the Robertson Panel became the final explanation for the films as the years passed. However, in the analysis that appeared after the Robertson Panel, one fact was left out. Newhouse saw the objects at close range. Fournet said, ". . . when you look at what Newhouse said when he was interviewed after that . . . When you put all that together, the seagull hypothesis becomes flimsier and flimsier."

Ruppelt, in fact, mentions that fact in his book. According to him, no one had asked Newhouse what the objects looked like because there were pictures of them. It was only later, after Ruppelt left the Air Force, that he talked to Newhouse about what he

---

[6]Donald H. Menzel and Lyle G. Boyd, *The World of Flying Saucers* (Garden City, N.Y.: Doubleday & Company, 1963).

[7]Hartmann was just one of many scientists who investigated the films. It is interesting that he believes the seagull theory, based on his personal observations.

had seen. According to Ruppelt, "He didn't *think* the UFO's were disk-shaped; he *knew* that they were."

The other movie, called the Great Falls film or the Montana movie, was, according to Ruppelt's book, made on August 15, 1950. Nick Mariana, the manager of the Great Falls minor league baseball team, was inspecting the field prior to a game with his secretary, Virginia Raunig. He was talking to her when a bright flash of light caught his eye and over Great Falls he could see two bright, silver objects. He said something to Raunig as he ran to his car to get his 16mm movie camera.

Mariana was able to film what he claimed were two circular UFOs as they passed over a building and behind a water tower. In the short film, the objects seemed to flash brightly, then move away from the camera. In less than twenty seconds, according to Mariana's estimate, the UFOs disappeared. Raunig saw the UFOs as Mariana filmed them, but she said that she watched them for only five to ten seconds.

Mariana, understandably excited by the film, called the local newspaper to report the incident. Processing took something over a week in 1950, and it was probably late August before the developed film was returned. During September and October, Mariana showed the film to various civic groups. At one of the meetings, a man suggested that Mariana allow the Air Force analyze the movie.

In October 1950, the Air Force entered the case, sending an officer from Maelstrom Air Force Base (formerly Great Falls AFB) to interview Mariana. During that interview, Mariana claimed the objects were in sight for twenty seconds, but later measurements, with Mariana running to the car for the camera, showed that the sighting lasted for nearly a minute.

Early analysis of the film proved nothing. Air Force officers said that two jet interceptors that had been in the area when the film was taken might be responsible for the sighting. Sunlight, reflecting brightly from the silver fuselages of the fighters, might have washed out the other details and that was why Mariana hadn't been able to identify them. The Air Force returned the film to Mariana, its analysis completed.

In 1952, the Air Force decided to review some of the old cases that had not been identified. Officers at Wright-Patterson AFB asked Mariana if they could look at the film one more time. He agreed and sent the film to the Air Force in Ohio.

Again, the Air Force analysis failed to find a solid explanation. Air Force records did show two F-94 fighters had landed at the air base at about the time the UFOs were seen by Mariana and Raunig. Air Force analysts believed that sunlight from the fuselage could cause the images on the film, but only if Mariana's estimate of time was right. If he was wrong—and the tests showed that he was—the jets had passed through enough arc that the sunlight should have faded and the identity of the jets should have been clear.

There was one additional problem with the case. Both Mariana and Raunig claimed they had seen the jets in another part of the sky. That would rule them out, if the witnesses weren't lying. Even with that information, the Air Force still labeled the case as "possible aircraft" and returned the film to Mariana.

When he got the film back, he was angry. According to him, the Air Force had removed more than thirty frames from the beginning and it was in those frames that showed the UFOs as elliptical shaped. Mariana demanded the return of the missing film.

Air Force records, however, don't corroborate this. Project Blue Book files show the analysts had removed one frame because of damaged sprockets. They had advised Mariana of this. Although Mariana said he had a letter from the Air Force proving the analysts removed the thirty frames, he was never able to produce it.

Through the years more analysis of the film was made. In the 1960s, the Condon Committee reexamined the film. Committee scientists discovered there were no home baseball games for the Great Falls team between August 9 and August 18. Early Air Force records note that both the August 5 and August 15 date were suggested. If the August 15 date is eliminated, then the "possible aircraft" explanation is also eliminated.[8]

All of the studies failed to produce any data that showed the film had been faked. Data indicated, as mentioned, that the objects were disk-shaped and the images on the film are consistent with high-polished metal surfaces. If Mariana estimated the length of the sighting wrong and the objects were in sight for nearly a minute, aircraft are effectively ruled out. If the twenty-second estimate is right, then it is possible for the jets to have caused the sighting.

In 1969, Dr. Robert M. L. Baker, after analysis, said that the physical evidence available on the film shows that it was not birds, balloons, mirages, or meteors and

---

[8]This means, simply, that the records show no aircraft in the proper location at the proper time.

he didn't think they were reflections from jets. In that respect, he was at odds with the Air Force.

It finally boils down to the point where no one can be sure if Mariana filmed two spacecraft, or two aircraft, or something else. The hard data on the film indicates that the aircraft explanation doesn't work, but that doesn't prove the objects are of extraterrestrial origin. It leaves the film as "unidentified."

Ruppelt's briefing took most of the first day and there was no time left for questions and answers when he finished. Those took place the next day. Dewey Fournet also made a presentation to the Robertson Panel.

According to Ruppelt, the last day was reserved for the films. That was the best evidence that Blue Book had. No one suggested that the Tremonton or Montana movies were faked. But in and of themselves, they proved nothing conclusively. Fournet said, "But you can knock out the seagulls and then where are you?"

It meant simply that one more mundane explanation had been eliminated, but that didn't lead directly to the extraterrestrial hypothesis. There was nothing on the films that allowed that explanation to be positively put forward. The films might be interesting, and they might not be explained to the satisfaction of investigators, but that was all they were.

Swords said that the last afternoon, Friday, with Hynek invited to stay, was when Robinson was given, or took, the task of writing the final report. Swords said, "I can't imagine that H. P. Robertson, a guy like him, is going to sit down late into the evening and bang out a draft of the report on his own that somehow, mysteriously, the next morning is already read by Lloyd Berkner and has already been taken by Marshall Chadwell to the Air Force Directorate of Intelligence and been approved. So when they show up on Saturday, Robertson presents this draft to the rest of the committee and the rest of the committee does minor revisions . . . There is some remarks that are out of line that they decided are not going to be included."

According to Swords, "It seems an amazingly cut-and-dried deal that by the time Saturday shows up, here's this mildly to be revised draft that has already been seen by one of the other committee members who wasn't even there for the first two and a half days. It's already been seen by Chadwell and the U.S. Air Force."

Fournet, who had a chance to review the data, who had been present during some of the sessions, and who now has a forty-year perspective, says that the scientists had no choice in their conclusions. The evidence, although somewhat persuasive, was not conclusive. There was little evidence other than the testimonies of witnesses. The Condon Committee would later reduce the testimonies to "anecdotal gossip."

Over the years, there are those who have claimed the Robertson Panel was a whitewash, but a thorough examination of the record suggests that panel scientists did the best they could within the framework of their orders. They were not experts in the UFO phenomenon and they had not spent months or years investigating and reviewing the sighting reports. They spoke to no witnesses[9] and the only evi-

---

[9]Hynek has said that he felt as if he had been treated as a witness by the panel members. Although the panel members wanted to see the films, they didn't try to get either photographer to appear before them to describe the scene.

dence they saw were films that showed bright lights moving through the sky that could, unfortunately, be interpreted as almost anything.

One other thing must be understood to keep the Robertson Panel in perspective. The panel's first concern was to determine if UFOs posed a threat to national security. That was a question panel members could answer. They decided, based on the number of UFO reports made through official intelligence channels through the years, that UFOs did, after a fashion, pose a threat.

Fournet mentioned it in his interview with me and Ruppelt mentioned it in his analysis. Too many reports at the wrong time *could* mask a Soviet attack on the United States. Although hindsight shows us this threat was of little importance, especially when the sorry state of Soviet missile research in 1952 is considered, it was a major concern to those men in the intelligence field in the early 1950s. A sudden flood of UFO reports, not unlike what had happened during the summer of 1952, could create havoc in the message traffic so that critical messages of an imminent attack would be hidden or lost.

With that as a concern, the Robertson Panel, who had seen nothing to suggest that UFOs were anything other than misidentifications, hoaxes, and weather and astronomical phenomena, needed to address this concern. That was the motivation behind some of the panel's recommendations. These recommendations, then, were born of a need to clear the intelligence reporting channels and not of a need to answer the questions about the reality of the UFO phenomena.

The panel report stated, ". . . although evidence of any direct threat from these sightings was wholly lacking, related dangers might well exist resulting from: a. Misidentification of actual enemy artifacts by defense personnel. b. Overloading of emergency reporting channels with 'false' information ('noise to signal ratio' analogy—Berkner). c. Subjectivity of public to mass hysteria and greater vulnerability to possible enemy psychological warfare."

The panel report continued, "Although not the concern of the CIA, the first two of these problems may seriously affect the Air Defense intelligence system, and should be studied by experts, possibly under ADC. If U.F.O.'s become discredited in a reaction to the 'flying saucer' scare, or if reporting channels are saturated with false and poorly documented reports, our capability of detecting hostile activity will be reduced. Dr. Page noted that more competent screening or filtering of reported sightings at or near the source is required, and that this can best be accomplished by an educational program."

Of all the suggestions in the panel report, this is the area that has caused the most trouble with interpretation. The panel was suggesting that if people were more familiar with what was in the sky around them, if they were familiar with natural phenomena that were rare but spectacular, then many sighting reports could be eliminated. How many UFO sightings are explained by Venus, meteors, or bright stars that seemed to hover for hours? In today's environment, with video cameras everywhere, how many times has Venus been taped and offered by witnesses as proof they saw something?

Under the subheading of "Educational Program," the panel recommended, "The Panel's concept of a broad educational program integrating efforts of all concerned agencies was that it should have two major aims: training and 'debunking.' "

The panel explained, "The training aim would result in proper recognition of unusually illuminated objects (e.g. balloons, aircraft reflections) as well as natural phenomena (meteors, fireballs, mirages, noctilucent clouds). Both visual and radar recognition are concerned. There would be many levels in such education . . . This training should result in a marked reduction in reports caused by misidentified cases and resultant confusion."

The problem with the next paragraph came from the use of the word "debunking." Many read something nefarious into it, while the use of it and the tone of the paragraph suggest something that was, at the time, fairly innocuous, at least according to Condon sixteen years later.

"The 'debunking' aim would result in reduction in public interest in 'flying saucers' which today evokes a strong psychological reaction. This education could be accomplished by mass media such as television, motion pictures, and popular articles. Basis of such education would be actual case histories which had been puzzling at first but later explained. As in the case of conjuring tricks, there is much less stimulation if the 'secret' is known. Such a program should tend to reduce the current gullibility of the public and consequently their susceptibility to clever hostile propaganda. The Panel noted that the general absence of Russian propaganda based on a subject with so many obvious possibilities for exploitation might indicate a possible Russian official policy."

The panel then discussed the planning of the educational program. Some have seen that as a "disinformation" program designed to explain UFOs as mundane. The real reason behind it, however, seems to be to end sighting reports made by those who are unfamiliar with the sky. The educational program was suggested as a teaching tool.

Seventeen years later, Edward Condon addressed a similar concern. He wanted an educational program that would discourage interest in UFOs. Again, he wasn't addressing the problem of the reality of the situation but was concerned with a symptom of it. The code word was "education," but the result would be the same: to hide the truth about UFOs behind the cloak of superior education, convincing the unenlightened that flying saucers were the realm of the unschooled, the ignorant, and the drunk.

The UFO information presented, according to those who were at some or all of the panel's sessions, was managed. Panel members had a limited amount of time and were unable to examine all of the aspects of the UFO field in the time they had. It can be suggested that a careful management of the data supplied would provide a biased picture and that the conclusions drawn from that specific data would be accurate, but those conclusions would be skewed. It could be argued that the panel was designed specifically so that time would not allow those embarrassing questions to be asked. And it can be suggested that the panel was loaded with scientists who had already made up their minds about the reality of UFOs.

A careful study of the data supplied to the Robertson Panel does suggest that UFOs are little more than anecdotal gossip. The exceptions supplied to them are the movies and the data from radar. However, without another piece of data, without some kind of physical evidence that would lead to the extraterrestrial hypothesis, no other conclusions could be drawn. The films were interesting, but there were alternative explanations that, while not as satisfactory in the long run, were certainly no less valid. And radar cases are open to the interpretation of the radar operators. Their training, talent, and expertise are all important factors.

The question then becomes: Was someone in the government confident enough in his own abilities to micromanage the data that he could influence the conclusions? Could he be sure that there wouldn't be a wild card on the table that might jerk his carefully prepared plan off the rails? The study was going to be classified, so the potential damage was limited for a time. But what would happen if the study concluded that UFOs were from other planets and that information leaked into the public arena?

It seems to be a very big risk to undertake. It also implies that there was someone managing these things at the top who was brilliant beyond description. If someone conceived of this plan as a way of convincing the vast majority of the people in the intelligence and scientific communities that UFOs were little more than illusion, misidentification, and hoax, it worked brilliantly. According to Swords, Robertson, Chadwell, and the others at CIA were just the sort of men who could design such a plan. Besides, they were the ones who selected the panel members. The only member of the panel who seemed unbiased was Thorton Page, and he was overwhelmed by the prestige of the other, high-powered members.

It must be pointed out there is some interesting evidence to support this scenario. The evidence suggests that the panel was empowered as a fact-finding commission and because the extraterrestrial evidence the panel received was weak to nonexistent, the panel concluded that UFOs posed no threat to national security, but not that UFOs were not extraterrestrial.

If the Robertson Panel was a part of the conspiracy of silence, some of its recommendations must have irritated those inside the intelligence community. Instead of suggesting that Project Blue Book be closed, the panel recommended that it be expanded. The panel suggested that the investigative staff be quadrupled and that fully trained specialists in various fields be employed. The panel said that the project should not be classified, but that every phase of it be open to public scrutiny. This is the way the Robertson Panel wanted to debunk the flying saucers. The panel wanted to tell everything that was publicly known about them.

It would seem that if, as many have suggested, the Robertson Panel was just another in a long line of manipulated investigations with foregone conclusions, that the recommendations would be to cease the operations. If the members of the panel knew the truth and were hiding it, they were recommending the path that could expose that data to all. But the reality of the situation seems to be that only one or two of the top men knew the truth. The others just thought they did. And although they recommended that Blue Book be open to public scrutiny, Blue Book was about to become little more than a shell of its former self. Air Defense Command regulations were already written that would move UFO investigation from Blue Book and ATIC to another classified unit. The public would not know the difference.

Dewey Fournet, who was present during the Robertson Panel meetings, who briefed panel members on the sighting reports, and who answered their questions about the investigation, said that it was a legitimate effort. The panel was searching for answers. But Fournet had not been present for all the sessions, and he thought that Durant had authored the report at the conclusion of the discussions late on Friday. Fournet did not know that the report, in draft form, existed before Friday and possibly before the panel was even convened on Wednesday.

But the question that seemed to be foremost in the minds of those on the panel was if there was a threat to national security. That is the angle that has been overlooked too often. Robertson might have wanted to answer the question about the nature of the phenomenon, but that's doubtful. Instead, he answered the one he had to. UFOs, at that point, posed no threat to national security. After more than five years of UFO sighting reports, no hostile intent had been observed.

The emerging documentation, the minutes of the meetings, diaries, and notes kept by the participants,[10] and discussions held with them in later years provide us with several important clues. The Robertson Panel, then, becomes just another chapter in the conspiracy of silence. It was scripted from the very beginning without those who made presentations aware that the final conclusions were drawn before they even sat down.

The story of the Robertson Panel isn't quite as open as some researchers have wanted to believe. It also indicates when the conspiracy of silence kicked into high gear.

---

[10]The vast majority of this material has been reviewed by Dr. Swords. Much of it is available in various archives and repositories for review by independent researchers.

CHAPTER 7

The 4602d and the
New Conspiracy of Silence

IT MIGHT BE SAID THAT THE CONSPIRACY OF SILENCE operated in two stages: an initial wave when the first flying saucers were reported and a second stage that came about because of the summer of 1952. Those in positions of power at the end of 1947 might have believed that the interest in flying saucers had vanished. Periodically, there were magazine articles and a few sightings, such as the Lubbock Lights in 1951, received some national publicity, but for the most part, public interest in UFOs had evaporated. Most people believed there was nothing to them.

The military, after the code name Sign was compromised, claimed that the UFO investigation had been closed. But the military had merely changed the name and kept the project going under the code name of Grudge. Then, in December 1949, the military announced that Project Grudge had been ended.

But the project continued, still using the code name Grudge. Later that code name was changed and Blue Book was born.

In the beginning, Blue Book was a solid investigation of UFOs. But after the summer of 1952, that situation changed. Clearly, UFOs were not going to go away. Clearly, the public interest, after more than five years, was at an all-time high. Newspaper reporters and magazine writers were trying to learn everything they could about UFOs. Books on the topic sold well and more were scheduled to be published that year. Something had to be done to end the interest.

One of the responses was the CIA's Robertson Panel. The other was a new set of regulations and a change in the way the UFO investigation was going to be handled. ATIC and Project Blue Book, the main "action" addressees on UFO-related items of intelligence, were about to lose that distinctive status. New regulations, issued by the Air Defense Command on January 3, 1953, created the 4602d Air Intelligence Service Squadron (AISS). Other new regulations, including Air Force Regulation 200-2, dated August 1953,[1] tasked the 4602d with the investigation of UFOs. All UFO reports would pass through the 4602d AISS prior to transmission to ATIC. That was a major change in the UFO investigation.

It is interesting to note that Ed Ruppelt, after briefing the members of the Robertson Panel, was on his way to Ent Air Force Base near Colorado Springs, the headquarters of the 4602d. He was scheduled to

---

[1]Various drafts of the regulation had been proposed. The August 1953 date comes from the draft that had been accepted by various Air Force commands. It would be officially published a year later.

arrive on January 24, 1953, to "present a one hour briefing at Officers Call."[2] The trip was arranged by Major Vernon L. Sadowski on January 7, 1953, or about a week before the Robertson Panel began its meetings.

But Ruppelt, in describing how the 4602d entered into the UFO investigation business, seemed to think it was the result not of manipulation at the top, but because of his pushing from the bottom. He wrote, "Project Blue Book got a badly needed shot in the arm when an unpublicized but highly important change took place: another intelligence agency began to take over all field investigations . . . the orders had been to build it up—get more people—do what the [Robertson] panel recommended. But when I'd ask for more people, all I got was a polite 'So sorry.' . . . I happened to be expounding my troubles one day at Air Defense Command Headquarters while I was briefing General Burgess, ADC's Director of Intelligence, and he told me about his 4602d Air Intelligence Squadron, a specialized intelligence unit that had recently become operational. Maybe it could help . . ."[3]

Ruppelt explained that he didn't expect much from Burgess. Ruppelt expected to write memos and letters and seal "it in a time capsule for preservation so that when the answer finally does come through the future generation that receives it will know how it all started."

---

[2]Based on the unit history of the 4602d AISS and correspondence available in the Project Blue Book files.

[3]Ed Ruppelt, *The Report on Unidentified Flying Objects* (New York: Ace Books, 1956).

This time things were different. Ruppelt wrote, "But I underestimated the efficiency of the Air Defense Command. Inside of two weeks General Burgess had called General Garland, they'd discussed the problem, and I was back in Colorado Springs setting up a program with Colonel White's 4602d."

In Ruppelt's book, he implied that all of this happened late in the summer of 1953. Ruppelt's tour at Blue Book was scheduled to end in February 1953, and he departed for two months of temporary duty in Denver. He wrote, "When I came back to ATIC in July 1953 and took over another job, Lieutenant Olsson was just getting out of the Air Force and A1/c (Airman First Class) [Max] Futch was now it . . . In a few days I again had Project Blue Book as an additional duty this time and I had orders to 'build it up.'"

So Ruppelt is talking to General Burgess at the end of the summer, and within weeks he is told that the 4602d is available to investigate UFOs. Documentation, however, doesn't bear this out.

On March 5, 1953, months before Ruppelt met with General Burgess, a letter, headed "Utilization of 4602d AISS Personnel in Project Blue Book Field Investigations," was sent to the Commanding General of the Air Defense Command and to the attention of the Director of Intelligence at Ent Air Force Base. The plan of action outlined in the letter was approved on March 23, 1953.

In the letter, it was written, "'During the recent conference attended by personnel of the 4602d AISS and Project Blue Book, the possibility of utilizing 4602d AISS field units to obtain additional data on reports of Unidentified Flying Objects was discussed.

It is believed by this Center that such a program would materially aid ATIC and give 4602d AISS personnel valuable experience in field interrogation. It would also give them an opportunity to establish further liaison with other governmental agencies, such as CAA, other military units etc., in their areas."

The interesting statement here, as in many of the other documents relating to the 4602d, is the idea that the field teams, by interrogating witnesses to UFO sightings, can gain valuable experience. Ruppelt pointed out that the 4602d had a primary function of interrogating captured enemy airmen during war. In a peacetime environment, all they could do was interrogate "captured" Americans in simulations. According to Ruppelt, "Investigating UFO reports would supplement these problems [wartime simulations] and add a factor of realism that would be invaluable in their training."

All of this went on while Ruppelt was on temporary duty and someone else was heading Project Blue Book. It would seem that some correspondence between the ADC and ATIC would have been on file at Blue Book. Ruppelt, when he returned to ATIC, should have been aware that negotiations between the 4602d and ATIC were in progress, yet Ruppelt's book suggests that he didn't understand that.

Upon publication of Air Force Regulation 200-2 in August 1953, a briefing about implementation of the regulation was held at Ent Air Force Base for members of the 4602d. Publication of a regulation suggests that the changes had been in the planning stage for a long time. It suggests that the implementation of ADC Regulation 24-3, published on January 3, 1953, was part of a larger plan.[4] It was probably all an outgrowth of the wave of sightings from the summer of 1952.

During the briefing, one of the officers asked, "What is the status of the 4602d in regards to this new UFOB[5] regulation?"

Major DeBruler said, "I want to say that on this UFOB regulation that ADC will designate the 4602d as the agency to discharge its responsibility for field and certain preliminary investigations. Secondly, there will be a criteria established as a guide to determine when the field units will conduct a detailed follow-up investigation and when they will not."[6]

This is important because it marks the shift in the UFO investigations. The Robertson Panel recommended no secrecy. The panel wanted to share everything with the public to prove there was nothing to hide. But that didn't happen. Instead, Blue Book was stripped of its investigative function and became little more than a public relations clearing house. The real investigations were conducted by the 4602d AISS, an intelligence agency of which no one outside a limited circle inside the intelligence community knew. Public questions about UFOs went to Blue Book, but no one asked the 4602d what it was doing. The 4602d operated outside the spotlight of the media.

---

[4] It seems to be too much of a coincidence to believe that after the summer sightings of 1952, that both the Air Force, in the form of the Air Defense Command, and the CIA began meetings about UFOs. These efforts seem to all be part of a larger plan designed to hide the truth from the public.

[5] UFOB is the term used inside the military for UFOs. They, for some reason, kept the "b" from "object."

[6] 4602d unit history.

From the documentation available, it is clear that
he investigative function after 1953 rested with the
602d.[7] UFO sighting reports were transmitted elec-
ronically to the closest of the field units for investi-
,ation. Once that investigation was completed, the
ightings that were not identified were transmitted
n to ATIC and supposedly provided to Project
lue Book.

Although AFR 200-2 was first published in August
953, its implementation seems to have lagged until
August of the following year. Reports available in
he 4602d unit history, originally classified "secret,"
how that there was some reluctance to take on the
ask of UFO investigation.

This is not to suggest, from some of the early re-
orts, that the 4602d was operating to suppress UFO
ata, though that was the effect. The men at the
neetings, from the questions asked, seemed more
oncerned with the logistical support available to
nem to complete their mission rather than hiding
nything about their work. The regulations at squad-
on and flight levels had not yet been written.

During the initial briefing held in 1954, Lieutenant
'aughn said, "General Carey is very vehement in
is desire to see these reports before they are sent
nywhere. What will be done about that? He has
een this AFR 200-2, but before they are sent in, he
till wants to see them."

Colonel White answered, "I see no objection to

Air Force regulations and the directives being passed from office to
ffice in the Pentagon make this clear. Ruppelt, in his book, complained
out the lack of support for Blue Book. After the new ADC regulations
ere passed in January 1953, no one in power expected Blue Book to
● any real work.

that, if they don't get tied up. There is nothing in 200-2 that says that written reports (AF 112) should go to General Carey. Again, this is in his division area of responsibility. General Carey is one of the sharpest officers in the Air Force today, and if he wants you to do something like this in his area, it, of course, should be done. The one arrangement that I would make is that you should hand-carry the reports to him."[8]

The question that begs to be asked is if this was in some way an attempt to circumvent AFR 200-2 by General Carey. And why should the reports be hand-carried to him?

The simplest answer is that General Carey, because the UFO program was moving into his area of responsibility, wanted to be kept apprised of what was happening in the field. Hand-carrying the reports just expedited the process. There seems to be nothing underhanded or nefarious in the operations as they were being established by the 4602d. The 4602d was tasked with a job and was attempting to carry it out to the best of its abilities.

What is important here is the shift of investigative responsibility. Ruppelt complained that his tiny shop was overworked and undermanned, and a splendid compromise was found. In reality, since none of this was made public until long after the fact, it is clear that it was one more aspect of the conspiracy of silence.

A review of the magazine articles and books released in 1947 and 1948 when Project Sign was created speak of Project Saucer. Once the real name,

---

[8] 4602d unit history.

Project Sign, was compromised, the public name of Project Saucer was scrapped. Officials then suggested that Project Sign had been closed and no new investigation had been undertaken. Of course, it was only a name change. The project still existed.

This time the name was left in place, but the location of the investigation shifted. Blue Book would issue press releases and reporters would call the project for information, but the investigation was now housed in the Air Defense Command and conducted by the 4602d.

While it can be argued persuasively that military secrets are necessary and since Blue Book was well known by the beginning of 1953, the policy makes sense. But it can also be argued that the policy is an outgrowth of a desire to mislead the public about the reality of the situation. The question that can be asked (and frequently was): "How can anyone suspect the Air Force takes UFOs seriously if the investigation consists of an officer, an NCO, an enlisted man or two, and a secretary?" The answer is, of course, not very.

But, of course, that wasn't the true picture. Investigation was continuing at a very high level with the addition of the 4602d's intelligence teams. More information comes from the unit history (originally classified as "secret") and dated from January 1 to June 30, 1955. "The 4602d Air Intelligence Service Squadron continues to conduct all field investigations within the zone of the interior to determine the identity of any Unidentified Flying Objects." The unit history also noted, "The responsibility for UFOB investigation was placed on the Air Defense Command, with the publication of AFR 200-2, dated 12 August 1954.''

This merely confirms what we had suspected before. There was a secret study of UFOs conducted by the Air Force that was not part of the Blue Book system. Clearly, ATIC was involved because regulations demanded it, but there is nothing to suggest that every report forwarded to ATIC made its way down to Blue Book.

There is a historical precedence for this belief. Colonel William Coleman eventually served with Project Blue Book. In the summer of 1955, Coleman and a crew were flying a B-25 from Miami, Florida, to Mississippi. The entire crew saw a round shadow of an object at treetop level.

During a maneuver, Coleman lost sight of the object, so he climbed to 1,500 feet. From that altitude he found the object again as it crossed a fresh-plowed, dried Alabama field. The object was kicking up twin voracities of dust as it raced along at low level. When Coleman gave chase, he lost sight of the object but could still see the trail it was leaving. As he began his landing in Mississippi, he caught a final glimpse of it at 25,000 feet.

Following regulations, Coleman and the crew made a report. According to AFR 200-2, in effect in the summer of 1955, that report would have gone to the 4602d with investigators dispatched from the nearest field office, probably Dobbins Air Force Base in Georgia.

When Coleman arrived at Blue Book some years later, he asked Robert Friend, then head of Blue Book, if he could see his sighting report. It was not in the Blue Book files. We can speculate, then, that the report was filed, as required by regulation, with the 4602d. When the 4602d failed to identify the source of the sighting, the report was forwarded to ATIC, as required by regulation. It went, however, no farther than that. It never reached Blue Book.

Dr. J. Allen Hynek, the Air Force astronomy consultant for Blue Book, has confirmed that situation. According to many former colleagues at the Center for UFO Studies, Hynek told them that the really good, really hot reports never reached Project Blue Book. They were stopped somewhere up the line.

While that demonstrates one level of the conspiracy, the attitude at the 4602d, not as unbiased as it should have been, demonstrates another level of the silence. In volume two of the unit history, there is a "UFOB Summary" that contains some disturbing remarks. The author of the report wrote, "First recorded instances of genuine UFOBs occurred in 1948 [sic] with the appearance of the 'Flying Saucer' in different parts of the United States. Rapid diffusion to all parts of the world, including the Soviet Union and its satellites . . . Birth of a new literary genre 'Science Fiction' which in most cases is entirely fictitious and unscientific [Do I really need to point out that science fiction is, by definition, *fiction*?] . . . Emotional stimulus of speculation on the fantastic . . . General Public not qualified to evaluate material propounded in science fiction. Absurd and fantastic theories given credence solely on the basis of ignorance . . . UFOB reports even though patently ridiculous receive undue attention through latent fear, etc."

Even with that attitude, something was getting done. According to the report, "The 4602d AISS had received a total of 306 preliminary UFOB reports from 12 August 1954 to 30 June 1955. Of this total, 198 reports were resolved by analysis at Squadron Headquarters; 48 were resolved from follow up investigations. Sixty (60) reports were forwarded to Air Technical Intelligence Center as unresolved, 37 for lack of sufficient data for evaluation and 23 as unknowns."

There is another aspect to this shift from Project Blue Book to the 4602d that must be examined. UFO researchers and believers had suggested for years that there were quick-reaction teams with a mission of retrieving crashed flying saucers. Clearly, there is no documentation to support this allegation. The 4602d, with a mission of interrogating downed enemy crew members, had qualified parachutists, skiers, mountain climbers, and personnel skilled in using unconventional transportation. The members of the 4602d were experts in survival, communications, and even photography who could reach a downed aircraft faster than anyone else. It other words, the 4602d was a highly trained quick-reaction team that had been assigned the additional mission of interrogating UFO witnesses.

All of these skills and training, for which the 4602d was known, would be the ones necessary for reaching the site of a crashed alien spacecraft quickly. If the Roswell crash as described earlier was of an alien craft, then it would be expected that some sort of recovery team would be established in case it happened again. The 4602d mission of aircrew recovery provides the perfect cover.

Or it can be considered from another point of view. The reason for creating the 4602d might be the one laid out in the various documents. It was started as a way of reaching airplane crash sites to capture enemy pilots. Such a mission could be easily adapted to the retrieval of an alien spacecraft, if one crashed anywhere in the world. The 4602d, although deployed only to sites inside the United States, according to the documentation, had personnel who could parachute into the remotest parts of the world on very short notice.

Although it has been suggested that the 4602d began to participate in the UFO program as a way of obtaining training in field interrogation techniques, Captain J. Cybulski, at an annual commanders' conference, reported, "The primary reason for our participation in this program is to solve a very perplexing problem for the Air Force and the country as a whole. To the Air Force the investigation of the UFOB is very important."[9]

This despite the fact that some of those writing reports didn't see the UFOB problem as particularly mysterious. The unidentified author wrote, "UFOB reports even the patently ridiculous receive undue attention . . ."

By the mid-1950s, Project Blue Book was no longer an investigative agency. Its authority had been stripped and although Blue Book did participate in the highly visible cases—those that were considered high-profile—it is clear the vast majority of the investigation was completed by the 4602d.

It is also clear from the documentation that the Air Force had a rather large staff working the UFO problem. While many of the investigators had other

---

[9]4602d unit history.

duties to perform, they also researched UFOs, as the number of investigations between August 1954 and July 1955 alone demonstrate. They investigated more than 300 UFO reports, one of which must have been Coleman's UFO sighting.

There is one other sighting that took place in this time frame, but for which I don't have precise information. Brigadier General Arthur Exon, who would later become a base commander at Wright-Patterson Air Force Base and who would corroborate some of the Roswell testimony, was a colonel at the Pentagon in the mid-1950s. During that time, the Air Force suffered, according to Exon, one of its biggest losses in UFO history. Four aircraft disappeared while chasing a UFO over Kentucky or Tennessee. They had been scrambled, but none of them ever returned. Exon said, "There were four of them that were scrambled. They were all lost."

He said that the incident was thoroughly investigated, but no one ever found a clue as to what happened. Exon pointed out that it didn't happen over water, where the aircraft could have crashed into a deep lake or into the ocean. To his knowledge, no wreckage was ever found. He did say, "It's a matter of record and it's kind of a mysterious thing."

This is, of course, exactly the sort of case for which the 4602d had been trained. The 4602d could have been on the scene in a matter of hours, if there was any sort of crash site to be explored. If not, the investigators for the 4602d would have been there trying to learn all they could about the disappearance.

While ATIC would have been kept informed about the investigation, it is just one more example of Blue Book being left out of the loop. And if what Exon said is accurate, the secrecy extended into the Pentagon. Granted, Exon would have had no need to know about the fate of the aircraft. What is interesting is that he heard about the disappearance but nothing about the outcome of the investigation.

What this shows is that the conspiracy of silence extended into the Pentagon. There are those who knew what was happening, those who knew that UFOs were taken seriously at the highest levels, and those who knew nothing at all about the situation. How better to keep a secret than to convince most that the topic was ridiculous? If you don't believe there is a secret, then you do not search for it.

CHAPTER 8

The End of Blue Book and the Condon Committee

THE TONE IN OFFICIAL CIRCLES CHANGED IN THE late 1950s and early 1960s. Many in high places began to see the Air Force's official UFO investigation as a burden the Air Force was forced to carry. After General Vandenberg's rejection of the extraterrestrial hypothesis in 1948, there had been little support for it until Ruppelt and the beginning of Blue Book. That situation changed in 1953, as new regulations took effect and the real UFO investigations were slipped out of Blue Book and into the Air Defense Command's 4602d.

That does not provide the whole story of the changing situation. After 1953, it was clear that Blue Book was considered of little importance. Manpower was reduced, and at one point an airman first class, the equivalent to a low-ranking NCO, had command of the operation. There were attempts to take Blue

Book out of ATIC (later Foreign Technology Division, FTD) and move it to SAFOI (Secretary of the Air Force, Office of Information).

On April 1, 1960, in a letter to Major General Dougher at the Pentagon, A. Francis Archer, a scientific advisor to Blue Book, commented on a memo written by Colonel Evans, a ranking office at ATIC, about Blue Book. Archer wrote, ". . . [I] have tried to get Blue Book out of ATIC for 10 years . . . and do not agree that the loss of prestige to the UFO project is a disadvantage."[1]

In 1962, Lieutenant Colonel Robert Friend, who headed Project Blue Book, wrote to his headquarters that the project should be handed over to a civilian agency that would word its report in such a way as to allow the Air Force to drop the study. At the same time, Edward Trapnell, an assistant to the Secretary of the Air Force, when talking to Dr. Robert Calkins of the Brookings Institution, said pretty much the same thing. Find a civilian committee to study the problem, then have them conclude it the way the Air Force wanted it concluded. One of the stipulations, of course, was that this civilian group say some positive things about the way the Air Force had handled the UFO problem for the last fifteen or twenty years.

Correspondence from various experts and agencies in the Blue Book files suggested the study be shut down. Some of those offering the advice realized that the public would have to be "educated to accept the closing." They wanted stronger suggestions by experts that UFOs were nothing more than mirages, misidentifications, and outright hoaxes.

---

[1]Administration files from Project Blue Book.

By 1966, the Air Force had managed to get Project Blue Book's press release issued through Secretary of the Air Force, Office of Information. Letters to the public no longer carried the prestigious ATIC letterhead but only the information office stamp. The Air Force was making its attempt to eliminate the UFO headache once and for all.

The major stumbling block was a new wave of sightings that began in April 1964 and lasted for nearly three years. First up was a report from Socorro, New Mexico,[2] that received national attention, including mentions on various network evening news programs as well as national front-page newspaper coverage.

Lonnie Zamora, a police officer in Socorro, was chasing a speeder in the early evening when he heard a loud roar and saw a flash of light. Believing that a dynamite shed had exploded, he broke off the chase, altering his course to take him by the shed.

Zamora was driving near a gully when, over 400 yards away, at the bottom of the gully, he spotted a bright white object. At first he thought it was an overturned car, but as he neared it, he could see two "people." Zamora stopped short and got out of his car. He couldn't see the individuals in the gully very well but thought they were shorter than normal adults.

Studying the scene, Zamora realized that the object wasn't an overturned vehicle but something else entirely. As he started forward, the figures apparently saw him. The figures ran into the UFO and Zamora ran toward his patrol car.

---

[2]Based on the Project Blue Book files and various other published accounts.

Seconds later, in a roaring of flame, the UFO disappeared. Zamora called his superior, Sergeant Sam Chavez. Although Chavez was not involved in the sighting and saw neither the craft nor the aliens, he did see the markings left behind. One bush was burning and some clumps of grass were burned. Four holes, apparently from landing gear, were pressed into the soft earth.

During the next several days, the official Air Force investigation was started. Air Force officers examined the landing site, interviewed Socorro residents, and took photographs. Air Force consultant Dr. J. Allen Hynek made a one-day investigation. Hynek, impressed with the sincerity displayed by Zamora and the physical evidence in the form of landing gear markings, said that he found no evidence that Zamora was capable of creating such an elaborate hoax.

A few months later, Hynek returned for another short investigation. He visited Zamora, Chavez, and the editor of the Socorro newspaper. In his final report, Hynek wrote, "The more articulate Sergeant Chavez still firmly believes Zamora's story . . . although I made a distinct attempt to find a chink in Zamora's armor, I simply couldn't find anyone, with the possible exception of a Mr. Philips, who has a house fairly near the site of the original sighting, who did anything but completely uphold Zamora's character."

Hynek's full report continues for eight pages but does not once suggest how the sighting could have been faked or why it would have been. He mentioned that Felix Philips lived close to the landing site but did not hear anything strange, even with the windows and french doors of his house open. Hynek wrote that he was not concerned with this seeming discrepancy because "the wind was blowing down the gully" and the Philips house is in the opposite direction. "This, of course, can make a tremendous difference in the ability to hear."

The final conclusion by Hynek was that he could not identify what had landed in Socorro. He didn't like Philips' claim of a hoax because "there are just too many bits of evidence that militate against this hypothesis."

Philip Klass, who entered the UFO community sometime after the Socorro sighting, made his own investigation. He wrote in *UFOs Explained*, "My investigation led me to disagree sharply with Hynek's statement that the Socorro case was 'one of the soundest, best substantiated reports.' Contrary to Hynek's observation, I found many 'contradictions or omissions.'"

Klass interviewed the same Socorro residents interviewed by Hynek, but he also interviewed others to whom Hynek never spoke, all of which led him in a different direction. He talked to several "scientist-professors" at the New Mexico Institute of Mining and Technology in Socorro. Klass was surprised that the scientists, with a single exception, were not interested in the Socorro UFO event. He wrote, "If the story was true, the most exciting scientific event of all time—a visit from an extraterrestrial spacecraft—had occurred almost within sight of the institute. How could these scientists be so uninterested?"

Then he shifted gears because one of the scientists told him to "nose around a bit." Klass asked for more information and was told that Socorro had no industry other than the institute. Tourists passed through on the main highways (one of which is now Interstate 25, which goes from Albuquerque to El Paso, Texas), but they never stopped, except to buy gas and to eat. Before the Air Force offered its Project Mogul explanation in 1994 for the Roswell crash, I had driven through Socorro a number of times, stopping only to eat or buy gas.

Klass quoted from the local newspaper that he read that night, " 'One of the best ways a community can boost its economy is to attract new industry. *Today, the fastest, most effective way to attract new industry is by first attracting tourists.* The reason is that industrialists, in selecting plant locations, are seeking for their employees the same kind of "community atmosphere" that appeals to tourists. [Emphasis added by Klass.]' " He had found his answer.

A year after the Socorro landing, on April 24, 1965, an article in the *El Paso Times* written by Jake Booher, Jr., reported that the town officials were quick to realize the significance of the UFO landing. Although Booher reported that Zamora wanted to forget the sighting, the town's seven thousand residents didn't. They were going to turn the landing site into the tourist attraction that would also attract industry.

Klass wrote, "The place where the UFO reportedly landed was especially convenient—almost midway between the two highways that bring tourists through Socorro—so it was relatively easy and inexpensive for city officials to provide an improved road that connected the site to the two highways."

In the next paragraph, Klass exposes the real story. The land next to the landing site was worthless. But if the site was developed as a tourist attraction, then the worthless land would suddenly become valuable. It could become the site of hot dog stands, souvenir shops, and maybe even a motel or two. This property, according to Klass, ". . . by a curious coincidence . . . was owned by Mayor Bursum, officer Zamora's boss."

The Socorro sighting, according to Klass, was the result of the mayor attempting to create a tourist attraction.[3] Of course, the tourist attractions were never developed, and the cars still flash by Socorro unless someone is hungry or needs gas. If someone stops, it is to find directions to the Very Large Array, a radio telescope on the Plains of San Agustin some fifty miles to the west, along Highway 60.

Just over a year later, a set of sightings came from Exeter, New Hampshire, that produced more national headlines and at least one book. Early on the morning of September 3, 1965, Norman Muscarello, then only eighteen, was hitchhiking home when a huge glowing object came at him across an open field. Frightened, Muscarello jumped into a ditch and watched as the object drifted around a house. Muscarello said the object was about eighty feet wide and had red pulsating lights.

As the object slipped away, Muscarello leaped from hiding and ran to another house. He banged on the door, but the residents thought he was drunk and wouldn't let him in. He spun around, ran to the road, and flagged down a car. The couple in the car took him to the Exeter police station.

The desk officer called Patrolman Eugene Bertrand,

---

[3]This is a recurring theme in the skeptical writings. We don't believe the witnesses because there is a suspected profit motive involved. Rarely has a UFO sighting been turned into a successful tourist attraction. There is no evidence of a profit motive in this case.

who had heard a similar story from a nearly hysterical woman he'd found parked by the side of the road. She told him she had been followed by a large, silent, airborne object with flashing red lights. It had passed within a few feet of her car.

Bertrand convinced Muscarello that they should return to where he'd seen the object. Bertrand thought he could convince the distraught young man that he'd seen some kind of helicopter or aircraft if they returned. Muscarello insisted that he knew an airplane when he saw one, especially when it was as close to him as the object had been.

Within minutes of their arrival, the object began a slow ascent from behind two pine trees. Bertrand thought about his revolver but left it in the holster. Instead, he watched as the object, wobbling slightly, bathed the area in a bright red light.

Bertrand ran back to his car and radioed the desk that he could see the object. Immediately, Bertrand was joined by another patrolman, David Hunt, who corroborated the sighting.

Later, Air Force investigators would report that "Operation Big Blast" was being conducted at the time. Descriptions by the witnesses suggested that refueling operations or photo recon missions. The Air Force admitted that the operations had been suspended by the time the witnesses claimed they saw the flying saucers.

The point here is not whether the sightings were explained adequately by the Air Force but that they received national publicity. John Fuller published *Incident at Exeter* in 1966, which provided more information about flying saucers for the general public. In fact, the Condon Committee, which would be formed about a year later, noted the explosion of UFO literature in the mid-1960s.

According to the final Condon report (issued in 1969), "By the early 1960s, the pattern for UFO books and magazine writing had become quite clearly established: the text consisted of a stringing together of many accounts or reported sightings with almost no critical comment or attempts at finding the validity of the material reported, mixed with a strong dash of criticism of the Air Force for not devoting more attention to the subject and for allegedly suppressing the startling truth about visitors from outer space."

But the sightings from Dexter, Michigan, that began on March 19, 1966, were the final straw, the inspiration for the Condon Committee. Those sightings involved police officers from Milan, Michigan. At one point, according to witnesses, the whole town was lit as an object flew over.

The next night the UFOs visited a swamp near the house of Frank Mannor, who later told reporters that "it was no hallaboolation." More than 50 people, including a dozen police officers, made sightings. Dr. Hynek, noting the close proximity of a swamp, the mild weather conditions, and the lack of wind, thought swamp gas might be an adequate explanation.

On the following night, March 21, the UFOs shifted to Hillsdale, Michigan, and a college campus. Nearly 100 people, including the local civil defense director, who was also an undertaker, saw the lights as they hovered above a nearby swamp. Hynek again suggested swamp gas.

Those who made sightings rejected Hynek's explanation outright. They suggested that the objects were huge and that some of them made sound. When some of the police officers used their binoculars, they thought they could see a shape behind the bright lights.

The response to Hynek's swamp gas theory was immediate. No one believed it. The explanation sounded too much like a guess that had little foundation. It was an explanation offered just to explain, without any thought given to the facts. Hynek was seen as the "chief debunker" paid by the Air Force, who had been hiding the information ever since the first UFO wave back in 1947. It doesn't matter if any of this is true because it was what was believed by the general public. The Air Force was not believed when it offered any explanation about UFOs.

Hynek was so savaged by the press that documents from the Project Blue Book files suggested that he no longer offer explanations. The documents suggested that the Office of Information issue the statements as a way of insulating Hynek from public criticism.

Public pressure was mounting. For three years in a row, a series of UFO sightings had grabbed national headlines. The explanations offered were found by the press to lack credibility. Congressman Gerald Ford of Michigan was demanding Congressional hearings about UFOs.

The outgrowth of this pressure by the public and Congress is one of the most blatant examples of the conspiracy of silence. Heralded in the beginning as just what the UFO phenomenon needed by those inside the civilian flying saucer community, the Condon Committee, organized at the University of Colorado, was funded by more than half a million dollars of Air Force money. Several universities had been approached, but they had all turned down the research grant. The University of Colorado had been way down the list of possible sites.

The scientific director of the project, the man who received the Air Force grant, was Dr. Edward U. Condon, a professor of physics and astrophysics and a fellow of the Joint Institute for Laboratory Astrophysics at the University of Colorado. As a career scientist, Condon had the sort of prestige the Air Force wanted.

Condon, prior to the Air Force assignment, had a distinguished career as a scientist. He was a former director of the National Bureau of Standards and was a member of the National Academy of Sciences. In 1941, he was named to the committee that established the atomic bomb program. He was a scientific advisor to a special Senate atomic energy committee for naval atomic bomb tests in 1946. Twenty years later, Condon was at the University of Colorado.

As noted by the documentation that appeared after the declassification of the Project Blue Book files, the formation of the Condon Committee was part of an already existing plan. Find a university to study the problem (flying saucers) and then conclude it the way the Air Force wanted it concluded.[4] It is obvious that the first universities approached did not agree to the conditions placed on them by the Air Force contracts. It is clear that the Air Force was beginning its attempt to get out of the UFO investigation business.

Jacques Vallee, writing about the Condon Committee in *Dimensions*, said, "As early as 1967, members

---

[4]Various letters from the administration files of Project Blue Book.

of the Condon Committee were privately approaching their scientific colleagues on other campuses, asking them how they would react if the committee's final report to the Air Force were to recommend closing down Project Blue Book." This tends to confirm the real mission of Condon was not to study the phenomenon but to study ways to end Air Force involvement in it.

A rebellion began inside the Condon Committee when a small group of scientists complained about the lack of scientific standards. A private memo written by Dr. Robert Low, which was discovered by the group, laid out the plan and provided evidence that the Condon Committee never intended to study UFOs. Key members of the research team set out to systematically debunk the subject. After the memo was published, the scientists in the rebellion group were fired. Details of this were laid out by Dr. David Saunders in *UFOs? Yes!*, a book written with R. Roger Harkins.

Dr. Michael Swords has spent the last several years studying the history of the Condon Committee and confirms the view that the Air Force used Condon. But Condon was a willing participant in the deception. According to a letter discovered by Swords and written by Lieutenant Colonel Robert Hippler to Condon, the plan was laid out in no uncertain terms. Hippler told Condon that no one knew of any extraterrestrial visitation and therefore there "has been no visitation."

Hippler also pointed out that Condon "must consider" the cost of the investigations of UFOs and to "determine if the taxpayer should support this" for the next ten years. Hippler warned that it would be another decade before another independent study could be mounted that might end the Air Force UFO project.[5]

Condon understood what Hippler was trying to tell him. Three days later, Condon delivered a lecture to scientists in Corning, New York, including those members of the Corning Section of the American Chemical Society and the Corning Glass Works Chapter of Sigma XI, telling them, "It is my inclination right now to recommend that the government get out of this business. My attitude right now is that there is nothing in it. But I am not supposed to reach a conclusion for another year."[6]

Robert Low responded to Hippler's letter a day or so after Condon's Corning talk, telling him that the committee members were very happy now that they knew what they were supposed to do. Low wrote, ". . . you indicate what you believe the Air Force wants of us, and I am very glad to have your opinion." Low pointed out that Hippler had answered the questions about the study "quite directly."[7]

In the UFO literature, Low had become nothing more than Condon's hatchet man, but Swords believes this to be an unfair characterization. In fact, according to Swords, Low had a rather brilliant plan for the investigation that would have entailed the creation of a "casebook" containing both new cases

---

[5]Correspondence (letter from Hippler to Condon 16 January 1967, letter from Low to Hippler 27 January 1967) filed at American Philosophical Society Library.

[6]Dick Olive, "Most UFO's Explainable, Says Scientist" *Elmira Star-Gazette*, January 26, 1967.

[7]Correspondence filed at American Philosophical Society Library.

and reinvestigation of some of the "classics," that is, cases that were extremely puzzling. Low hinted to those around him that he believed UFOs were a subject worthy of study.

Condon, it seems, agreed and was having fun with the UFO phenomenon at the beginning of the study in late 1966 through the summer of 1967. He attended UFO conventions and was seen with the most outrageous of the devotees, according to Dr. Swords. The crazier, the better. But in the summer of 1967, late June or early July, his attitude began to change.

For some reason, Condon began to fear UFOs. The theme of his discussions with others after June 1967, according to Swords, was that UFOs could be harmful to children. There was something wrong with an interest in UFOs. Even in the summary to the report, Condon wrote, "Therefore we strongly recommend that teachers refrain from giving students credit for school work based on their reading of the presently available UFO books and magazine articles. Teachers who find their students strongly motivated in this direction should attempt to channel their interests in the direction of the serious study of astronomy and meteorology, and in the critical analysis of arguments for fantastic propositions that are being supported by appeals to fallacious reasoning or false data."

This is a theme that he came back to frequently. Condon told colleagues that the Betty and Barney Hill[8] case pointed out the problem with a belief in UFOs. Condon believed that "all this kooky" stuff was the product of some sort of mental instability

---

[8] The Barney and Betty Hill case is the first abduction report to receive widespread coverage in the United States. It set the standard for the thousands of such reports that would follow.

and not just boys having fun. Because of that, he saw UFOs as dangerous.

In 1969, the Condon Committee released its findings. The Condon Committee found, as had all of the previous committees, that UFOs posed no threat to the security of the United States. Edward U. Condon wrote, in "Section I, Recommendations and Conclusions," that "The history of the past 21 years has repeatedly led Air Force officers to the conclusion that none of the things seen, or thought to have been seen, which pass by the name UFO reports, constituted any hazard or threat to national security."

After suggesting that such a finding was "out of our province" to study and that the committee would pass any such evidence it did find on to the Air Force, Condon wrote, "We know of no reason to question the finding of the Air Force that the whole class of UFO reports so far considered does not pose a defense problem."

Included in the recommendations was the idea that "It is our impression that the defense function could be performed within the framework established for intelligence and surveillance operations without the continuance of a special unit such as Project Blue Book, but this is a question for defense specialists rather than research scientists."

That seems to have taken care of most of the requirements. Condon confirmed that national security wasn't an issue, said some positive things about the Air Force handling of the UFO phenomenon, and recommended the end of Project Blue Book. He did his job.

Finally Condon wrote, "It has been contended that the subject has been shrouded in official secrecy. We conclude otherwise. We have no evidence of secrecy concerning UFO reports. What has been miscalled secrecy has been no more than an intelligent policy of delay in releasing data so that the public does not become confused by premature publication of incomplete studies or reports."

It is impossible to understand how Condon could write those words after being handed a stack of Blue Book files stamped SECRET that had been held by the Air Force for more than a decade. It is impossible to understand this when there was documentation that proves secrecy on the part of the Air Force. It was in 1969 that Brigadier General C. H. Bolender wrote, "Moreover, reports of unidentified flying objects which could affect national security are made in accordance with JANAP 146 or Air Force Manual 55-11 and are not part of the Blue Book system."

Air Force Regulation 200-2, which guided the investigation of UFOs by the military, made it clear that reports of UFOs were investigated by the 4602d AISS after 1953. More importantly, the regulation ordered, "For those objects which are not explainable, only the fact that ATIC will analyze the data is worthy of release, due to the many unknowns involved."

In other words, documentation existed to support the claim that there was secrecy. While a case can be made that the regulations and the secrecy are warranted by the circumstances, it can also be argued that the secrecy did exist, contrary to what Condon wrote.

What this does is demonstrate that the Condon Committee was not an unbiased scientific study of UFOs, but a carefully designed project that had a single objective: to end public Air Force involvement in the UFO phenomenon. After all, according to Hippler, should the taxpayers fund another ten years of UFO research?

The Condon report suggested that there was no evidence of extraterrestrial visitation and that all UFO reports could be explained if sufficient data had been gathered in the beginning. This is exactly what Hippler wrote in his January 1967 letter to Condon. Yet, even when the committee selected the sightings it would investigate, it failed to explain almost 30 percent of them. In one case (over Labrador, 30 June 1954), the committee wrote, "This unusual sighting should therefore be assigned to the category of some almost certainly natural phenomenon, which is so rare that it apparently has never been reported before or since."[9]

In other cases, the "possible" or "probable" labels that had been attached to sightings were removed. The Tremonton, Utah, film of July 1952 switched from possible birds to being definitely explained as birds.

The Washington National sightings, also of July 1952, as detailed by the Condon Committee, bore no resemblance to the unbiased reports offered by other investigators. In the Condon report, it was suggested that very few of the pilots sent to look for UFOs on those nights saw anything. Most of the sightings were made on radar and the radar end was explainable as weather-related phenomena.

The problem here is the idea there were few visual sightings. The report did quote from a few Air Force personnel who talked of seeing stars, but even Ed Ruppelt, head of Project Blue Book during the sightings, admitted that those "confessions" seemed coerced.

---

[9]Daniel S. Gillmore (ed.), *Final Report of the Scientific Study of Unidentified Flying Objects* (New York: Bantam Books, 1968), p. 140.

Dewey Fournet and Al Chop, who both were present on the second Saturday night set of sightings, knew that visual sightings had been made. Fournet said, "When you combine radar reports with [Lieutenant] Holcomb's explanations to me about solid returns with reports of the pilots, I think you can conclude they were not reflections from the atmosphere or temperature inversions."

Aware that the Condon Committee had virtually overlooked the visual sightings made by both civilian airline and military interceptor pilots, as well as lockons by onboard radars, I asked about the Condon Committee's suggestion that there were few visual corroborations. Fournet said, "The reports we got from at least one of the fighter pilots was pretty gory." He wouldn't elaborate, just saying that "It was pretty interesting."

Fournet made one other point that I found interesting. Although the Condon Committee had spoken to a number of the controllers who had been in the radar room during the Washington Nationals, the investigators didn't search for Fournet. Finding him from scratch was incredibly easy. I asked if he would have told the Condon Committee investigators what he had just told me. Fournet said, "Yes, I would. In fact, I think I would have told them more had I known what they were doing."

During my interview with Al Chop, I asked him if he had been contacted by the Condon Committee during its research. He said that he hadn't been. He would have, of course, provided the committee with as much information as he had given to me if the investigators had called.

During his investigation in December 1966, Michael Wertheimer spoke to many of the people who had been involved in the sightings, including some of the air traffic controllers and the Air Force personnel who reported sightings. He was aware of the visual and radar sightings, that targets were seen, at least once, on radars in three separate locations, and that onboard radars had locked on to the targets.

Wertheimer makes it very clear in his preliminary report that the controllers believed they were watching solid targets. They were aware of the explanation of weather-related phenomena, but they didn't believe it to be accurate. Paul Petersen, one of those controllers, told Wertheimer that he had not seen targets like those he saw in July 1952. He also mentioned that he had only seen similar targets on a couple of occasions after.

It becomes clear here that the conspiracy of silence is in full operation. Both Fournet and Chop were easy to locate. I did nothing special to find them. Had Wertheimer wanted to speak to them, he could have found them as easily. Since he didn't, the question becomes: "Why not?" Was he—or someone else on the Condon Committee—afraid of what they would say?

Timing here is critical. Wertheimer made his preliminary investigation at the beginning of December in 1966. Six weeks later, Hippler told Condon exactly what the Air Force wanted. The Washington Nationals investigation apparently ended at that point. And even though they had information that there were visual- and radar-coordinated sightings, when the final report was written, that information disappeared.

To fully understand this, we must examine the contract that was given to Condon. According to Swords, Condon was the "grantee" and the chief scientist. He had the job of writing the conclusions. He was not required to allow the "committee" to review them. In fact, Condon wrote his conclusions based on his personal opinion rather than the scientific facts surrounding UFOs as revealed by the investigation— what little there had been.

Discussing this with Dr. Swords, I asked about that and he said, "The chief scientist will write the summary and he can say whatever he wants in it. The summary for the Condon report is a disaster."

The casebook was never written. Low's plan for reviewing a number of cases in-depth is something that never happened. According to Swords, fifteen or so cases were written up for the casebook, but those treatments had been written by Tad Foster, a graduate law student. These were not technically oriented, and the plan called for the scientists to rewrite them in the proper format. That never happened.

The draft of the Washington Nationals, written by Foster for the ill-fated casebook, seems to be quite comprehensive. It lays out the weather data, interviews with the primary participants with the important exceptions of Fournet and Chop, and describes the complex events of July 1952 chronologically. What is interesting is the difference in the draft for the casebook and the final description as it appeared in the Condon report.

Another thing Condon did was refuse to investigate any of the past "classic" cases.[10] Whenever it was suggested, Condon said that they had been investigated and what could they learn that was new?

---

[10] Many on the Condon Committee thought that a careful reexamination of these cases would produce positive results. Condon refused. The only exceptions seem to be the radar cases and the photographic cases.

Even the Zamora case, the Exeter sightings, and the Michigan sightings were considered old cases. No need to review them.

Condon, then, did the job he was hired to do. He attempted to bury the questions about UFOs under a blanket of scientific jargon and supposed objectivity. The committee report, structured the way Condon wanted it, was, then, a prime example of the conspiracy of silence. It stopped many scientists and journalists from speaking about UFOs in a positive light, and that is exactly what it was designed to do.

The question that can be asked (and should be): "Was there something sinister about Condon and his report?" The answer isn't simple. Swords believes that Hippler and Condon, acting in concert, were sinister. The rest of the committee members, the men hired to do the work, did what they could under the conditions that presented themselves. Swords said, "I think that Condon and Colonel Hippler are nefarious and I think that Condon goes from being just simply nefarious to being paranoid."

It is quite clear from the evidence at hand that the Condon investigation of UFOs was not the unbiased report it was supposed to be. Almost no one accepts, as genuine, the conclusions it draws. Had Low's plan been used, then, according to Swords, ". . . there were a whole lot of people on the project, including Bob Low, who weren't whitewashing. Condon, because he was the grantee and it was a typical Air Force contract, he had the right . . . [as] the chief scientist [to] unilaterally . . . write the summary . . . Condon just takes control." Swords believed that if Low's plan had been used, "You would have had a hell of a lot different UFO history . . ."

With the report in hand, with the recommendations of an "independent" group of scientists, the Air Force found it could now end Project Blue Book. On December 17, 1969, the Air Force announced that it had completed its twenty-two year study of UFOs. There just was nothing to them. In fact, after investigating more than 12,000 sightings, only 701 were "unidentified."

A study of the Project Blue Book files, however, reveals just how misleading those statistics are. While it is true that only 701 sightings are listed as "unidentified," there are many others labeled as "identified" in which the explanation is less than perfect. As noted, Colonel Edward H. Wynn had written in 1960, "Probable causes for sightings based on limited information should be accepted."

Overlooking that, simply because a debate over the explanations for sightings that are thirty or forty years old would be counterproductive, we can draw other conclusions. For example, over 4,000 sightings are marked as "insufficient for a scientific analysis."[11] This means there is no explanation, but the label keeps the sighting out of the "unidentified" category.

Granted, some of the sightings contain very little information. If a man sees a bright light in the night sky at 3:00 A.M., it would be very difficult to explain the sighting if he can't himself. If it was a meteor, how many others would be awake at that hour to see it and identify it as such? And how many of those would misidentify the meteor?

There are other sightings that were labeled as "insufficient" that were not single-witness and where the object was in sight for several minutes. In one case, the

---

[11]Based on an analysis of the Project Blue Book file master index.

witness, learning that his sighting had been put into the "insufficient" category, wrote to ask what additional information the Air Force needed. If he had left something out of the report he'd provided to the officer who interviewed him, the witness wanted to know what it was. After further consideration by the Air Force, the sighting was relabeled as "unidentified."

But the Air Force was happy with the results of the Condon study. If a civilian now called an air base with a UFO sighting, he or she was told that the official UFO project had ended. If the witness felt threatened by the sighting, he or she could call the local law enforcement authorities. If investigation was desired, then a call to a university might provide the solution. Some law enforcement agencies passed UFO sightings on to local amateur groups. Others merely listened politely but did nothing with the report.

But the conspiracy had reached a new level. The government could deny any interest in UFOs. It had been announced that the Air Force was no longer investigating flying saucers. If there was a UFO case that interested the government, it could investigate without having to worry about being followed by the media. As happened when Project Sign was reorganized into Project Grudge, the government could now claim there was no longer any official interest. But the investigation did continue. Project Moon Dust and Operation Blue Fly would provide the manpower, the funds, and the umbrella under which to operate. Blue Book is gone, but the investigation continues.

CHAPTER 9

—

After Project Blue Book

WITH THE END OF PROJECT BLUE BOOK, THE
conspiracy of silence was in full swing at last. The
official word was that the Air Force and the government were now out of the business of investigating
UFOs. Twenty-two years and millions of dollars had
been wasted on a topic that posed no threat to national
security. Further study would produce no results that
would add to scientific knowledge. No solid reason
could be found to waste more time and money on an
effort that had failed to produce any tangible results.

After the end of Blue Book, when anyone asked,
the Air Force would reply that it had ended its study.
The records of Project Blue Book were housed in the
National Archives. Any and all questions relating to
UFOs were answered the same way. Ask the Na-
tional Archives.

Members of Congress were treated no better. Congressman Steven Schiff of New Mexico, seeking an-

swers after members of his constituency asked him questions about the Roswell crash in particular and UFOs in general, forwarded a request to the Air Force, who sent it on to the National Archives. Schiff thought he should have gotten a better answer than he did. Schiff, with the power of Congress behind him, asked the General Accounting Office (GAO) to look into the situation.

But the truth of the matter is that the Air Force and the government were not being completely honest. UFOs were a topic that was still of interest to the Air Force. The requirement for UFO report investigation had not been lifted. The Air Force just changed the criterion so that it was not required to investigate all the UFO reports coming from the public. Or to alert the public that such investigations had continued beyond the end of Project Blue Book.[1]

About four years after Blue Book was closed, another wave of sightings hit the United States. It differed from earlier waves because there were so many occupant reports. Rather than lights in the night sky, people were reporting craft on the ground, often leaving evidence behind them. And with so many craft on the ground, witnesses were also reporting the beings from inside now on the outside.

The sighting that first gained the national attention during the wave and alerted the newspapers happened on October 12, 1973, in Pascagoula, Mississippi. According to Charles Hickson, he and a friend,

---

[1] Even if we had no documentation, this is the conclusion to be drawn. The Air Defense Command must investigate all overflights of American territory. To suggest it doesn't have a mission to investigate UFO sightings is ridiculous. The Air Force is no longer required to report those investigations to the public.

Calvin Parker, were fishing from an old pier on the west bank of the Pascagoula River when a bright blue light attracted their attention. At first it was high overhead, but then it dropped toward the ground. Hickson later told investigators that it stopped only a few feet above the surface of the bayou. There was a buzzing noise coming from it, but there was no wind or blast like that from a jet engine.

As he watched, one end of the object, an egg-shaped craft, opened and three creatures floated from it. Hickson believed them to be about five feet tall, covered in wrinkled gray skin, with long arms that ended in lobsterlike claws and legs that seemed to be fused together. The creatures, which seemed to be buzzing slightly, headed for the men, the three beings separating so that one could pick up the now-unconscious Parker while the other two lifted Hickson, floating him toward the dimly glowing ship.

A door seemed to appear in the side of the craft, and the men were floated through it. According to Hickson, he and Parker spent about twenty minutes on the ship. The interior was bare, except for a device that Hickson thought looked like a big eye. Eventually he was floated back off the ship and deposited on the riverbank with Parker.

Hickson didn't see the UFO take off. He reported there was a buzzing sound and the UFO vanished. For a few minutes, Hickson didn't know what to do. The story was so fantastic that he didn't think anyone would believe him. Besides, Parker, now conscious, was still terrified.

After several drinks in a local bar, Hickson decided that someone in authority should be told. He tried the Pascagoula newspaper office, but it was closed.

Next he tried Kessler Air Force Base and received the now-standard reply that the Air Force no longer investigated UFO sightings. It was suggested that possibly the local sheriff or university would be interested.

Hickson opted for the sheriff, telling him that he had no desire for publicity, despite the fact that he had visited the newspaper office first. Within hours, however, the story was national news and Hickson had more publicity than he ever dreamed possible.

The next morning Jim and Coral Lorenzen of the civilian Aerial Phenomena Research Organization (APRO) learned of the abduction and began making plans. All three of their consultants in psychology were busy, but James A. Harder, their director of research,[2] could travel to Pascagoula. Harder, although a civil engineer, was versed in the use of hypnosis.

Dr. J. Allen Hynek had also heard the news reports and called APRO headquarters to find out if there were any plans to investigate. Learning that Harder was being dispatched, Hynek made his own plans to fly to Pascagoula.

On Saturday morning, the whole cast was assembled in the offices of the J. Walker Shipbuilders Company. Along with Hickson, Parker, Hynek, and Harder were Hickson's attorney, Joe Colingo, Dr. Julius Bosco, Deputy Sheriff Barney Mathis, and police detective Thomas Huntly.

Over the next days, the details of the abduction were examined. Hickson confirmed much of his

---

[2]Dr. Harder is a civil engineer who had been trained in the use of hypnosis.

story, adding that the alien spaceship was sixteen to eighteen feet long and had a "trap door" in the back. He described the creatures for the assembled men.

Harder was impressed and told APRO headquarters that it would be nearly impossible for the men to simulate their feelings of terror (an erroneous conclusion)[3] while under hypnosis. Newsmen asked both Hynek and Harder for their opinions. Hynek suggested that what the men experienced, although frightening, didn't translate into an extraterrestrial event.

Reporters weren't as reserved in their opinions as Hynek and Harder had been. Headlines the next day screamed: SCIENTISTS BELIEVE UFO STORY. That wasn't exactly right, but before the claim could be corrected, reporters were off chasing another UFO event.

Late in the month, after Harder and Hynek had completed much of their investigation, a polygraph examination was arranged in New Orleans for Hickson. According to several sources, Hickson passed the test, which took nearly two hours to complete. Newspapers claimed that the "lie test" proved the case.

Philip Klass, who launched his own investigation some days later, believed there was something wrong with the test. He wondered why the operator, a man who had yet to finish his training, conducted the test when other more qualified polygraph operators could be found closer to Pascagoula. To Klass, this suggested the test had been rigged in Hickson's favor.

But Klass, Harder, and all the rest overlooked a

---

[3]Psychologists now say that the emotions displayed under hypnosis, while real, are no measure of the reality of the situation. Hypnosis is poorly understood and is not a pathway to the truth.

couple of important points. The lie detector test could only suggest to a reasonable certainty that Hickson was telling the truth as he believed it. It could not prove that Hickson and Parker were abducted and it certainly could not prove that the abduction had been at the hands of alien beings.

Two years later, in October 1975, Hickson attended a UFO conference held at Fort Smith, Arkansas. He had been invited to tell his story, on the condition that he submit to another lie detector test arranged by the conference organizers. Hickson agreed, but when the time came, Hickson said his attorney had advised him not to take the test. Although many attorneys routinely advise their clients against taking such tests because the tests are so open to human interpretation, the controversy was stirred again.

There were other minor controversies in the story. Hickson seemed to have no real idea when he had seen the UFO, telling researchers and investigators at different times that it was about seven in the evening, or maybe about eight, or even as late as nine. Hickson told me that he never wore a watch because it would not keep the proper time. No matter how many he tried, they either ran fast, slow, or stopped altogether. That does provide him with a good excuse for not having a good feel for the time.

The controversy about the Hickson-Parker abduction continues to rage today. But what is important is not the wave of sightings or the final conclusions drawn based on those sightings, but what the government reaction to them was. Although the government claimed to have no interest, telling all who called that the UFO investigations had been completed, evidence suggests that this wasn't the truth.

Hynek, who had started the private Center for UFO Studies and who was now in the private sector, teaching astronomy at Northwestern University near Chicago, was called to Wright-Patterson Air Force Base. Colleagues at the center suggest that Hynek, who was there to brief a group of high-ranking military officers about the October 1973 wave of sightings,[4] thought he was finally going to learn the answers.

Hynek did brief the officers, telling them what he had discovered during the most recent wave. There were more than 100 reports of occupants, there were abductions, and there seemed to be a worldwide nature to the reports. The wave matched, in intensity, the largest of the UFO waves from twenty years earlier.

But when he was done, he was thanked and escorted off the base. No revelations were made to him. Just requests by military officers for information.

Those at the center, having reviewed Hynek's papers after his death in 1986, learned that Hynek was still a paid consultant to the Air Force in 1973. Although the contract didn't mention UFOs by name, the implication was clear. Hynek's role as a consultant in unusual aerial phenomena continued after the official end of Project Blue Book.

The paper trail, however, doesn't end there. UFO researchers had spoken of another secret investigation that paralleled Project Blue Book. It seems that the field work was carried out by the 4602d AISS,

---

[4] Dr. Mark Rodeghier, scientific director of the J. Allen Hynek Center for UFO Studies, has suggested that Hynek was called to Wright-Patterson AFB for consultation in a subject unrelated to UFOs and that he was questioned about the status of the subject before he left the base.

which by 1973 had evolved into the 1127th Air Activities Group, with a headquarters, not at Ent Air Force Base, Colorado, but at Fort Belvoir, Virginia. The code name for the project leaked as UFO researchers began to use the Freedom of Information Act (FOIA) to continue their investigations.

Project Moon Dust, begun, according to the documentation, in 1953 to interrogate captured enemy crew members (where have we heard that before?), was still active after the end of Blue Book. Although the Air Force claimed that Moon Dust never existed, documentation proved otherwise.

Clifford Stone, a retired Army sergeant who resides in Roswell, New Mexico, began researching Project Moon Dust and Operation Blue Fly a number of years ago. Documents available from various sources, including the Department of State, have corroborated the existence of Moon Dust.

According to a document recovered by Stone, a proposal was made for the creation of "AFCIN Intelligence Team Personnel" in November 1961. Like everything else in the UFO field, the authenticity of the document is in question. Two versions have been released, one claiming that the document was only a draft that had never implemented.[5]

The document, however, did refer to Project Moon Dust and Operation Blue Fly under Paragraph 5, Subsection F. It said, "Blue Fly: Operation Blue Fly has been established to facilitate expeditious delivery to FTD of Moon Dust or other items of great technical

---

[5]Cliff Stone suggests that the function was already in operation and that the draft nature of the proposal was to replace the members of the teams who were about to be released from the service.

intelligence interest. AFCIN SOP for Blue Fly operations, February 1960, provides for 1127th participation."

Subsection G. said, "Moon Dust: As a specialized aspect of its overall material exploitation program, Headquarters USAF has established Project Moon Dust to locate, recover and deliver descended foreign space vehicles. ICGL #4, 25 April 1961 delineates collection responsibilities."

Unidentified flying objects were brought into the discussion in the document under Paragraph 5, Definitions. It said, "Unidentified Flying Objects (UFO): Headquarters USAF has established a program for investigation of reliably reported unidentified flying objects within the United States. AFR 200-2 delineates 1127th collection responsibilities."

Other parts of the document explained how the collection teams were to be organized, what the requirements for membership on those teams was, and a discussion about the falling numbers of team members. The recommendations were suggested as ways of ensuring the missions would be accomplished in the future.

What is important about this document is that it mentioned both Moon Dust and Blue Fly. Whether it was a draft that was never implemented or a document that was forwarded to a higher headquarters isn't important to our discussion. The verification of Moon Dust and its relationship with UFOs is what is relevant.

However, even with the documents in hand, those inside the Air Force were denying the existence of Moon Dust. Senator Jeff Bingaman from New Mexico, at the insistence of Stone, wrote to the Air Force

Congressional liaison office with questions about Project Moon Dust. Lieutenant Colonel John E. Madison of the Congressional Inquiry Division, Office of Legislative Liaison, wrote, "There is no agency, nor has there ever been, at Fort Belvoir, Virginia, which would deal with UFOs or have any information about the incident in Roswell. In addition, there is no Project Moon Dust or Operation Blue Fly. Those missions have never existed."[6]

Never existed? Documentation suggested that they had, indeed, existed. They were mentioned by name in the 1961 document. It could be argued, since the handwritten note on one version said, "This draft proposal was not approved and not forwarded for action," that Moon Dust had never been an active mission. In that respect, it could be claimed that Lieutenant Colonel Madison was right when he told Bingaman that the missions had never existed. He hadn't said they weren't proposed, only that they hadn't existed.

But other documents showed that Moon Dust had been put into effect. On July 26, 1973, about four years after the shutdown of Project Blue Book, a classified document originated by the department of State was sent to "All American Diplomatic and Consular Posts." It ordered that "the designator 'MOONDUST [sic] is used in cases involving examination of non-US space objects or objects of unknown origin."

Tying Moon Dust to UFOs on the basis of that document is difficult. It can be argued that "objects

[6]Letter from Lieutenant Colonel Madison to Senator Jeff Bingaman, copy supplied by Cliff Stone. See also *The Truth About the UFO Crash at Roswell* (Kevin Randle and Donald Schmitt, New York: Avon Books, 1994).

of unknown origin" could be interpreted as meaning extraterrestrial. It can also mean objects from foreign nations that have nothing to do with UFOs. Other Moon Dust documents do mention UFOs and UFO sightings, which demonstrates that investigations of UFOs were part of the Moon Dust mission.

And there are documents that mention the retrieval of "space fragments," some of which are post-Blue Book. For example, in a document dated October 7, 1970, the Department of State sent a report to 1127th Field Activity Group that said, "Subject: (U) Moon Dust. DATT called by Minister of Interior to inspect object found . . . Minister said object fell in area with three loud explosions and then burned for five days . . . The object resembles a pressurized fuel tank."[7]

There is little doubt that the object was anything other than what was reported. However, it does show that Moon Dust was in operation after 1969. In other cases, such as one dated August 17, 1967, a large cube-shaped object found in the Sudan could easily be the retrieval of a terrestrially manufactured satellite. The object, weighing about three tons, was found about fifty miles from Kutum. According to the documents, authorities "in El Fasher have photographs and with difficulty cut samples."

This all becomes important because it establishes the existence of Moon Dust as an active government mission. There are other examples, and in fact, through Freedom of Information Act requests, UFO researchers, including myself, have received micro-

---

[7]Microfiche records available through the Department of State, topic of Moon Dust.

filmed records from the Department of State concerning Moon Dust. More than 6,000 such documents have been recovered from the microfilm.

It is important to remember that very few of the documents use the term UFO, but there are some. Many times the reports are from foreign newspapers, telling of UFO sightings in various countries. It establishes the connection between Moon Dust and UFOs and that the interest has continued after the end of Blue Book.

Many documents recovered under Moon Dust FOIA requests deal specifically with UFOs.[8] A series of documents, sent electronically to various military command and intelligence functions, including the CIA, told of the UFO sightings over Belgium beginning in November 1989.

One special document referred to sightings on the night of March 30 and the early morning hours of March 31, 1990. Belgian F-16 fighters attempted to intercept the objects, using onboard radars to track them. Radar information showed the object moving slowly, about twenty-five miles an hour, before accelerating at tremendous speed. It dived from 7,000 feet to below 750 feet in the space of a second.

According to the documents, the F-16s got radar locks on the UFO on three separate occasions. And on each of those three separate occasions, the UFO took evasive action, breaking the lock.

The Belgium Air Force Chief of Operations, Colo-

---

[8]Many of the documents, while clearly related to UFOs, fail to mention the term specifically. Others, available on the mircofiche, are labeled as UFO sightings. These include newspaper clippings from various foreign countries. These clippings were transmitted under the main heading of Moon Dust.

nel W. De Brouwer, according to the document, ". . . noted the large number of reported sightings, particularly in Nov 89 in the Liege area and that the BAF [Belgian Air Force] and the MOD [Ministry of Defense] are taking the issue seriously. BAF experts have not been able to explain the phenomena either . . . DeBrouwer [sic] specifically addressed the possibility of the objects being USAF B-2 or F-117 stealth aircraft which would not appear on Belgian radar, but might be sighted visually if they were operating at low altitude in the Ardennes area. He made it quite clear that no USAF over flight requests had ever been received for this type mission and that the alledged [sic] observations did not correspond in any way to the observable characteristics of either U.S. aircraft."

The report contained another UFO sighting, this one by a Belgian Air Force officer and his wife who ". . . were alledgedly [sic] blinded by a huge bright flying object as they were driving on the autoroute. They stopped their car, but were so frightened they abandoned the vehicle and ran into the woods. They could not provide a detailed description but whatever it was definitely appeared real to them."

In the comments section of the report, it said, "The BAF has ruled some of the sightings were caused by inversion layers, lazer [sic] beams and other forms of high intensity lighting hitting clouds. But a remarkable number occurred on clear nights with no other explainable activity nearby . . . The BAF is concerned to a point about the UFO issue and is taking action to investigate the information they have . . . The USAF did confirm to the BAR and Belgian MOD that no USAF stealth aircraft were operating in the Ardennes area during the periods in question."

No matter how you slice it, this demonstrates an interest in UFOs by government agencies that postdates the end of Project Blue Book. If we accept Air Force statements, then we can assume that sightings, regardless of geographic location, would be of no interest to the military. Clearly, if a UFO appeared over an important military installation, such as an atomic weapons storage facility, we can assume the Air Force would attempt an intercept. Military officers would require an immediate identification of the intruder. Any other policy would be nothing short of negligent.

But UFO sightings in Belgium have no relevance to the safety and security of the United States. Even if the objects were "painted" on radar and interceptors also locked on to the target, there is no real need for the sightings to be reported through official channels. Yet, they were reported, not only to the Department of State, but to a large number of military offices, including the Chief of Staff of the Air Force, the Chief of Naval Operations, and various commands around the world. The CIA and the DIA, as well as the White House, were also alerted.[9]

This seems to be strange routing on a topic that, according to the Condon Committee and the Air Force, didn't even exist. While the routing for the message might be considered routine, it is interesting that the message existed at all. Why alert anyone to UFO sightings in Belgium? The phenomenon just didn't exist, according to all the officials who bothered to make statements on the subject.

---

[9]Various Department of State documents, topic of Moon Dust.

There are other examples of an official interest in UFOs after the end of Blue Book. In other documents uncovered by Cliff Stone, dated December 9, 1989 and sent to FM Detachment 21 at Fort Belvoir, Virginia, the only addressee on the message, is a report on "Soviet Aircrew Sightings of Unexplained Phenomena." Although some of the message has been deleted "per 5 U.S.C. 552(b) (1)," it is clear that the unexplained phenomena were UFOs.

The report said, "[Name deleted] report provides information concerning unexplained phenomena which the source has either personally observed or has heard about from friends/acquaintances. The observations (exact dates not recalled) consisted of domes of light, points of light, and ellipse or cylindrically shaped objects."

The text of the report continued, "[Name deleted] Domes of light. On one occasion a silver-colored light was observed in the Azerbajdzhan region of the USSR. A bright center point emitted light in all directions which slowly increased the size of a dome which was less bright. The dome continued to grow even after the light in the center had been extinguished. The center light continued for about 15 minutes. The emitted light (dome) lasted much longer (over 30 minutes.) (Field comment—The light could have been caused by the launch of a strategic rocket, but the source did not think so.) Source also observed this phenomena near Kuybyshev//GEOCOORDS: 5241N05326E//, USSR. The details were the same as mentioned above, except the center light and resultant dome were orange in color."

After another short deletion, the text went on. ". . . Points of light. During the springtime, source observed four points of light over the Caucuses Mountains . . ." Then the note "Deleted per 5 U.S.C. 552(b) (1)." The text continues, "The points were greenish in color and the light was spreading. The points were approximately 150 to 200 kilometers (KM) from source. Each point emitted a separate light. Deleted per 5 U.S.C. 552(b) (1). Source could see the lights from the air, but cloud cover prevented their being seen from the ground."

More of the document was deleted and then, under Paragraph 3, Subsection A., it said, "Personal sighting." There was a blank space and then "Near the Black Sea, source observed an object flying in vertical circles. The bright silver-colored object was approximately 50 to 60 KM from source. The object moved away from source as he approached. When source [blank space] away from object, it moved back toward him. It was difficult to determine the dimensions and exact shape of the object. (Field Comment—Source could not recall . . . Deleted per 5 U.S.C. 552(b) (1) . . . at the time of the sighting."

In the next paragraph, Paragraph 8, there was no indication that anything was deleted. Paragraph 8 began with a blacked-out space and then said, "Unidentified Object. In the spring of 1984, A friend of the source was sent." There was a large section blanked under 5 U.S.C. 552 (b) (1) and the final words of the paragraph were ". . . unidentified object approached the coastline of the Black Sea." More deletions under the same U.S. code and then the statement "The pilot never acquired a visual identification of the object."

In the past, UFO researchers have held up documents obtained under the Freedom of Information

Act that contained huge sections that were blacked out.[10] It is a great visual tool. It shows exactly how much of the document has been deleted prior to release. With these documents, it is clear that sections have been deleted, but there is no visual impact. All we can tell is that some parts of some paragraphs have been removed. The best clue to the amount of material missing is the jump from Paragraph 3 to Paragraph 8. The impression is that very little has been removed. The reality is that a great deal is missing.

It is clear from the documents, and contrary to the statements by Lieutenant Colonel Madison to Senator Bingaman, that Moon Dust did exist. It is clear that Madison was less than candid with the senator.

Stone challenged the Air Force response on two counts, providing documentation that Madison had not been as complete in his answer to Bingaman as he could have been. The evidence clearly proved there had been a Project Moon Dust, an Operation Blue Fly, and there was a unit at Fort Belvoir that had an active interest in UFOs.

George M. Mattingley, Jr., a full colonel and chief of the Congressional Inquiry Division, Office of Legislative Liaison, responded. Mattingley wrote, ". . . we wish to amend the statements contained in the previous response to your inquiry."

Mattingley then reconstructed a history of Moon Dust and the 4602d AISS that is not quite accurate. "In 1953, during the Korean War, the Air Defense

---

[10]Many of these documents, released under FIOA requests, contained no useful information. In some cases, only headings at the top of the document were not blacked out. In a few cases, there were only random words that were not blacked out.

Command organized intelligence teams to deploy, recover, or exploit at the scene downed enemy personnel, equipment, and aircraft. The unit with the responsibility for maintaining these teams was located at Fort Belvoir, Virginia. As the occasion never arose to use these air defense teams, the mission was assigned to Headquarters, United States Air Force, in 1957 and expanded to include the following peacetime functions: a) Unidentified Flying Objects (UFOs), to investigate reliably reported UFOs with the United States; b) Project MOON DUST, to recover objects and debris from space vehicles that had survived re-entry from space to earth; c) Operation BLUE FLY, to expeditiously retrieve downed Soviet Bloc equipment.''

While it certainly seems clear that these activities began in 1953, and all the various Air Force documents and histories indicate that the original purpose was to exploit downed enemy flight crews, there are some problems. The documentation available, including the first version of AFR 200-2 of August 1953 and the published version of August 1954, show that UFO investigations were always a part of the 4602d's mission. As early as the summer of 1953, plans were being made to use 4602d personnel to interrogate UFO witnesses.

Mattingley implied that the UFO mission didn't begin until 1957, but the documentation refutes that. The 1957 date is important simply because there would be little reason to develop a team to recover returning space debris because there was little to recover. The Soviets succeeded in putting a small satellite in orbit in October 1957. Prior to that, very little debris from rocket launches would be falling to Earth to be retrieved by Moon Dust teams.

Mattingley wrote, "These teams were eventually disbanded because of a lack of activity; Project MOON DUST and Operation BLUE FLY missions were similarly discontinued."

But that, too, doesn't seem to be quite right. Documentation dated from the mid-1980s suggests that both Moon Dust and Blue Fly survived until then. On July 1, 1987, Robert Todd, in response to a Freedom of Information Act request of April 17, 1987, was told by Colonel Phillip E. Thompson, Deputy Assistant Chief of Staff, Intelligence, that "The nickname 'Project Moondust' no longer exists officially. It has been replaced by another name which is not releasable."

In other words, this mirrors the transition period between the end of Project Grudge and the beginning of Project Blue Book. Public affairs officers told reporters that Grudge had been concluded. They were suggesting that the UFO project had been ended, which wasn't the case. The name had been changed, but the investigation continued.

Now Mattingley was suggesting that Moon Dust had been discontinued because the teams were not used. Thompson, however, was suggesting that the mission continued under a new, still-classified name. Again, Mattingley was being less than candid with a United States senator.

Mattingley ended his letter, reporting, "Since the Air Force discontinued its investigative interest in UFOs in 1969, reports of UFO sightings are now recorded and forwarded only if there is prior interest in the source of the UFO sighting. For example, Enclosures 3 and 4 of Mr. Stone's letter pertain to debriefings of two Soviet sources who were being interviewed for possible military information of interest. Their recounts of UFO sightings, even though they had occurred many years earlier, were included in the report for historical interest and were incidental to the main purpose of the report."

But that makes no sense because there is a single addressee on the document and that addressee is at Fort Belvoir. The information might have been developed out of an interview conducted into Soviet military operations, but someone thought it had significance. If the information was unimportant, then it wouldn't have been transmitted to Fort Belvoir. To suggest otherwise is to suggest that valuable time is being used to study trivia. Mattingley's response to the senator makes no more sense than did Madison's.

What we see is that both Mattingley and Madison were less than candid. Madison got caught because Stone had sufficient documentation to refute the points raised by Madison. Mattingley took over, throwing out more information, all of which was skewed slightly. Mattingley's letter gives the appearance of being complete and comprehensive when it is more of the same. The facts recited by Mattingley are not in agreement with the facts developed through other outside and independent sources.

The conspiracy of silence, then, is still alive and well. With the Condon Committee and the end of Project Blue Book, the Air Force took steps to give itself ready answers to difficult questions. When sighting reports mounted, when reporters returned with more questions, the official spokesman could deny that UFOs were important. The investigation had ended. The truth is that Blue Book ended, but the investigation did not.

The theme that runs through all the documentation

and letters is that UFOs pose no threat to the security of the United States. It can be argued that such a finding was all that the Air Force was required to do. Once the question of national security was answered, its mission was complete. It might not be able to stop the overflights of UFOs and that might damage the reputation of the Air Force, but the security of the nation was tight. The UFOs were doing nothing to harm us.

The Air Force, then, does not want to admit that it does not control the skies over the United States. That too is one of its missions. If there are extraterrestrial craft flashing through the sky, then the second mission of the Air Force is not being accomplished. The Air Force has attempted intercepts, including those over the capital of the United States, Washington, D.C., but it has failed to stop those overflights or alter the situation.

One of the motivations for the conspiracy of silence is that problem. The Air Force will not admit that it does not control the sky. To admit otherwise is to admit failure. Since there is no apparent threat to the security of the United States, the Air Force ignores the second mission.

What is clear from all of this is that the Air Force had the motivation to cover up the truth. The Air Force contributed to the conspiracy of silence with its actions. Part of it might have been incompetence, but a large part of it was carefully planned.

The question that has yet to be asked: "Is the Air Force alone or does the conspiracy go higher into the executive branch of the federal government?" That has always been the question. The answer, however, is no longer a matter of speculation.

CHAPTER 10

General Exon and
the Crash/Retrievals

THIS CONSPIRACY OF SILENCE TAKES MANY SUBTLE and simple forms. It can be as simple as a rhetorical question or as insidious as a conspiracy at the top. The history of the conversations and interviews with Brigadier General Arthur Exon is illustrative. It also demonstrates that many aspects of this conspiracy are designed by those who wish to keep the truth hidden from the general public. Sometimes, though, it is the politics of the UFO community that hide the truth. To completely understand everything that is happening around UFOs, it is also necessary to understand the small internal workings of the UFO phenomenon.

Brigadier General Arthur Exon surfaced in 1990 as a witness to some of the events surrounding the crash of the craft near Roswell in 1947. Exon, a lieutenant colonel in 1947, was assigned to Wright Field.

He was on hand when the material and the bodies arrived at that base. Though he now claims no first-hand knowledge of those events, that he was, in fact, speculating about them when Don Schmitt and I interviewed him beginning in May 1990, the situation as described by Exon was considerably different than what he claims today.

It is clear from the various published documents and histories of the Air Force that Exon rose to the rank of brigadier general and that he, at one time, commanded the sprawling Wright-Patterson Air Force Base complex. There is no question that Exon is who he claims to be and the information he provided about his career has been corroborated by various public sources.

It should be noted here that a base commander does not directly command all of the units on a base. It is not unlike the organization of a city with a mayor at the top as the person in overall charge. Under the mayor, directing various functions, may be a streets commissioner, a chief of police, a water commissioner, and so forth. In some cities, a city manager is responsible for the functioning of various city departments and various city-owned facilities. As the base commander at Wright-Patterson, General Exon's job was similar to the job of city manager.

Earlier in his career, Exon had a long stint at the Pentagon. He held various procurement assignments, including Deputy for Procurement and Production and Deputy Chief of Staff for Materiel.[1] That information becomes important when many of the statements made by Exon are carefully examined.

---

[1] Information from a variety of sources, including Exon's official Air Force biography.

Exon was, because of his assignments and the locations of those assignments, in a position to see and hear things about flying saucers. These he reported to both Schmitt and me during our initial interviews with him, drawing on his memories and what he had seen himself. From the tone of those interviews and from the language used by Exon during each of them, the area for speculation is relatively small. That point, too, has become important.

During the interview I conducted with Exon on May 19, 1990, Exon, talking about the whole UFO phenomenon, said, "Well, there were probably more than that. I don't know how many. I know that while I was there [at Wright-Patterson] I was . . . I had charge of all of the administrative airplanes and had to assign priority airplanes to members who would go out and investigate reported sightings. This was anyplace in the States. I remember several out in Wyoming and Montana and that area in the '60s—'64 and '65. Now that was all the responsibility that I had. I knew there were certain teams of people there representing headquarters USAF as well as the organizations there at Wright-Pat, FTD, and so on . . . when a crew came back it was their own business. Nobody asked any questions that I know of, nor would they probably have gotten answers had they asked them."

Exon clarified this by saying, "The way this happened to me is that I would get a call and say that the crew or the team was leaving and they knew . . . there was such and such a time and they wanted an airplane and pilots to take X number of people to wherever. They might be gone two or three days or might be gone a week. They would come back and that would be the end of it. So there were certain people in FTD that would lay the missions on. Of course I knew who they were."

It is apparent from Exon's comments here that he is talking from firsthand experience. Part of his job at Wright-Patterson was to assist those flying off the base to investigate UFOs. While it is true that Exon did not investigate those sightings himself and it is true that he wasn't told of the results of those investigations, it is also true that he knew, based on his experience, what was happening. The men were flying out to investigate UFO sightings.

From what Exon said, it is clear that he was not referring to officers assigned to Project Blue Book. We know from the records that Blue Book was a small operation in 1965. Two officers, a sergeant, and a secretary were assigned and that was it. There is no indication that Blue Book conducted many, if any, field investigations in 1965. In fact, other documentation shows that another project inside the Air Force held the investigative responsibility in 1965. Various regulations and other Air Force records point to the 1127th Air Activities Group as the responsible agency.

During his June 18, 1990, interview with Exon, Schmitt asked specifically if these investigators were assigned to Wright-Pat.

Exon said, "No. They were, they would come from Washington, D.C. And they would ask for an airplane tomorrow morning and that would give the guys a chance to get there [Wright-Patterson] by commercial airline . . . The airplane would take off at such and such a time. Sometimes they'd be gone for three days and sometimes they'd be gone for a week. I know they went out to Montana and Wyoming and the Northwest states a number of times in a year and a half that I recall. There probably were other places. They went to Arizona once or twice."

The tone of Exon's statements and his responses to the specific questions make it clear these were not speculations as now claimed. He ordered the aircraft, he knew they had been authorized by regulations and an officer in the Washington, D.C., area. We can speculate, based on what we know, that the men came from the 1127th Air Activities Group at Fort Belvoir, Virginia.

The only area of speculation by Exon is his statement that they probably went places other than Montana, Wyoming, and the Northwest. The statements reflect his firsthand knowledge of the situation at Wright-Patterson.

During the course of my May 19, 1990, interview and in Schmitt's June 18, 1990, interview, Exon talked of a sighting over Kentucky. Exon mentioned that four aircraft had been scrambled because of a UFO report. All four of the aircraft disappeared. Exon didn't have much additional information, but it was clear that the aircraft had vanished. Exon said, "They don't know what happened. If they went out overseas or out over water, which is not likely . . . There were four of them that were scrambled. They were all lost."

I asked, "Nobody ever found any wreckage or have any clues as to what happened to them?"

"Not that I know of," said Exon. "That's been investigated before and it's a matter of record and it's kind of a mysterious thing."

When Schmitt spoke to Exon in person on June

18, he mentioned the disappearance again. Exon told Schmitt, "I was in the Pentagon. I was there five and a half years from '55 to '60. That was the time period that we lost four airplanes down there . . . [Kentucky or Tennessee]."[2]

It's clear from Exon that he learned much of this information because of who he was and where he was stationed. Clearly, he was not on the scene when the four aircraft vanished, but he was in a position to know about it. He had access to the classified data that was transmitted to the Pentagon. And he was in communication with those responsible for the investigation of this event.

During these interviews, Exon kept referring to a group of high-ranking officials, both governmental and military, who controlled access to all of the data as "The Unholy Thirteen."

As the information about the Roswell UFO crash came to light, various conclusions were drawn by researchers. Everyone agreed that if the crash happened, there would have been a research project designed to exploit the find. Men to the top level of the government would have been informed and would have been appointed to oversee the study of the recovered craft. There is no question that the events at Roswell would have precipitated such a response.

In the early 1980s, it seemed that documents confirming this speculation had been discovered. These papers, labeled as MJ-12, suggested that a government study had been initiated after the crash outside Roswell. The first and most detailed of the MJ-12

---

[2]This is a case that should be researched further. Preliminary work on it has been very disappointing.

documents listed twelve men who were appointed by President Truman: government officials, scientists, and military officers. There were those inside the UFO community who believed that the documents were authentic—and those who believed them to be fraudulent. Neither side could provide a provenance for the documents, and without that, good research demanded that they be treated as fakes.

That debate has been carried out in various public arenas. It now seems, and most inside the UFO community agree, that the documents are phony. Exon, however, becomes important in the debate because he ran into the oversight committee while he was serving in the Pentagon. He remembered some of the names of committee members and provided them to us during the first interviews we conducted.

As these data were reported by Schmitt and me, there were challenges to the validity of the information. Some suggested that we had misquoted Exon or that we had misunderstood what Exon was saying. Then Exon himself began to suggest that he had been speculating about the situation and that he didn't know anything firsthand.

Of course, the tapes of the interviews and the letter that Exon sent to me on November 21, 1991, make it clear that most of what Exon told us was not speculation. It was information that he gained because of who he was and where he was. The areas of speculation were small.

One of the reasons for those allegations, which surfaced from inside the UFO community, was that Exon's testimony destroyed much of MJ-12. Exon, a source who could be questioned by others, who could speak of his personal knowledge, and who had access to the inside information, provided data suggesting the MJ-12 documents were faked. Because of that, those who believed the MJ-12 documents were authentic felt that they had to do something about Exon's testimony. If he was right, MJ-12, as such, didn't exist. That was the motivation behind efforts to belittle or destroy the information provided by Exon.

Now, however, we continue to hear those who say that Exon told them he was only "speculating."[3] Though I had quoted him as a source of information about the events at Roswell, and it was clear that he did know many things, others claimed that Exon knew nothing firsthand. Exon did say, however, that he had flown over the crash area later. Others who spoke to him heard him say that he had flown over many points that could have been the actual impact site where the craft was found or the debris field reported by rancher Mac Brazel. In other words, it was again being suggested that we had blown the importance of the Exon testimony all out of proportion and that what he knew personally was virtually nothing.

This change, I believe, is the result of the situation that developed *after* we had spoken to Exon, and after we reported what he had told us. Remember, we interviewed Exon both in person and on the telephone. All of those interviews were recorded, with the exception of the last, held at the Officers' Club at Wright-Patterson AFB.

---

[3]This is a politically motivated comment because of the data supplied by Exon. Here is a high-ranking source, talking on the record. If what he says is accurate, then the UFO situation is much different than we had believed. Those conspiring to keep the data away from the public have no recourse but to suggest this.

And, I believe, the resulting rejection of some of Exon's testimony is politically motivated. In other words, some of those suggesting that we had misquoted General Exon or taken his statements out of context were saying that because the information he provided suggested that certain theories, such as MJ-12, were in error.

Exon told me, for example, that he had been at Wright Field when the staff heard the material found at Roswell was being brought in. He said that he knew it was coming in. He said that the bodies had been brought to Wright Field and that he believed that one of those bodies had been sent to Lowry Army Air Field because the Army's mortuary service was based there. Obviously, they were sent there for study and to learn the best way to preserve the tissues.

During the interview conducted on May 19, 1990, I asked Exon, "You've heard the rumors about the little bodies and all that stuff, haven't you?"

Exon responded, "Well, yes, I have. In fact, I know people that were in photographing some of the residue from the New Mexico affair near Roswell."[4]

Exon then said, "As a result of that, I know they saw the one sighting and then where . . . a good bit of the information came down. There was another location where it was where apparently the main body of the spacecraft was . . . where they did say there were bodies there . . . I've got special information, but it may be more rumor than fact about what happened to those bodies, although they were all

---

[4]He is referring to J. Bond Johnson, the *Fort Worth Star-Telegraph* photographer who was in General Ramey's office on July 8, 1947.

found apparently outside the craft itself but were in
fairly good condition. In other words, they weren't
broken up a lot."

Let's look at those statements closely. Exon, a retired Air Force brigadier general, is saying that he
heard about the rumored bodies and the "residue"
from New Mexico. He is not laughing it off but is
discussing it seriously. It is clear that he *did not* see
the bodies but had heard of them. He speaks of his
special knowledge, suggests it might be rumor, but
then he describes the discovery of the bodies in a
serious light.

Talking of the bodies and if they were taken to
Wright-Patterson, he said, "Well, that's my information. But one of them was that it went to the mortuary outfit . . . I think at that time it was in Denver,
where these people were being identified. But the
strongest information was that they were brought
into Wright-Pat. But whatever happened to the metal
residue, I imagine it's still in the . . . someplace."

Here Exon is saying that his information is that one
of the bodies went to Denver. His best information is
that the bodies were taken to Wright-Patterson and
then he speculates. He believes that the metal has
remained at Wright-Pat. However, there is no question from his statements that both the bodies and the
metal were taken to Wright Field.

Now, it can be argued that Exon has yet to see
anything himself. However, he is in communication
with those who had seen something themselves. The
only real area of speculation in that statement is that
the metal is still housed somewhere at Wright-
Patterson.

Exon continued, saying, "But back in that '47 time

period, everybody was, it happened and why wasn't there more information and who kept the lid on it. Well, *I know* [emphasis added] that at the time the sightings happened it went to General Ramey [commander of the Eighth Air Force] who is now deceased, who was at Carswell Air Force Base [Fort Worth Army Air Field in July 1947] and he along with the people out at Roswell decided to change the story while they got their act together and got the information in to the Pentagon and in to the president."

There is no speculation here. Exon is telling us what he knew from his conversations with the people directly involved. Notice that there is no hint of speculation anywhere, but Exon, in fact, uses the term "I know" instead of anything suggesting that he was guessing based on who he was and what he had heard through the grapevine.

"Of course President Truman and General Spaatz [commander of the Army Air Forces], the Secretary of Defense who has now passed away, and other people who were close to them were the ones who made up the key investigative teams in relation to the released information. One of my officers who did some research who worked for me at Wright-Patterson, who had done some research on this as part of his school, came up with a deal that there was great concern at that time and there was fear that people would panic if the sketchy information that they had, such as what was it and where did it come from and what was their mission and so on and so on, got out. So they decided to make it a national cover-up . . . *I did know* [emphasis added] that their numbers one and two people were at the top of the staff including the Secretary of Defense and the Chie of Staff and the intelligence circle including the President, I don't know whether anybody outside the President's office, I never heard of any elected officials."

He then qualified the statements, saying, "This is stuff I've heard from '47 on to the present time, really. About why wasn't it . . . about who was responsible and it was no problem to find out who was in those positions in '47 and '48 and I just happen to remember them because the Air Force was being formed and I was in the Pentagon and worked around a lot between the Pentagon and the field so I knew these people."

I then said, trying to clarify the situation, "But what you know personally is that the information is going to be held until . . ."

"Until these people have expired," finished Exon.

Again, however, what we were discussing was what Exon knew from conversations held with those on the inside. At no point was he speculating about this. The tone of the conversations made that clear. While he might not have witnessed all of the events himself, he had discussed them with those who had.

That point becomes clear when the discussion moved to the material that had been recovered. Although he speculated about the location of the metal, meaning he believed that it was still at Wright-Patterson, he did know what happened once it had arrived at the base in 1947. He said, "I think it was there because there was quite a bit of effort to take it to the labs and try to analyze it chemically and metallurgy and everything else involved in trying to find out what the material was because some of it was very flimsy and was tougher than hell and other was almost like foil but strong. It had them pretty puzzled so I *know* [emphasis added] people were investigating trying to find out what it was. And it wouldn't surprise me if some of the material wasn't still around. Certainly the reports."

So Exon was aware of the various laboratory tests that were conducted. It is not necessary for him to have witnessed the tests to know what had transpired during them. It is not unlike an attorney using expert testimony in a trial. The attorney might not have personally witnessed the tests, but he could interview the scientist who had conducted them. So Exon might not have seen the tests, but he spoke to those who had. He was not speculating but reporting exactly what he had heard from those who had.

And he knew about the material, describing it using the same terms that so many others had used. While Exon does not confirm that he had seen the material himself, he knew the people involved in the analysis of it. He was not speculating about that but telling me exactly what he had learned from those he knew at Wright-Patterson.

In fact, the only area of speculation was that the material would still be around somewhere. And if the material itself couldn't be located, then the reports and analysis of the debris would be available. Reasonable speculation considering who he was and what he had already admitted to knowing.

We then began to speak of the alien bodies. This had always been the area hardest to penetrate. Those who saw metal were easy to find. While metal is metal and can be explained in the mundane if the extraordinary properties are ignored, once the discussion turned to the bodies, the area for mundane answers shrinks to nothing.

I mentioned the bodies to Exon, saying that I knew the bodies from Roswell had been taken to Wright-Patterson. Exon answered, saying that he knew it, too, and then added, "Well, I don't know that."

Exon then said, "People I have known were involved in it and they're the ones that told me they [the bodies] got to Wright-Patterson. But what I've been trying to do is try to imagine what could have been done with them scientifically from a storage standpoint for future investigation. It's one thing to kind of have an autopsy and another thing to keep them. I know there were facilities available that could have done that, but I don't believe they were at Wright-Patterson."

In other words, Exon's speculation wasn't about the bodies arriving at Wright-Patterson or even the fact that bodies were recovered. Instead, he was speculating on the tests that could be conducted on them when they arrived at Wright-Patterson.

Later, as we were wrapping up the conversation, I asked about other UFO crashes. I had been told that Exon was aware of four others, but he said, "Well, I don't know they were crashes. The only crash I *really* know about is the one in Arizona . . . I mean New Mexico. The rest of it is all rumor."

Exon was now telling me that he knew of one UFO crash and that was the one in New Mexico. He wasn't speculating here but telling me what he had learned through his fellow officers at Wright-Pat and from his firsthand observations while in the Air Force.

His knowledge of the event went far beyond what

he had been told by those he trusted. Again, in the last few months, Exon has suggested that the situation isn't as we have reported it. He had flown over many areas of the New Mexican desert and during those flights he had speculated about the location of the crash. Notice that he is not denying there was a crash, only that he had personally seen the site, though that is exactly what he told both Don Schmitt and me during our interviews with him.

But this reading of the situation simply isn't the case. On June 18, 1990, Schmitt had the opportunity to visit Exon at his home. Schmitt was able to record most of the conversation, although he had trouble with his tape recorder and a gardener who decided that it was time to mow the lawn. Schmitt also made notes to back up the tape.

Again, Exon explained about the oversight committee that controlled access to the information about the crash. Exon was telling Schmitt what he knew, based on his position as the base commander at Wright-Patterson.

Schmitt asked, "Was there any name for the operation?"

Exon answered, "Well, I . . . no, I don't recall that there was. Our contact was a man, a telephone number. He'd call and he'd set the airplane up. I just knew there was an investigative team. There probably was a name but I . . ."

There was a slight break in the tape and then Exon said, ". . . Stuart Symington, who was Secretary of Defense [actually he was Under Secretary of War for Air in July 1947], Joe [actually Carl] Spaatz [commander of the Army Air Forces] . . . all these guys at the top of the government. They were the ones who knew the most about Roswell, New Mexico. They were involved in what to do about the residue from that . . . those two findings."

Schmitt said, "You say 'those two'."

Exon answered, "It was probably part of the same accident, but there were two distinct sites. One, assuming that the thing, as I understand it, as I remember flying the area later, that the damage to the vehicle seemed to be coming from the southeast and northwest but it could have been going in the opposite direction, but it doesn't seem likely. So the farther northwest pieces found on the ranch, those pieces were mostly metal . . ."

Here again there is nothing that suggests that Exon was speculating. There is nothing to suggest that he had flown over many areas and that some of them could have been part of the accident and some of them just desolate areas on the New Mexican landscape. He was telling Schmitt on audiotape that there had been two distinct sites and that he had specifically flown over them. He told Schmitt that the one farthest away, the one we labeled as the debris field (the Mac Brazel site near Corona), contained mostly metal fragments. This testimony is accurate and corroborates, after a fashion, the testimony that we had received from other firsthand witnesses, including Major (later Colonel) Edwin Easley, Master Sergeant Lewis. S. Rickett, Sergeant Thomas Gonzales, and Dr. W. Curry Holden.

He then described the debris that had been found, saying, ". . . couldn't be easily ripped or changed . . . you could change it. You could wad it up . . . you could change the shape, but it was still there and . . . there were other parts of it that were very thin but awfully strong and couldn't be dented with heavy hammers and stuff like that . . . which at that time were causing some people concern . . . again, say it was a shape of some kind . . . you could grab this end and bend it, but it would come right back. It was flexible to a degree."

Since Exon is now claiming that he had flown over many sites and was only speculating, a letter he sent to me on November 24, 1991, becomes important. At that time we had been accused of misquoting Exon. After I supplied a copy of his taped interviews, a copy of the book, and other data, I asked in what area he believed we had misquoted him.

He wrote back, "I'm sorry that a portion of my interview has caused you trouble. I will acknowledge that the 'quick' quote does have me saying that my flights later, *much later*, varified [sic] the direction of possible flight of the object. I remember auto tracks leading to pivital [sic] sites and obvious gouges in terrain."

What becomes clear upon reviewing the tapes and the letter is that Exon was not speculating about these events and activities as he now claims. There is nothing in the statements he made or in the letter he wrote that suggests that he wasn't telling us what he knew from either firsthand observation or communication with those who were directly involved. The speculations revolved around what happened *after* the debris or bodies had arrived at Wright-Patterson, not about the recovery of the craft, material, or bodies. In fact, he wasn't even speculating about some of the testing. He said that he received the information about the tests from technicians he knew personally.

During the last few years, we have heard from others that Exon was saying that he had been speculating, that he knew nothing firsthand, and that we had put emphasis on his words that didn't belong. This simply isn't true and we have all the quotes used here on tape. We can prove that the things we claimed he said were the things he actually said and that we haven't taken anything out of context.

We can, however, take all this even further. First, we know from the public documentation and records that Exon is who he claims to be. He is a retired brigadier general who was, at one time, the base commander at Wright-Patterson. That lends a certain force to his words. Generals don't normally say radical things because it can undercut their credibility. In fact, it is sometimes difficult to get generals to admit to things that everyone else knows are true. Because Exon is a retired general, he has one level of credibility.

However, he said many things to both Schmitt and me during the interviews that could be checked against the testimony of other witnesses. When the facts check, then another level of corroboration is added. The facts provided by Exon have been carefully examined and even that is an interesting story by itself.

For example, Exon said that he knew Stuart Symington was one of those on the oversight committee he labeled "The Unholy Thirteen." But he also said that elected officials, because of who they were, would never be brought into the circle. The lone exception, of course, was President Truman. There would be no way to keep the President out of something like this. But other than the President, those in the legislative branch, those voted in by the civilian population, would not be included.

How, then, to explain Stuart Symington? Exon had clearly named the senator from Missouri as one of those who knew the truth. As mentioned, Symington was the Under Secretary of War for Air in July 1947. That made him the first civilian encountered in the chain of command for the Army Air Forces.

As the information moved up the chain of command, from Roswell, to Fort Worth, to SAC headquarters in Washington, D.C., and finally on to Army Air Forces headquarters, the information would then be passed to Symington as the first civilian encountered in that aspect of the chain of command.

Of course, the information would also go to the office of the Chief of Staff of the Army, General Eisenhower, who would pass the data to the Secretary of War, and then to the President. In July 1947, the military branch of the government was being redefined. James Forrestal, at the end of the month, would be named the first Secretary of Defense. In early July, Truman, among others, knew what was going to happen and it is conceivable, in fact likely, that Forrestal would have been briefed on the events outside of Roswell.

When the oversight committee was formed, those people in the top levels of the military and government were assigned the duties. Given what we now knew, Exon's claim that Symington was one of those makes perfect sense. The creators of the MJ-12 documents hadn't done their homework properly, nor did they understand the chain of command. Had they, then Symington surely would have been listed rather than ignored.

Other names provided by Exon made the same kind

of sense. He mentioned General Carl Spaatz. In July 1947, Spaatz was the commander of the Army Air Forces. Naturally, he would have been alerted and would have been on the oversight committee. Again, the MJ-12 briefing failed to mention him because in early July 1947 he was absent from Washington, D.C. According to the record, he was in Washington State and did not attend various meetings and briefings at the White House. Instead, those were attended by Spaatz's deputy, Lieutenant General Hoyt S. Vandenberg. Interestingly, Vandenberg's name appears on the MJ-12 briefing, but Spaatz's does not.

If someone was researching who was where in July 1947 and did not understand the significance of the chain of command, then he or she might have placed Vandenberg's name on the document. However, if someone was relating what had happened in July 1947 and who was involved from memory, he or she would have selected Spaatz because of who Spaatz was. In other words, it seems that Exon's recollections are more accurate, based on who held what positions in July 1947.

Other aspects of the corroboration aren't quite as esoteric. Exon mentioned that the bodies had been taken to Wright Field. There have been many who said the same thing. Frank Kaufmann said that he had been on one of the aircraft that eventually flew into Wright-Patterson.

Exon said that the material, the metallic debris, was flown on to Wright Field. Pappy Henderson, a pilot with the 1st Air Transport Unit at Roswell, said that he was one of the pilots who flew the debris to Wright Field.

Exon described the debris in the same terms used by a dozen other witnesses, including Bill Brazel,

Major Jesse A. Marcel, Master Sergeant Lewis S. Rickett, Sergeant Robert Smith, Frankie Rowe, Sallye Tadolini, and Loretta Proctor.

There is no indication that Exon was personally acquainted with any of these people, though it is clear that he was aware of the Roswell case before we interviewed him.

Exon's somewhat vague description of the location of the impact site agrees with what Schmitt and I have been able to uncover in the last several years. Remember, it was originally believed that the debris field found by Mac Brazel was related to claims of an impact site near the Plains of San Agustin. The original theory was that the craft had come apart over the Brazel ranch and fallen to the ground some 150 miles to the west, near Magdalena, New Mexico. When I interviewed Exon in 1990, no one was questioning this scenario. In other words, if Exon was relying on previously published material, then he would have made similar claims.

But Exon was telling us what he *knew* from his experiences at Wright Field. In fact, if we go back to his statement about two distinct sites, we find another clue about the validity of the statements made by Exon. He said, "So the farther northwest pieces found on the ranch, those pieces were mostly metal."

He was speaking of flying over the two sites, and if we followed the conventional wisdom, if we followed the scenario developed in the late 1970s, then Exon's statement should have read, "So the farther east pieces found on the ranch . . ."

Clearly, Exon was not speculating, nor was he drawing on what he might have read elsewhere. He was describing a situation he had witnessed firsthand. And as we continued to investigate, drawing on the testimonies supplied by Frank Kaufmann, Edwin Easley, Lewis Rickett, W. Curry Holden, Thomas Gonzales, and the secondhand information from Frankie Rowe and Barbara Dugger, we learn that Exon's claim that the impact site was to the southeast of the Brazel ranch was correct. This suggests an inside and intimate knowledge of the events near Roswell, just as we have claimed. Exon was not relating what he believed to be the truth or was speculating to be the truth, but the situation as he had lived it in 1947. The statements are on tape and the words are clear.

The question to be asked, then: "If Exon was speaking to us candidly, and if the information is accurate, then why now the claim that he was speculating?" The answer is threefold.

First, it seems that the change in Exon's attitude was precipitated by outside events. Exon gave us many facts that he should have kept to himself. I believe that we caught him off-guard, speaking of events that were more than thirty and forty years old. He assumed that the information was no longer classified and no longer important. Because of that, he spoke freely of events that he should have kept to himself.

Second, some of the controversy around Exon's statements was the result of the politics inside the UFO community. If Exon was telling us the truth, if his information was accurate, then clearly the MJ-12 documents were fraudulent. The wrong people were named on the oversight committee. Because of that, proponents of MJ-12 claimed that we had misquoted Exon. They didn't want any information that suggested MJ-12 was fraudulent. Rather than suggest where Exon was wrong, they attacked the accuracy of the quotes, ignoring the fact that we had the statements on tape.

Finally, and most telling, is the information given to Schmitt near the end of his interview with Exon. Schmitt said, "We still have witnesses involved with Roswell that tell us they are sworn to secrecy or at least that's still their perception . . . they will go to their graves honoring their commitments."[5]

Exon, telling us something that becomes important when all is considered, said, "I'd do the same thing. You'd just be hazed and hassled by everybody who was trying to reconstruct the thing . . ."

Exon, now being "hazed and hassled" and probably having been reprimanded by someone inside the Air Force, is trying to subtly "rewrite" history. He is claiming that his statements were speculations, but that, as we've seen, isn't the case. Exon might not like it, but his words are on tape and taken in context. He let quite a bit of information out of the bag, probably not realizing what he was doing. Now those words have come back to haunt him. We cannot let the skeptics and the Air Force twist this information around. With the tapes and letters from Exon, we can prevent that from happening. He knows the truth, and he knows that we know it. And now everyone knows the truth, too. It is all part of the conspiracy of silence.

---

[5]This conversation was held at Exon's home and the specific quotes used are on audiotape.

CHAPTER 11

———

Is There Still a Conspiracy of Silence?

IT COULD BE ARGUED THAT THERE NEVER WAS A conspiracy of silence. It could be argued that the investigation into the phenomenon known as flying saucers was riddled with incompetence and indifference. When flying saucers first appeared in late June 1947, no one knew what was happening. Reports of unidentified flying objects penetrating American airspace would be of great concern to the Army Air Forces. Intelligence officers would want to identify the objects as quickly as possible to determine if they were hostile or benign.

By the end of the summer of 1947, it could be argued that the military had, in fact, identified the objects as little more than mass hysteria, misidentification, and outright hoaxes. There was nothing extraterrestrial about the flying saucers. And, more importantly to the military men, there was no threat

223

to the security of the United States. Because of that, the military let the subject slide. The military no longer cared about flying saucers.[1] The government's mission had been completed.

The evidence, in the form of documentation available through declassified records and through Freedom of Information Act requests, reveals that the military didn't believe its mission was complete, however. Instead, it created a priority project with the expressed purpose of learning the truth. Those same officers who were suggesting that flying saucers were nothing more than illusion were, in fact, lying to the very public they were supposedly trying to protect.

A secret project with a high priority was created to investigate the phenomenon. Although it was called Project Saucer in the public statements, it was, in fact, Project Sign. During its life, the military would suggest that it had been shut down more than once. In the end, it was never closed but evolved into Project Grudge, which the military also claimed to have shut down and which, in turn, evolved into Project Blue Book.

Statements from those on the inside of the investigation were less than candid. Often witnesses who claimed to have seen a flying saucer were ridiculed as drunk or crazy or less than bright.[2] These state-

---

[1] Once they had determined there was no threat, many military officers believed their responsibility had ended. That drove the decision-making processes and not the reality of the situation.

[2] Although this is what is claimed, nearly every survey suggests that those reporting flying saucers are well educated, have not been drinking, and are not mentally unstable. This is a good example of rejecting data rather than dealing with it because the facts are too difficult to ignore otherwise.

ments, designed to limit interest in the topic, were frequently not true. Many of the sightings came from trained observers or individuals with high-level security clearances. These people couldn't be publicly labeled as "nuts." The solution was to bury the reports under the umbrella of national security, even when the investigations always claimed that UFOs posed no threat to national security.

Clearly, there is a contradiction here. How can the officers suggest no threat to national security, yet refuse to release information because it might jeopardize national security? During the Washington National sightings in 1952, reporters were chased from the radar centers by military officers who claimed that classified intercept techniques,[3] radio procedures, and radar sets were being used. Captain Edward Ruppelt, himself the head of Project Blue Book, maintained that this was not true. It was just an excuse to chase the reporters out because, if they watched, they might learn that the situation concerning UFOs was not as ridiculous as the military would have them believe. Clearly, those military officers were afraid that the conspiracy of silence would be penetrated on that night in July 1952.

Incompetence, then, doesn't seem to be a viable explanation. Too many bright people were learning too many things. The best cover for them was to look as if they didn't know what they were doing, all the while gathering their data. Incompetence is the perfect cover for the conspiracy. Incompetence has always been the perfect cover for just about everything.

---

[3]Al Chop gave me the same explanation for chasing the reporters from the radar room. There were classified procedures being used.

Those in the military are not stupid. They can read the signs as well as the rest of us. They can see which way the wind is blowing. They are not going to jeopardize careers when it is clear that the man at the top, in one case the Chief of Staff of the Air Force, has made his opinion very clear.

In 1948, after those in the trenches had an opportunity to review the data, they created an "Estimate of the Situation." Much has been written about this document, which was, according to the official history of the UFO field, destroyed shortly after it was created. But an examination of the situation shows us how the conspiracy worked, at least in part.

According to those involved, the "Estimate" reviewed a number of important UFO sightings. The officers putting it together concluded that the flying saucers were extraterrestrial in origin. They forwarded their "Estimate" up the chain of command until it reached General Hoyt S. Vandenberg, then Chief of Staff of the Air Force. According to Ruppelt, the report was "batted" back down, with a note suggesting that the evidence did not support the conclusions drawn.

But Vandenberg's or the Air Force's actions after the report had been written were important. Everyone associated with Project Sign disappeared. They were all reassigned, with the exception of two of the lowest-ranking members. The message from the top was clear. Flying saucers were not real and those who thought otherwise could find themselves at odds with the Chief of Staff. The quickest way to end a promising career was to come into conflict with the Chief of Staff, who had the power to destroy even the strongest opponent with a single word to friends or subordinates in the right places at the right times.

From that point on, the conspiracy of silence might not have always been a verbalized policy. Those entering into the conspiracy were doing so only as a career move. The reality of flying saucers meant nothing to them. Flying saucers did not affect their lives unless they expressed a belief in them publicly. Those assigned to projects investigating flying saucers had seen the carnage after the "Estimate" was batted back down the chain of command. No one had to verbalize the orders. The message was clear—abundantly clear—to everyone.

In the five years that followed the summer of 1947, flying saucers behaved themselves. There were no spectacular headline-grabbing sightings. When something happened, the Air Force had its flying saucer project to publicly investigate. The situation appeared to be well in hand. The Lubbock Lights, for example, were explained to the satisfaction of those on the outside of the conspiracy. The explanation wasn't particularly good, but it worked. People wanted to believe that the Air Force was doing a good job and accepted that it was honestly searching for the truth. No one questioned the Air Force except the "flying saucer nuts."

In fact, when the code name for Project Sign was compromised, the Air Force changed it to Grudge but told the public that the "Saucer project" had been ended. The real truth was that the investigation continued as before but at an inconspicuous level. The conspiracy of silence had little to do.

Before the summer of 1952, the situation inside the Air Force changed. Project Grudge, operating at a low level, was suddenly expanded and revitalized. Blue Book was born of Grudge. And solid investigations were attempted.

The Lubbock Lights appeared as the transition was being completed. The original investigation was an attempt to learn the truth about the lights. But it is clear now that the only push from the Air Force was to explain the sightings. Forget the truth; put out an explanation.

And then came the summer of 1952. UFOs, a term invented by Ruppelt to eliminate the melodramatic and slightly derogatory "flying saucer," were suddenly swarming over the United States. Reports, hundreds of them, were coming from everywhere. Experts, such as those charged with the safety of air travelers at Washington National Airport, were seeing flying saucers on their radars. If UFOs were illusions and misidentifications, it meant that the men at Washington National Airport were not competent to handle their jobs. Safety should not take a backseat.

The Air Force announced that something was seen, but nothing more dangerous than "temperature inversions." The conspiracy closed ranks to provide what seemed to be a solid explanation for the sightings. Never mind that the men involved were experts who could recognize weather-related phenomena when they saw it on their radarscopes. Never mind that airline crews and fighter pilots who were vectored into the area saw lights where the radar showed them to be. Never mind that multiple radars were used, showing the objects right where pilots said they were. And never mind the Air Force pressured, according to Ruppelt himself, military witnesses into changing their testimony to support the natural phenomena explanation being offered by Major General John Samford at the Pentagon.

The conspiracy of silence, which had been relatively dormant for five years, was suddenly active again. Major General Samford, who should have known better,[4] was telling the public that there was nothing to the UFOs. They could all be explained by the mundane.

But the conspiracy had fallen apart for a while. Now that was about to be changed. Project Blue Book was too public, its investigations too open to public scrutiny, even with many of the files classified as "secret." The investigative team at Blue Book was stripped of its main role and became little more than a public relations outfit.

After January 1953, the real investigation was conducted by the 4602d AISS, part of the Air Defense Command. The conspiracy had buried the UFO investigation in a newly formed unit and published the regulations to provide the authority for that unit to take over the investigation. All the while the Air Force was claiming that Blue Book was the agency to investigate UFOs, the reality of the situation was that the ADC was conducting the investigations with its semisecret 4602d AISS.

Repeatedly, Air Force officers and government officials were telling the public that no secret investigation of UFOs existed while that secret investigation

---

[4]Samford was the head of Air Force intelligence in 1952. As such, he knew more about the UFO situation than he was letting on to the press. He was less than honest during the July press conferences, though Ruppelt, in his book, suggests that Samford was caught ill-prepared for the press.

continued. The documents now prove it. There is no question that a conspiracy of silence was in place at the time.

In fact, the CIA, which often has claimed no interest in UFOs, formed its own advisory panel in 1953 to review the situation. It could be said that the scientists assembled knew virtually nothing about UFOs, the Air Force did a poor job of presenting its case, and the physical evidence—what little there was—did not prove UFOs to be extraterrestrial.

It's a nice scenario, but completely wrong. The scientists seemed to have been selected because of their hostility to the subject. Their conclusions seemed to have been drawn from the very beginning, possibly before the first session was convened. And the documentation available proves that the conspiracy of silence was still functioning at a high level as the Robertson Panel met.

It can argued that the final report, which says little, was written *before* the panel convened. Although on the last Friday it was suggested that a report should be drawn up for review by the next morning, the draft was available. Not only was it available, but it seems to have been reviewed by the Air Force and one of the panel members before the Saturday session started. In other words, there was no discussion of the UFO problem, but a stage-managed conference that had its conclusions written for it before anyone sat down at the conference table.[5]

---

[5]The evidence for this is based on a review of the final day, when Robertson said he would write the draft of their report. The timing is such that it is nearly impossible for him to have created the report, circulated as it was apparent he did, and still make the Saturday morning session. Maybe not a smoking gun, but certainly a cold pistol found in the room.

As public interest waxed and waned, the Air Force took the necessary steps to prevent a solid investigation by outsiders into the phenomenon. It issued explanations for sightings that made little or no sense, but the Air Force could see positive results. Top-line journalists, scientists, and military officers were not going to risk their careers over a topic like flying saucers. Provide an explanation that looked good and everyone would accept it. Or at least everyone who mattered would accept it.

The situation in the mid-1960s changed again. A series of impressive sightings that produced some physical evidence and, more importantly, got national attention forced the government's hand. Too much was being said about the flying saucers. The conspiracy of silence jumped back into high gear. A plan that had been kicked around for years was implemented. A supposedly objective academic investigation was proposed. The University of Colorado accepted the grant and Dr. Edward U. Condon, a scientist of some stature, was appointed as the project leader. Finally America would learn the truth.

But the reality was different. At no time was it planned that the report would be objective. Scientists on the Condon Committee soon learned that truth. Lieutenant Colonel Robert Hippler told them exactly what their conclusions were to be. He laid it all out in a letter to Condon. There was no evidence of visitation and therefore they were to conclude that flying saucers had not visited Earth. Hippler was also concerned about taxpayers funding continued UFO research. All Condon had to do now was mount the investigation and spend the money appropriated.

The Condon Committee found explanations for

sightings that were at odds with the facts. Condon made it clear what he was supposed to do: End the interest in UFOs. At a lecture in Corning, New York, Condon told a scientific fraternity, "It is my inclination right now to recommend that the government get out of this business. My attitude right now is there is nothing to it. But I am not supposed to reach a conclusion for another year." That was just days after he had received the Hippler letter.

The conclusion Condon reached was the one that everyone expected. The UFO phenomenon was nothing that threatened the United States. Project Blue Book was closed and an era ended.

The impression was that no further investigation was necessary, but that was just another page in the book. The conspiracy of silence was alive and doing well. A part of the investigation continued under the code name Project Moon Dust. Sure, Moon Dust had other more mundane missions, but that is irrelevant to the discussion because one of those missions was the investigation of UFOs.

All of this can be proven by the documents that have been found by researchers over the last several years. There is no doubt about any of this. The documents prove it all. Even officers assigned to Blue Book tell us that not all sighting reports went there. Many were forwarded to another unit that no one has identified yet, though many believe that Project Moon Dust was controlled by the 4602d.

The Air Force, when challenged with these facts by a United States senator, denied that Moon Dust had ever existed. The Air Force denied that a unit at Fort Belvoir, Virginia, with an interest in UFOs had ever existed. Documentation proved that the Air

Force was not telling the truth to the American public.

The investigation by the government continues, though the government denies it. The government claims, when challenged, that all investigations ended in 1969, but the documentation shows military and government interest in UFOs long after 1969. And when challenged under the Freedom of Information Act, the government said that Moon Dust no longer existed *by that nickname*. The officer, Colonel Phillip Thompson, didn't say the project had ended, only that the code name had been changed. The new name, according to him, was properly classified and would not be released. It was a trick the government had used before with a great deal of success.

The conspiracy of silence still exists today. The Air Force, in September 1994, issued a report on the events outside of Roswell, New Mexico. The Air Force said that it lied in 1947 about the crash there— just a little white lie, told because of national security considerations. On review of its records, the Air Force determined that the event was caused by a weather balloon, but this one from the then top secret, according to the Air Force, Project Mogul.[6] All the Air Force did in its new report was change the name of the balloon. Its mission was to present a somewhat plausible explanation for a case that was gaining widespread public and Congressional attention. By offering an explanation that sounded good to those who had neither the time nor the inclination

---

[6] There is some documentation that suggests that Project Mogul was not as highly classified as Air Force investigators would have us believe. I have documents classified as ''confidential,'' the lowest classification, that refer to the balloon project and Mogul.

to engage in in-depth research, the Air Force could end some of the speculation about the Roswell crash. The Air Force learned that lesson beginning in 1947 and had it reinforced a dozen times since then.

The news media joined the conspiracy by filling their pages with the Air Force explanation for the crash. None of the journalists bothered to call the UFO investigators named in the Air Force report. After all, according to the Air Force, the UFO investigators were all making a living on the Roswell case. They were nothing more than "commercial writers."

And the conspiracy is alive and well today. Some may ask what the motivation for it would be. Why continue the lie today? People are more sophisticated. Millions of adults, including those in their forties and fifties, were raised on the idea of life on other planets and even flying saucers. Movies from 1950 onward have suggested that flying saucers are real and they can get here. Even the fictional *Star Trek* taught us of a multitude of life throughout the galaxy. To learn that we were not alone would not be a time of panic but a time of joy. Interstellar flight was possible. We could go to other planets and other stars.

Yet the Air Force continues to suggest that UFOs are not real, even today. The question that is so often asked: "Why do they continue to deny it today?" Many people have told me that they wouldn't panic. They don't believe that others would panic.

The answer, I believe, is simple. Those at the top do not want to admit that there is something going on out there. Something over which they are powerless. They can't stop the UFOs. They can't force them down. They can't prevent them from flying through our sky. They can do absolutely nothing about them. To admit that is to admit they cannot do their job.

Is this sufficient reason for the Air Force to deny the truth? In May 1995, Alan Diehl, a former safety official, in a confidential report to Secretary of Defense William Perry, documented thirty cases of botched probes by the Air Force.[7] Although Diehl suggested that part of the reason was incompetence, he also accused the Air Force investigators of seeking to please superiors, hide culpability, and avoid embarrassment. In other words, the accident investigations were influenced by factors other than wanting to learn the truth. The truth was not as important as protecting careers and saving the reputations of high-ranking officers.

Now, if we begin with an idea that is somewhat incredible—that is, that UFOs are extraterrestrial—and we examine the history of the Air Force investigations, we see the same pattern. Officers (those who weren't incompetents, charlatans, and sycophants) were conducting their investigations to please those above them. There is no doubt that such considerations were a huge factor in the investigation of UFOs. In other words, the conspiracy of silence, when not a result of incompetency, was a consciously applied program to keep us from learning the truth about UFOs and the Air Force investigation of them.

No, incompetence and indifference does not fully explain the situation. There was a conspiracy of silence, begun in 1947 after the Roswell crash, that con-

---

[7]Diehl's investigation was related to accident reports and not UFOs, but the policy at the top is illustrative. They want to do nothing to rock the boat. There is no reason to believe that this policy wouldn't apply to other aspects of Air Force operations.

tinues until today. We can see it in the actions of the Air Force when it enters the arena claiming Roswell was nothing more than a neoprene balloon and radar target. We see the results as we try to convince some that UFOs deserve, at the very least, a rigorous investigation. We see it as ridiculous explanations for sightings are used time and again without a single shred of evidence. We see it as scientists and journalists ask, "Where is the evidence?" when that evidence is massed all around them. The Air Force just refuses to see it.

The conspiracy is beginning to unravel now. We can see it for what it is. Conspiracies do not survive the light of day. They do not survive scrutiny by those who open their eyes. Now that we can see it exists and understand how it works, we can finally stamp it out.

CHAPTER 12

The Air Force and
Project Mogul

FURTHER EVIDENCE THAT THE CONSPIRACY OF SI-
lence is alive and well came on September 8, 1994,
when the United States Air Force, in an almost un-
precedented move, issued a statement about the
events outside of Roswell, New Mexico. After nearly
five decades of claiming that the artifacts found were
nothing more spectacular than the remains of a neoprene weather balloon with a radar reflector, the Air
Force finally identified the material. It was a . . .
weather balloon. It was not an ordinary weather balloon, but a special one assigned to the then top-secret
Project Mogul. In its twenty-three-page report, the
Air Force laid out the evidence for its conclusion.

At the beginning of their research, Air Force investigators decided that they were not going to attempt
to interview all the various witnesses who have been
identified by UFO researchers as participants in the

Roswell events. Given the numbers, this isn't surprising. What is disturbing, however, is that the investigators only interviewed five people in the course of their investigation: three retired military officers and two civilians involved with Project Mogul.

One of the most important of those retired officers is Lieutenant Colonel Sheridan Cavitt. According to Major (later Lieutenant Colonel) Jesse A. Marcel, Sr., Cavitt accompanied him out to the debris field reported by W. W. "Mac" Brazel. Of those three, only Cavitt is still alive and he certainly holds one of the keys to the case.

I first interviewed Cavitt in January 1990 while he wintered in Sierra Vista, Arizona. During that visit, he told me that he had not been in Roswell in July 1947 and that he had participated in no recoveries of a flying saucer, V-2 rocket, or any type of weather balloon. He didn't know why he had been identified as one of those people because he simply wasn't there and knew nothing about the event.

In March 1993, I visited Cavitt at his home in Washington State. During that interview, he showed me copies of his orders from 1947. According to Special Order No. 121, dated 11 June 1947, Cavitt was assigned to the counterintelligence office at Roswell and had five days to report, meaning he had to arrive by June 16. Once he arrived, he claims that he was given a leave so that he had been assigned to Roswell, but was not physically present, in early July 1947. Because of that, Cavitt said that he was not involved in any of the events now known as the Roswell Incident.

I interviewed him one more time in June 1994. He mentioned that he had been visited by a Pentagon colonel (Richard Weaver), but he wasn't any more candid about the events in Roswell. In fact, when I asked him why he thought both Marcel and Lewis Rickett, the former master sergeant who had served under him, had identified him as the senior counter-intelligence officer at Roswell, Cavitt said that he didn't know. Although he had told Weaver he was at Roswell, had recovered a balloon, and had, in fact, taken Rickett out to one of the sites, Cavitt still insisted to me that he had no real role in those events.

Now we learn from the Air Force report and the supporting documentation, including a transcript of Weaver's interview with Cavitt, that things were not as we had been told. Cavitt said, "So I went out and I do not recall whether Marcel went with Rickett and me, I had Rickett with me. We went out to this site. There were no, as I understand, checkpoints or anything like that (going through guards and that sort of garbage) . . . we went out there and we found it. It was a small amount of, as I recall, bamboo sticks, reflective sort of material that would, well, at first glance, you would probably think it was aluminum foil, something of that type. And we gathered up some of it. I don't know whether we even tried to get all of it. It wasn't scattered, well, what I call, you know, extensively. Like, it didn't go along the ground and splatter off some here and some there. We gathered some of it and took it back to the base and I remember I had turned it over to Marcel. As I say, I do not remember whether Marcel was there or not on the site. He could have been. We took it back to the intelligence room . . . in the CIC office."[1]

---

[1]Cavitt's quote is part of the supporting documentation from the "Report of Air Force Research Regarding the 'Roswell Incident,' " issued on July 27, 1994.

Cavitt told Weaver that he recognized the debris as the remains of a balloon immediately. He didn't explain why he had not bothered to communicate this rather vital piece of intelligence to Marcel, nor did Weaver ask him. Instead, Cavitt kept this secret so that Marcel misidentified the debris as extraterrestrial and Colonel (later General) William Blanchard ordered the press announcement that they had recovered one of the mysterious flying saucers.

Although Cavitt identified Rickett as the man he had taken to the site, the Air Force investigators never tried to learn what Rickett had said. Rickett died before the Air Force officers began their latest investigation, but he left both an audio- and videotaped record of what he had seen and done. Interestingly, Rickett talks of going out to the site with Cavitt, but he doesn't remember if Marcel accompanied them or not.

Rickett provided testimony refuting some of Cavitt's claims. During an interview conducted on October 29, 1989, Don Schmitt asked, "The roads were blocked?" Rickett said, "Yeah, they had . . . on the road we drove on . . . MPs standing there."

Rickett also described material that he had seen. He said that he didn't think it was metal, but that "It was damn hard." Describing it, he said, "It wasn't bright and shiny on one side like foil is, but it wouldn't wrinkle." Clearly, Rickett is discussing something tougher than the foil that would have been used on the radar targets attached to the Project Mogul balloons.[2] He certainly isn't discussing the foil used in the radar reflectors on a rawin target.

---

[2] Professor Moore makes it clear that this was the New York University balloon project. He didn't know the code name until forty-five years later. Like others, I use the terms interchangeably.

The video and audiotapes of Rickett's testimony are important only because they allow outside investigators to either watch or listen to the witness interviewed. The investigators would then see that statements by Rickett were not taken out of context or that the statements had been altered as the Air Force suggested in its report.

In the course of his interview with Cavitt, Weaver asked if he had been sworn to secrecy. Weaver wrote, "Lieutenant Colonel Cavitt also stated that he had never taken any oath or signed any agreement not to talk about this incident and had never been threatened by anyone in the government because of it."

The simple response is that Cavitt, because of who he was and the position he held, would not normally be told after an event that he couldn't talk about it. Those trained in intelligence work know that classified events are not to be discussed with those who don't hold the proper clearances. There is, however, a body of testimony ignored by Weaver and the Air Force investigators that suggests that others were, in fact, sworn to secrecy or threatened by representatives of the federal government.

In July 1947, Major (later Colonel) Edwin Easley was the provost marshal, the equivalent to a civilian chief of police, at Roswell. On January 11, 1990, I interviewed Easley for the first time. I told him who I was and verified that he was the provost marshal at the base in July 1947. When he confirmed it, I asked if he was familiar with the story of the flying saucer crash. He said, "I've heard about it."

I asked, "Do you have any firsthand knowledge of it?"

Easley said, "I can't talk about it."

When I changed my question and asked again Easley repeated, "I can't talk about it."

I finally asked, "Can you tell me if you were at the crash site?" Easley repeated, "I can't talk about it. I told you that . . . I've been sworn to secrecy. I can't tell you that."[3]

In later interviews, Easley spoke more in depth about what had happened, providing some interesting information, but he always felt that he had been sworn to secrecy. Prior to his death, he told family members that "I promised the President that I wouldn't talk about it."

But Easley clearly felt he had been sworn to secrecy and the event was of such importance that even the President was involved in it. Air Force investigators have belittled this idea, asking, "Do you really think that the President would talk to a major?"

That doesn't, of course, answer the question. If the events were important enough, and if a major was one of those on the scene, then yes, the President would speak to a major. History is filled with examples of the President gathering information from lower-ranking members of the military. A lieutenant colonel named Doolittle suggested to a President that he could bomb Tokyo.

What we don't know, however, is if Easley spoke to Truman personally or if he spoke to a representative of the President. That distinction isn't very

---

[3]The entire conversation with Easley was recorded on audiotape. Although it has been suggested by skeptics that Easley claimed it was classified as a way of terminating the interview, the entire conversation was friendly and Easley said that I was welcome to call with additional questions. Easley's interview proves that military officers were sworn to secrecy concerning these events in 1947.

important. Easley believed he had promised the President that he wouldn't talk about it.

Was Project Mogul considered so important that President Truman would personally make sure it wasn't compromised? There is testimony from others, such as Chester Lytle, who suggested that most scientists didn't think Mogul had a chance of working. In 1947, even project engineers were concerned. Professor Charles B. Moore, one of those engineers, told me that preliminary work, done during Operation Crossroads, the atomic test at Bikini, had suggested that the theory was flawed. Although Mogul scientists were at Bikini using their equipment, they failed to detect the detonation. Other information suggests that by July 1947 Mogul wasn't considered all that important.

Weaver, in his Air Force report, mentioned that he had reviewed *The Roswell Events,* which was created by Fred Whiting of the Fund for UFO Research. Included in that document is a complete transcript of my interview with Easley, but Weaver never mentioned it. He didn't ask for a copy of the tape, available at the Fund for UFO Research, nor did he ask me for one. Instead, he wrote that Cavitt had not been sworn to secrecy, suggesting that no one had been. Easley's taped statements suggest that military officers were, in fact, sworn to secrecy about these events. And Easley's statements suggest that many of the officers felt compelled to remain silent, even forty-five years after the events.

We can take the idea of this silence even farther. Colonel (later Brigadier General) Thomas J. DuBose was the Chief of Staff of the Eighth Air Force in July 1947. Interviewed on August 10, 1990, by Don

Schmitt and Stanton Friedman and recorded on videotape, DuBose said, "Actually, it was a cover story, the balloon part of it . . . The remnants that were taken from this location and [Colonel] Al Clark [base commander at Fort Worth (Eighth Air Force) in 1947] took it to Washington and whatever happened to them then, I have no knowledge. That part of it was, in fact, a story that we were told to give to the public and the news and that was it . . . We were told this is the story [balloon explanation] that is to be given to the press and that is it and anything else, forget it." Unfortunately, General DuBose has since died, but his statements are recorded on videotape for review by other interested researchers.

Joe Stefula, a researcher living in New Jersey, tracked down another of the officers who had been assigned to the MP company at Roswell in July 1947. The man told Stefula that Major Easley had told him to go out to the crash site. He said, "The military police had guards there."

Stefula also learned from the former military officer that he had also been told he was not to talk about what he had seen. According to Stefula, Easley reminded the officer that they were not to discuss anything about the incident. He remained quiet, not even telling his wife about it, until Stefula called him.

Not only did government officials attempt to keep military officers silent, they also shut down radio reports. George "Jud" Roberts was the minority owner of radio station KGFL in Roswell. Majority owner Walt Whitmore, Sr., had interviewed Mac Brazel and planned to broadcast that report. Instead, according to Roberts, representatives of the FCC and from the New Mexico Congressional delegation called the station, ordering KGFL *not* to broadcast the Brazel interview. If KGFL did play it, Roberts reports that he was told the station would lose its license the next day. There was no talk of hearings, just a threat to prevent the broadcast of the Brazel interview. Roberts has been interviewed on both audio and videotape. Had Weaver asked, I certainly could have put him in contact with Roberts so he could confirm, to his satisfaction, that Roberts had not been misquoted.

What this demonstrates is that there is a body of firsthand testimony suggesting that both military officers and civilians were sworn to secrecy and that the material recovered was not consistent with that from a Project Mogul balloon. Weaver had access to all this data, but refused to review it. While I certainly understand that he didn't want to interview everyone we had interviewed in the course of our extensive investigation, it would seem that he would have been interested in what retired high-ranking Air Force officers would have to say. He wouldn't have had to rely on the interpretations of those interviews as filtered through us, but could have reviewed them on tape, since those interviews were recorded. And it seems he would have wanted to interview, in person, one of those civilians, a radio broadcaster, who claimed to have been censored by orders from Washington, D.C. Although tapes are not as satisfactory as meeting the witness in person, they are a way of determining if, as Weaver suggested, those statements had been twisted, misrepresented, or taken out of context. There is no indication that Weaver made any attempt to review this material or to speak to Roberts or any of the other living witnesses to the threats. He rejected it out of hand because it would show the weakness of the Project Mogul explanation.

In examining the evidence for Project Mogul, it becomes clear that the case is not nearly as strong as the Air Force would have us believe. The links to Mogul are very weak and the Air Force investigators were unable to discover any documents that would prove their point. In the end, it is speculation based on a limited review of the evidence available and limited interviews conducted with a mission in mind. It is, in fact, just another page in the book of the conspiracy of silence.

For the Project Mogul explanation to work, we must believe that Major Marcel was unable to identify a rather common type of weather balloon. We must accept the idea that Cavitt did recognize the balloon, but said nothing to either Marcel or Blanchard or anyone else at that time. We must believe that Cavitt, having the answer to the Roswell riddle, sat on that answer, even though he was interviewed by various UFO researchers many times.[4] And we must accept the Air Force theory that there was something special about the Mogul balloon arrays that would have prevented easy identification by some, but obvious identification by others, including Mac Brazel's teenage daughter, Bessie.

In fact, if we accept the testimony of Bessie Brazel, as recorded by John Kirby and Don Neuman, there

---

[4]Cavitt, as have many others, claims that he has been misquoted or that his statements have been taken out of context. Yet, I have not misquoted him, nor taken his statements out of context. What I have reported is what he has told me. To suggest otherwise is nothing more than an attempt to retract his own statements without having to prove either allegation.

is another conflict. Bessie Brazel claimed that she and her father had collected all the material from the field. They stored it under the porch of their ranch house in three or four gunny sacks. If that is true, then there was no debris for Cavitt and Marcel to recover on July 7, nothing for them to have seen. In fact, there is no reason for them to have gone out to the Brazel ranch.

If we want to split hairs, as Weaver sometimes has, we can show that Bessie Brazel's description of the tape doesn't match that claimed to have been on the Mogul balloons, one of the keys to the identification. She said, "In Oriental art, the petals aren't connected . . . They were very, very light pastel . . . pinks and blues and yellows."

However, according to Charles Moore, the tape used on the balloons, while featuring the flowers described by Bessie Brazel, did not feature the wide range of colors.

Irving Newton, the Eighth Air Force weather officer ordered to Ramey's office on July 8, has maintained from the beginning that the debris in Ramey's office was a neoprene balloon and rawin target. There is no doubt that this is what he saw.

Newton is important for one other reason. He told reporters for the *San Antonio Express-News* that he didn't believe what he had seen was a balloon from Project Mogul. Newton said that the rawin targets were used in atomic testing in the Far East. He was referring to Operation Crossroads. Jesse Marcel was also a participant in those experiments.

So there are discrepancies with Bessie Brazel's testimony, just as there are discrepancies with the identity of the debris displayed for the press. Discrepancies that were overlooked by Weaver. But the most important point is raised by the testimony of both the neighbors and Bessie's brother, Bill Brazel. They don't remember Bessie being at the ranch that summer. And if she wasn't at the ranch, then all her testimony about the debris is useless.

Weaver also used several of the affidavits published in Whiting's report, but never used all the information available in them. While the Project Mogul material resembles, in a very gross sense, that found by Mac Brazel, it is not an exact match by any means. This is demonstrated by a number of statements made by those who saw and handled the debris.

Jesse Marcel, Sr., when he was shown two of the photographs of the alleged debris taken in Brigadier General Roger Ramey's office, said to Johnny Mann, a reporter at TV station WWL in New Orleans, "That's not the stuff I found." He recognized it as a balloon immediately from the photographs. Why, then, couldn't he recognize that same material on the Brazel ranch, if that was, in fact, what he had seen in 1947?

Linda Corley interviewed and recorded Marcel in his home in Houma, Louisiana, in the early 1980s. She had asked Marcel to provide her with information that had not been published in *The Roswell Incident*. One of the things that Marcel told her during the taped interview was that the material in Ramey's office, the material photographed by the reporters, was not the stuff that he had found on the ranch.

Coupled to DuBose's statements that he had been told to tell the press and anyone else who asked that what had been found was a weather balloon and that all this was a cover story, a real pattern begins to emerge. Clearly, someone had decided that information was not to be shared with the general public. The military in Roswell, as well as many other locations, was working very hard to make sure the information did not leak.

Jesse Marcel, Jr., when he saw the pictures taken in Ramey's office, said that they did, in fact, resemble what he had seen in a very gross sense. The pictures were of foil and sticks, but were definitely not of the debris he'd seen in 1947. He described many of the strange properties others had noticed. He also said that the symbols he saw on one of the small I-beams[5] were purple, not pinkish, and that they were about three-eighths of an inch high.

Professor Moore said the strange symbols had been printed on tape used to reinforce the balsa sticks that were part of the Mogul array. Weaver, among others, believed this to be one more area where Mogul easily explained the Roswell debris. But the symbols on the Mogul arrays were pink and three inches high. Again, a very gross resemblance to what both Jesse Marcel, Sr., and Jesse Marcel, Jr., had said, but not a close match.

Sallye Tadolini, a daughter of one of Brazel's neighbors, was also quoted by Weaver. He wrote that in her affidavit, dated September 27, 1993, she said, ". . . What Bill [Brazel] showed us was a piece of what I still think as fabric. It was something like aluminum foil, something like satin, something like well-tanned leather in its toughness, yet was not pre-

---

[5]Marcel's description of the I-beams is quite specific. I showed a mock-up to Professor Moore, who said that there was nothing like it on any of the New York University balloons. If the Marcel mock-up is accurate, this alone eliminates Mogul as the culprit in the event.

cisely like any one of those materials . . . It was about the thickness of very fine kidskin glove leather and a dull metallic grayish silver, one side slightly darker than the other. I do not remember it having any design or embossing on it . . ."[6]

Weaver didn't bother with the next paragraph in the affidavit because it would have created too many questions. Tadolini had continued, saying, "Bill passed it around, and we all felt of it. I did a lot of sewing, so the feel made a great impression on me. It felt like no fabric I have touched before or since. It was very silky or satiny, with the same texture on both sides. Yet when I crumpled it in my hands, the feel was like that you notice when you crumple a leather glove in your hand. When it was released, it sprang back into its original shape, quickly flattening out with no wrinkles . . ."

When I interviewed Tadolini, she said that she had spent part of the morning ironing. She was intrigued by the material's ability to resume its original shape without wrinkles. It would mean that she wouldn't have to iron anything again.

Bill Brazel had found similar material on the debris field on the ranch near Corona. When he showed it to his father, Mac said that it looked like "some of that contraption I found." That ties the material discovered by Bill with the debris reported by his father. It was representative of the strange debris.

Bill, interviewed by Schmitt and me in February 1989, said, "The only reason I noticed the tin foil . . .

---

[6]The affidavits used by everyone—the Air Force, other researchers, and myself—were collected by Fred Whiting as part of his assembling of a package of material on the Roswell case. Many researchers contributed to the collection of those affidavits.

[I] took it out [of my pocket] and put it in the box
and I noticed that when I put the piece of foil in that
box . . . the damned thing just started unfolding. Just
flattened out."

What all this demonstrates is that the situation in
New Mexico in 1947 wasn't as Weaver and the other
Air Force investigators would have us believe. There
were military officers sworn to secrecy, as demonstrated by Major Easley's statements; there was a
cover-up, as demonstrated by Colonel DuBose's
statements; and there was a suppression of the news
media, as demonstrated by the Jud Roberts's interview. It also suggests the debris recovered at the
Brazel ranch site was not the remains of a neoprene
balloon and rawin target device. All this opens the
door for questions, but it doesn't completely eliminate Project Mogul as the culprit in the events. It
seems to suggest that something other than a Project
Mogul balloon was recovered on the Brazel ranch
and there is additional information that underscores
that fact, the Air Force opinion to the contrary.

First, it must be remembered that the Air Force
claimed that Launch No. 4, made on June 4, 1947,
was responsible for the debris. The Air Force implied
in its report that these balloons were something special. In fact, polyethylene, a material that was invented in 1947, might have fooled some of the less
sophisticated witnesses because of its very nature,
but the descriptions provided by the eyewitnesses
suggest they were not. And the records show that
the first polyethylene balloon was not launched until
July 3, 1947, and therefore couldn't have been responsible for the material found on the Brazel ranch, if
the Air Force was correct about the launch date. Poly-

ethylene, then, cannot be suggested because the polyethylene just wasn't available until too late.

Balloon Launch No. 4, according to the diary kept by Dr. Albert Crary, one of the leaders of Project Mogul, was composed of a cluster of regular meteorological balloons made of neoprene. It did contain a "sonobuoy," or microphone, but no "official" record was kept because no data of scientific or atmospheric importance were recovered. Charles Moore told me that he believed they had lost track of Launch No. 4 near Arabela, New Mexico, which is twenty or thirty miles south of the Brazel ranch site. Unfortunately, there is no documentation to support this claim.

There is another point that must be made here. Dr. Crary's diary suggested there was no array train attached to Flight No. 4. Crary wrote, of June 4, 1947, "Out to Tularosa Range and fired charges between 00 and 06 this A.M. No balloon flight again on account of clouds. Flew regular sonobuoy mike up in a cluster of balloons and had good luck on receiver on ground but poor on plane. Out with Thompson P.M. Shot charges from 1800 to 2400."

Moore, trying to explain the contradictory information, wrote, "One interpretation of the June 4 entry is that the launch scheduled for making airborne measurements on Crary's surface explosions after midnight was canceled because of clouds, but after the sky cleared around dawn, the cluster of already-inflated balloons was released, later than planned."[7] There is no indication that this was anything other than pure speculation by Professor Moore.

---

[7]Professor Charles Moore, "The New York University Balloon Flights During Early June 1947" (Socorro, N.M.: The Author, 1995).

There is another interpretation to the data from Crary's diary, if we examine the entry for June 5, 1947. The first of the successful flights was recorded on that date by Crary, who wrote, "Up at 4 to shoot 2 charges for balloon flight. Whole assembly of constant altitude balloons sent up at 0500 . . . recovered equipment some 25 miles east of Roswell."

It is reasonable to believe, then, that the June 4 flight was nothing more than a cluster of balloons with a sonobuoy and no long array train. Crary noted that a "whole assembly" was flown on June 5, but mentioned only the sonobuoy of June 4. If there was no assembly, then there were no rawin targets to scatter the metallic debris. Had there been the whole assembly, it seems reasonable to conclude that Crary would have mentioned it, if only because it would have been the first flight of the whole assembly after the researchers arrived in New Mexico.

The other important point, though the Air Force didn't make it clear, is that there was nothing special about the balloons in Launch No. 4, nothing that would fool anyone. They were standard balloons, about fifteen feet in diameter and made of rubber, rubber that would turn from a tan to a black after exposure to sunlight. The color wouldn't be uniform. The portions directly exposed to sunlight would blacken faster than those in shadow. The point is that the rubber reacted to the heat and light from the sun. Attempts to cut it or to burn it would have been successful. And surely someone, if not Marcel himself, would have recognized the material as having come from a neoprene weather balloon.

What becomes even more confusing is the note that Flight No. 6, launched on June 6, was lost for a short time. A B-17 was used to search for the equipment, but failed to find it. Then on Sunday, June 8, rancher Sid West, according to the information supplied by Moore, found the "balloon train south of High Rolls in mountains. Contacted him and made arrangements to recover equipment."

This episode raises additional questions. How did Sid West know who to contact about the balloon array train? How did he recognize it as something mundane when Marcel and most of the officers at the 509th Bomb Group couldn't recognize similar debris for what it was? And why the effort to recover the balloon arrays in all cases but that of Flight No. 4? What was lacking from Flight No. 4 that made it of no importance?

The answers to these questions are illustrative. Moore told me that the balloon flights had been tagged so that ranchers would know where to report the discovery of the balloons. According to all the descriptions of debris found on the Brazel ranch, there was a great deal of it. So much that it seems reasonable, as it was collected, to assume that someone would have found the tag and reported the discovery to the researchers at Alamogordo and Project Mogul. Moore, however, says that there were no tags on Flight No. 4. He suggests that the researchers didn't begin tagging the flights until after Flight No. 4.

That certainly would explain why Brazel, when he found all the debris, didn't call the Mogul researchers. However, the explanation is inadequate unless Flight No. 4 was not a full array. This seems to be another suggestion that Flight No. 4 contained nothing more than the sonobuoy and the neoprene balloons.

The Air Force maintained that the balloon found by Brazel was in the field for more than a month. The *Roswell Daily Record* suggested that Brazel found the balloon first on June 14, ten days after the launch, but left it there for another three weeks. This is in conflict with what ranchers have told me.

According to the ranchers, this sort of debris is not left on the pastures because the livestock would ingest it. They wouldn't search out the debris, but would eat it when they found it. That sort of debris could kill the animals and a rancher wouldn't leave it where the livestock could get at it. If Brazel had found the material on June 14, as reported in the newspaper, he would have picked it up on June 14. The only reason to report it was left on the field was to provide explanation for what Marcel and Cavitt found on July 7.

The Air Force used the descriptions of the material as published in the July 9 edition of the *Roswell Daily Record* to suggest, again, that it was a Mogul balloon. But Brazel talked of debris that was smoky gray, not black. Once again, we have a description that is close, but not exactly right. And at the end of the article, Brazel said that he had found balloons on two other occasions, but this was nothing like those.

The Air Force also implied that the reason there was a cover-up was to protect Project Mogul. While the project itself was highly classified, according to the Air Force, the balloons, rawin targets, and other equipment were not classified. There was little of intelligence value to be recovered by Soviet agents if they knew that balloons were being launched from the Alamogordo Army Air Field or if they recovered one.

In fact, there was so little of importance attached to the balloons that a story about them was published in the *Alamogordo News*. If Soviet agents were interested in Mogul and balloon launches, that article provided more than enough clues for them. There were photos of the balloon clusters, but, more importantly, Watson Laboratories and some of the men involved in the launches were mentioned in the article.

Had what Brazel found been nothing more than a weather balloon, there would have been no reason for the elaborate events that took place around it. Brazel would have recognized it and disposed of it without having to consult the local sheriff or the military at the Roswell base.

If it was only a weather balloon, as Sheridan Cavitt now claims, why didn't he mention it to anyone, saving the 509th from the embarrassment of announcing it had a flying saucer, only to have that statement challenged by the officers of the Eighth Air Force?

In fact, if it was only a weather balloon, even one attached to the top secret Project Mogul, why would the President ask Edwin Easley not to discuss it? The balloon itself would not suggest to anyone what Mogul was about.[8] There would be no reason to bother the President with such trivia. A phone call

---

[8]The implication is that Mogul was so highly classified that it needed to be protected, but the reality of the situation is different. The purpose might have been classified, but the equipment used was not. There would be no reason for the extraordinary efforts to protect Mogul. The reactions of the participants were not consistent with the facts, if Mogul was the culprit. However, if Mogul was not the culprit, then the actions begin to make sense.

from General Ramey would have kept Easley from talking, if it was felt that such a reminder was necessary.

There are other sources of information and documentation, and these data eliminate Mogul once and for all. We know from the Mogul reports that Flight No. 4 was not documented other than in Dr. Crary's diary. The next flight, No. 5, launched on June 5, was tracked and found down about twenty-five miles east of Roswell. That fact becomes important when we review the winds aloft data.

Winds aloft data are available from the National Climatic Data Center in Asheville, North Carolina. These are measurements of the winds from the surface to 20,000 feet made every six hours. We know, then, what direction the winds were blowing on the dates in question. It is precise data that can provide us with good clues about the fate of Flight No. 4.

The winds at the beginning of June were blowing generally to the east or the northeast. Although the winds aloft charts tend to suggest that the winds would not have pushed the balloon toward the Brazel ranch,[9] which was north-northeast of Alamogordo, and the winds didn't shift during the twenty-four hours between Flight No. 4 and Flight No. 5, it is remotely possible that a Mogul balloon did fall on the Brazel ranch.

The path of Flight No. 4 would have been generally to the east, south of the Brazel ranch site. Moore told me that he seemed to remember having lost

---

[9] Professor Moore suggests that as the balloons popped up into the stratosphere, they would have been pushed back, toward the Brazel ranch. The weather and winds data are insufficient to prove this point.

track of No. 4 near Arabela, New Mexico, about twenty or thirty miles south of the debris field. If that is true, then Flight No. 4 was not responsible. If it was near Arabela, the winds would have driven it to the east or northeast, but not north to the debris field.

One other Mogul culprit has been named by other UFO researchers. They believe, because of the information Schmitt and I developed showing the crash on July 4, that Mogul Flight No. 9, launched on the evening of July 3, was responsible. Although one of the July 3 launches was made of polyethylene and because of that, it is possible that some misidentified this plasticized rubber as something extraterrestrial, Flight No. 9 was a cluster of neoprene balloons.

Like Flight No. 4, there was no official record for Flight No. 9. According to Professor Moore, there were a number of Mogul flights that weren't recorded because no data of scientific value was learned. Flight No. 9 was one of those.

Currently the only record available is from the personal diary of Dr. Crary. Flight No. 9 took place on the evening of July 3 and was to be sent up in conjunction with the scheduled launch of a V-2 rocket. The rocket, however, did not fly because of an accident on the pad.

Moore told me that they stripped all of the equipment from the balloon array train, but they couldn't put the helium back into the bottles. Because of that, they allowed the balloons to be launched. He said that he thought the Watson Lab people did not track the balloons because they had been at work from very early that morning.

Crary's diary, however, suggested the balloons

were launched with a dummy load. The diary also noted that it was a cluster of GM (General Mills) plastic balloons that was sent up. This was the mysterious Flight No. 9. The next entry mentioned Flight No. 10.

What we know from various documents, including declassified Project Mogul reports, Captain A. C. Trakowski's report published as part of Project Grudge, and personal interviews with the various Mogul personnel, is that Flight No. 8, launched on the morning of July 3, was found down in the Tularosa Valley to the northwest of Alamogordo. Those balloons, according to the various documents, were never recovered, but they were seen on the ground.

Flight No. 10, launched on the morning of July 5, was last seen near Albuquerque. That, too, is northwest of Alamogordo. It suggests that the winds were blowing from the southeast to the northwest, and if that is true, and there was no shift in the winds, then Flight No. 9 should have followed a similar path. And if that is true, then Flight No. 9 never came close to the Brazel ranch and therefore couldn't be responsible for the debris.

According to the winds aloft records, there was no appreciable change in the wind directions between the morning of July 3, when Flight No. 8 was made, and the morning of July 5, when Flight No. 10 was made. Although the flights reached to 150,000 feet or more, we do have the data from the flight paths of Flight No. 8 and Flight No. 10. We can conclude from the winds aloft data and the flight paths of the balloons sent up a matter of hours before and after No. 9 that it would have traveled to the northwest. That means it wouldn't have come within sixty to a hundred miles of the Brazel ranch.

The documentation available, then, excludes Flight No. 9 as the culprit. The winds aloft data underscores the proof that Flight No. 9 was not responsible.

But the final bit of information, one that completely excludes Flight No. 9, has been found. A series of photographs of the launch show Flight No. 9 without an array train attached to it.[10] And if there was no array train, then there was nothing to scatter the metallic debris.

What this demonstrates is that our assumptions, based on what was written by Dr. Crary, are accurate. The diary mentioned the composition of the array trains, if they existed. Crary's diary mentioned Flight No. 9 contained only balloons and a dummy load, which is what the photographs confirmed. His diary mentioned Flight No. 4 contained only a sonobuoy but no mention of a whole assembly. It was the next entry, Flight No. 5, that contained that mention. It seems reasonable to believe that Flight No. 4, because no data of scientific or atmospheric importance was recovered and because of the entries by Dr. Crary, had no array train. If that is true, then New York University balloons, which carried the various equipment aloft, had no role in the events surrounding Roswell.

In fact, all the documentation from various sources, including *Contributions of Balloon Operations to Research and Development at the Air Force Missile Development Center 1947–1958*, lists Flight No. 5 as the *first*

---

[10]Professor Moore received copies of the photographs from another member of the project. It is clear from the photographs that no array train had been attached to Flight No. 9.

research balloon launch at Holloman. Given that, other documentation, and Dr. Crary's diary, which mentions nothing of an array train but does mention the sonobuoy, there is but one conclusion. Flight No. 4 did not contain the material that would account for the debris found by Mac Brazel.

All of the other Mogul flights were accounted for in the various available records. If neither Flight No. 4 nor Flight No. 9 were responsible, then no Mogul flight was responsible. And the information available, including the most important winds aloft data, tends to exclude both Project Mogul balloon flights.

There is one other piece of evidence. Remember, Brigadier General Arthur Exon reported that in 1947 he had the opportunity to fly over the impact site and debris field. He said, "It was probably part of the same accident, but there were two distinct sites. One, assuming that the thing, as I understand it, as I remember flying the area later, that the damage to the vehicle seemed to be coming from the southeast to the northwest but it could have been going in the opposite direction, but it doesn't seem likely. So the farther northwest pieces found on the ranch, those pieces were mostly metal."

His testimony corroborates two sites, the orientation of those sites, and effectively eliminates Project Mogul. There is no way Project Mogul could have created two distinct sites as part of a single event. Weaver ignored Exon's testimony during his investigation because of the damage it does to the Project Mogul theory.

No, Project Mogul, although reportedly highly classified, does not explain the events on the Brazel ranch. There is too much testimony from too many firsthand witnesses. When all the data are examined, it is obvious that Project Mogul is inadequate as an explanation.

The Air Force, in the course of its investigation, and the many other researchers have done us one favor. They eliminated all other explanations for the events near Roswell. Normally, these alternatives are suggested by those who have done little or no research on the case themselves. John Keel, a writer who specializes in the strange, the unusual, and the paranormal, claimed that he had solved the case after discussing the situation with a historian living in Roswell. The answer, according to Keel, was a Japanese balloon bomb. Of course, Keel could not offer the name of the historian or any documentation to support his theory. Contrary to Keel's position, Japanese balloon bombs were not classified in 1947, so had it been one of those, there would have been no reason to misidentify it as something other than a balloon bomb. In fact, the *Roswell Daily Record* carried a story in July 1947 that mentioned balloon bombs, showing that the information about them was widespread and available in Roswell.

Ron Schaffner, a UFO researcher, suggested that it was an aluminum parachute assembly from a V-2 rocket that had strayed off course. According to Schaffner, there had been a moratorium on V-2 launches because of an accident in May 1947 when a faulty gyroscope caused a rocket to crash into a cemetery about half a mile from Juarez, Mexico. If the military had launched a rocket in violation of that moratorium and it had crashed into ranch land in New Mexico, those responsible might have initiated a cover-up to protect their jobs and themselves from prosecution.

Research, however, showed that the July 3, 1947, rocket, Schaffner's culprit, never left the ground. There was an accident on the pad, resulting in injuries to several technicians and soldiers. Newspaper reports from around the country announced the failure and the accident.

Schaffner's theory failed because the rocket never left the pad, so it could not have scattered the debris. There was no cover-up because the newspapers reported these events. The moratorium that had been in place in early June had been lifted by the time of the July 3 attempted launch. And finally, the records from the White Sands Proving Ground (later White Sands Missile Range) account for all rockets launched in that time frame. Nothing is missing from the record, so there is nothing that could have fallen on the Brazel ranch in New Mexico. V-2 rockets or any of the rockets launched from White Sands have been eliminated.

One UFO researcher believed he had found the solution, labeling the crash as the wreck of a Northrop Flying Wing. More specifically, he thought it was the N-9M, the two-engine version of the propeller-driven design. He believed that the unusual design might have caused the confusion, although the craft was constructed of plywood and steel tubing.

That theory failed when it was discovered that the last flight of the N-9M had taken place in 1946. The full-sized four-engine versions, designated XB-35, were not flying in July 1947, none of them crashed, and, in fact, they had been grounded by mechanical problems the year before. The jet-powered version, the YB-49, did not fly until October 1947, and was therefore eliminated.

In 1994, the Air Force reviewed its files on the events outside Roswell in a search for an explanation for the crash debris. Investigators agreed that a missile, balloon bomb, or an experimental aircraft did not account for the debris found by Mac Brazel. The investigators also reviewed aircraft accident files. They concluded, "USAF records showed that between June 24, 1947, and July 28, 1947, there were five crashes in New Mexico alone, involving A-26C, P51N, C-82A, and PQ-14B aircraft; however, none of these were on the date(s) in question nor in the area(s) in question."

Air Force officers also suggested that the events were not the result of any kind of nuclear accident, which, if it had been, certainly would have been classified in 1947. They wrote, "A number of records still classified TOP SECRET and SECRET–RESTRICTED DATA having to do with nuclear weapons were located in the Federal Records Center in St. Louis, MO. These records, which pertained to the 509th, had nothing to do with any activities that could have been misinterpreted as the 'Roswell Incident.' Also, any records of a nuclear-related incident would have been inherited by the Department of Energy (DOE), and, had one occurred, it is likely DOE would have publicly reported it as part of its recent declassification and public release efforts."

The Air Force, then, in its search for an answer that explains the events at Roswell, had eliminated all of the mundane explanations except one, the balloons assigned to Project Mogul. The records and documentation, along with the participants, have eliminated that final explanation. Looking at the Roswell case, there is no earthly explanation for it.

In 1994, the General Accounting Office, at the request of New Mexico Republican Steven Schiff, began an investigation to determine if there were any records that would answer questions about the events near Roswell. In the summer of 1995, the GAO issued its findings. The report was short, described by some as a poor high school book report, but it did nothing to suggest that Roswell could be explained as anything mundane.

There were two key points to the report. One, as GAO investigators searched for the outgoing messages from the Roswell base, they learned that all such messages had been destroyed without proper authorization. The report said, "Our search of government records was complicated by the fact that some records we wanted to review were missing and there was not always an explanation. Further, the records management regulations for the retention and disposition of records were unclear or changing during the period we reviewed." In other words, these messages, which were part of the permanent record, had been destroyed. No one could explain who did it or why.

Second, although the investigators mentioned the Air Force theory that balloons assigned to Project Mogul were responsible for the debris, the GAO didn't endorse that position.[11] The lone conclusion to

---

[11] Dr. Mark Rodeghier made a search of other GAO reports to determine if the GAO would draw conclusions if the data required it. He found that the GAO would endorse positions if it agreed with the findings. The fact the GAO investigators mentioned the Air Force report but did not endorse it becomes even more important when coupled to these other findings.

be drawn from that was that the GAO was not suitably impressed with the Air Force idea. The GAO mentioned it but didn't seem to believe it.

This is in contrast to the GAO position on MJ-12. The idea of a super-secret committee, known in UFO circles as "The Majestic Twelve," was explored by GAO investigators, but they found no evidence that it ever existed. Citing a number of different sources, documents, and agencies, all of which suggested that there was no evidence of a "Majestic Twelve," the GAO concurred. This demonstrates that the GAO investigators were not afraid of taking a stand on controversial topics. When the evidence impressed them, they drew conclusions. In this case, it was that the MJ-12 documents were fraudulent.

The GAO also missed one other bet. The investigators received a telex from the FBI, dated July 8, 1947, that referred to the events at Roswell. The copy they had was sanitized, leaving out a couple of names and other information. The reason that this is strange is because I, as well as many other members of the UFO community, have had the full text of the message for years. It has been published in a number of books. Why couldn't the GAO receive an unsanitized version of it?

That same message, which mentioned the balloon and radar reflector, also suggested that the FBI investigation has "not borne out this belief." The message then said, "Disc and balloon being transported to Wright Field." In other words, there is some documentation that suggests the balloon explanation offered in 1947 was not accurate, but the GAO didn't pursue this information at all.

More importantly, a second FBI document, with a

handwritten note by J. Edgar Hoover that mentions "discs recovered," seems to have been overlooked by the GAO. It is an ambiguous document that is relevant to the discussion.

The one thing the GAO report did do was confirm that some of the documentation from the 509th Bomb Group had been improperly destroyed so it could not be reviewed. The report also showed that some agencies of the government were being less than honest in their attempts to find documents. And finally, the GAO report did nothing to support the Air Force claim that a balloon was responsible for the Roswell case.

There were enough ambiguities in the GAO statements that Dr. Mark Rodeghier asked Jack Krieth of the GAO investigation team a couple of questions. Krieth told Rodeghier that he didn't find Professor Moore's arguments particularly convincing. Nor did the Air Force present any evidence that Mogul was responsible. Krieth, therefore, didn't believe that Mogul was responsible.

None of this, however, leads directly to the extraterrestrial explanation. Other evidence takes us in that direction. But it must be remembered that all terrestrial explanations have been eliminated by searches of military records, private industry's research and development programs, eyewitness testimony, and a failure to find any documentation to support these other answers. When the investigation is over and all of the evidence is examined, there is little room left for speculation and none for Mogul.

CHAPTER 13

——

How the Conspiracy
Works Today

IN TODAY'S ENVIRONMENT, THE GOVERNMENT NO longer needs to hide the truth and engineer diversions. At some point, we began doing it to ourselves and blaming the government for it. Or we are pretending to be government agents, as if this somehow increases the credibility of those making claims about UFOs. Or we are accusing each other of being government agents[1] who have some sort of hidden agenda, most probably to keep the lid down and the cover-up intact.

There is no question that a policy of debunking once existed. Hundreds of documents have surfaced showing this to be the truth. Statements by various government and military officials who contradicted

——

[1] In the UFO community, you are considered to have made it if you are accused of being a government agent. Some are now claiming that they are government agents, though the reason for this escapes me.

one another have proved this time and time again. In fact, in January 1953, the Robertson Panel recommended that all UFO sightings be explained. The panel even explained sightings that had defied Air Force experts, and "possible" or "probable" explanations became positive identification.

In other words, there was a policy of explaining sighting reports. The interpretation of that policy, whether it was suggested just to explain sightings that could be identified or if it was meant to explain all sightings regardless of the facts, is irrelevant. It demonstrates a policy of debunking established by a governmental body. Although there are other examples that predate the Robertson Panel, it seems to be the boldest of the statements. It establishes that originally there was a conspiracy of silence at the highest levels of the government by the documentation now available to UFO investigators.

By the early 1960s, the Air Force would be searching for a way to end its involvement in UFO investigation. To that end, as explored earlier, the Air Force tried to find an organization that would handle the problem as the Air Force wanted it handled. There is no question that the Condon Committee, formed in 1966 and sponsored by the Air Force, had only one real mission: to end the Air Force's public investigation of UFOs.

At the same time—that is, from the beginning of the modern flying saucer era—there have been suggestions that a campaign of disinformation has existed. UFO researchers have claimed for years that a committee at the highest levels is responsible for the climate of ridicule that currently exists. Someone at the very top of the government, either military or civilian, was orchestrating the silly information by planting articles in the tabloid press and by financing the antics of the lunatic fringe. In this fashion, those at the top are able to keep the real information suppressed because the scientific and the legitimate journalistic communities are repelled by the nonsense. Who would want to risk a reputation that has taken years to build when it seems that all the data is the result of invention, distortion, illusion, and outright hoax?

Some of this can easily be proved. Once again, the real mission of the Robertson Panel comes into question. From all the evidence and from the final report that was eventually released to the public and to UFO researchers, it seems reasonable to conclude that the panel wanted to end the interest in flying saucers. Although the use of the term "debunking," according to later analysis, seems to be innocent, it still raises many questions.

Of course, it can be claimed that the recommendations of both the Robertson Panel and the Condon Committee were nothing more nefarious than scientific conclusions based on objective research. It can be argued, with the lack of positive evidence, that no other conclusion was possible. Had positive proof for the existence of UFOs been found or offered, then other conclusions would have been reached.

And even if UFO researchers have been correct in their assumptions, that in no way translates into an organized attempt to suppress data, hide evidence, or fool the public. It could be that those at the top sincerely believed there is nothing to the phenomenon and have been trying to discourage interest in

UFOs for what they believe to be good scientific reason.

The question that must be asked now is if that policy, that debunking effort, is still in effect. Or, because of the structure of the UFO field, have those at the top of the conspiracy of silence stopped actively trying to debunk UFOs? It could be, as many have suggested, that the pettiness, jealousy, and egos of those in positions of power in the UFO community have created a climate where no outside influence is necessary. We continue to do it to ourselves.

There are many cases in point. The controversy over the MJ-12 documents—that is, a briefing and supporting documents prepared for President-elect Eisenhower—proves this. According to these papers, released in 1987, a high-level committee of top scientists, military officers, and politicians was formed within days of the discovery of the craft outside of Roswell. If the documents were authentic, then many of the questions asked by Ufology would have been answered, providing proof to the world that UFOs were real, they were extraterrestrial, and they crashed.

The controversy over the documents began immediately, with skeptics and believers lining up to argue. In the years that followed, the evidence proving that MJ-12 was a hoax has been found. Few researchers believe there is anything to MJ-12 now. Only a couple of people hang on to the belief that MJ-12 was anything other than a fraud.

But there is still an argument about who created the documents—and for what purpose. Some think that the oversight committee, the one alluded to by responsible witnesses, created to exploit the Roswell find, is still operating. One of its responsibilities is to create disinformation to fool the UFO community and keep the curtain of silence lowered.

Theories about the origin of the MJ-12 documents corroborate this. One group believes that the documents were created by UFO researchers themselves for one of two reasons. One reason was to present documentation to prove the case. If authorities would endorse the fakes, then it could be claimed the case was proved. UFOs existed as extraterrestrial spacecraft and they were landing on Earth. The government had information to prove this but was withholding it from the public.

A second reason to create the documents was to propel those who had them into the spotlight.[2] When the documents were released in 1987, opportunities for national publicity followed. Several UFO researchers, some of whom had nothing to do with the creation of the documents, appeared on national television programs. If that had been the plan by those who created the documents, it worked very well.

There is, however, another group that believes that the documents, if fake, were created by insiders to mislead the public. Those insiders, with access to the information held by the oversight committee, created documents that looked authentic on the surface. However, as researchers began to study them, they would find flaws that would eventually lead to the conclusion the documents were fake. In that way,

---

[2]It should be pointed out here that there is no evidence whatsoever that Stan Friedman had a hand in creating these documents, though he is one of the foremost proponents of them.

those who endorsed the documents would lose their credibility. And the UFO field as a whole would be viewed by the general public as a group of crackpots that couldn't be trusted to tell the truth if they knew it. The MJ-12 documents, according to these people, were disinformation rather than a hoax.

Ed Komarek, a cofounder of Operation Right to Know, believes that the disinformation agents are still operating. He not only suspects the government of engineering the MJ-12 hoax, but of planting stories in the tabloids, creating other hoaxes, and spilling disinformation into various public forums to keep us all in the dark. The great hoaxes of the UFO field, according to Komarek, are the result of the disinformation campaign.

Komarek might have a point, but it is more likely that the oversight committee has realized that the tactic is no longer necessary. MJ-12 was more likely a hoax created inside the UFO community by people who had never served in the military rather than disinformation engineered inside the government in an attempt to keep the lid clamped down.

But there have been claims of other hoaxes from the inside as well. Gerald Anderson, after seeing the Roswell segment on *Unsolved Mysteries*, called the toll-free number to tell his tale of a crashed saucer, several dead aliens, and of one who had survived. Later, he made his claims to both Stan Friedman and me. Although it was clear, almost from the beginning, that Anderson was a witness to nothing, but an opportunist trying for his fifteen minutes of fame, Friedman accepted the story as true. Later, as Anderson's report began to unravel, Friedman suggested that Anderson couldn't have known what he knew if not briefed by someone who did. If Anderson wasn't on the inside, meaning if Anderson hadn't witnessed what he claimed, if Anderson hadn't seen the crashed craft, then he talked to someone who had. Of course, there was no corroboration for this belief. It was an attempt to salvage something from the Anderson tale.

Others, however, believed that Anderson was an agent of disinformation. He worked for the government. His job was to divert attention from the Roswell case and lead it in strange directions. His story was not designed to hold up under close, professional scrutiny, but then most of the investigators inside the UFO community were far from professionals.[3] Often they accepted everything told to them by witnesses as the truth. Since Anderson had passed a lie detector test and had undergone hypnotic regression, that seemed to underscore the validity of his tale and there were those all too willing to accept everything he said about the case.

And one man, wanting to believe Anderson was telling the truth, suggested that the negative documentation about Anderson had been planted by the government to destroy his credibility. The man wouldn't consider the possibility that Anderson was merely an opportunist who managed to get himself featured in a couple of UFO documentaries, a couple of free trips to New Mexico, and his name mentioned in various books and magazines. Anderson even

---

[3]To prevent misunderstanding, I should point out that I mean nearly everyone in the UFO community has a "day job" that pays the bills. Few have been trained as investigators. This, by no means, reduces the importance of the work they have done.

made a little money on the deal, paid to him for expenses.

A case can still be made for government influence inside the UFO community if we accept as truthful the stories told by some of the researchers. At the 1989 MUFON Symposium held in Las Vegas, Nevada, researcher William L. Moore said that, as an unpaid agent of the government, he had spread disinformation. In the April 1991 issue of *Fate*, it was reported that Moore, at a meeting held on April 1, 1990, in Hollywood, said the disclosures he was about to make were a combination of true information and disinformation, for that was how the government worked with him.

At the MUFON Symposium and in the *Fate* article, Moore claimed to be responsible for some of the disinformation concerning animal mutilations, the underground alien bases, and the other wild rumors that had been circulating inside the UFO community for years. Moore's claims, then, seemed to suggest that the government was still participating in spreading disinformation about UFOs.

There was never any proof that Moore was receiving disinformation. It was his claim, but those inside the UFO community were willing to believe it. If Moore's claims were true, it offered validation for their own beliefs. If there was nothing to UFOs, there would be no need for the government to spread disinformation about them. If, on the other hand, UFOs were real and there was a government policy to suppress the information, then a planned program of disinformation made sense. It also proved that the government knew the truth and was trying to hide it in a backward sort of way.

Of course, all that is true if we believe what Moore was saying. But without proof and without additional testimony from others who were in the same place—that is, spreading disinformation provided to them by government agents—there is no reason to draw those conclusions. It is just as likely, if not more so, that the government was not involved with Moore.

MJ-12 suggests that the government is continuing that policy if we overlook some of the evidence. It is more likely that MJ-12 reflects the machinations of the UFO community. Solid arguments can be made in both directions. There are, however, other indications that the problem with the suppression of evidence comes from inside the UFO community rather than outside of it. It is the infighting that goes on as various personalities jockey for positions of power and prominence. It offers the real clues about the current conspiracy of silence.

During the 1995 MUFON Symposium in Seattle, Stan Friedman's lecture was not about the state of research, not about research he had conducted and the results of that research, or about how science could be applied to UFO research, but was entitled "Roswell Revisited." The title suggests that it was another examination of the evidence of the events in Roswell in 1947. In reality, it was an attack on various researchers and organizations who don't agree with Friedman's version of the Roswell case.

Friedman wrote in the abstract of his paper, "A great deal has been published and broadcast concerning the 1947 recovery of crashed flying saucers in New Mexico in the past three years. Much has unfortunately been nonsense or misleading. New imaginative, but false, scenarios have been created about the events and people involved in them. Careful research has taken a backseat to research by proclamation. Considering the past history of deceit on both sides of the UFO question, that isn't surprising. But when the U.S. Air Force, *The New York Times*, *The Washington Post*, the Associated Press, and Showtime all disinform the public with misinformation which they are unwilling to correct, it is time to set the record straight. This paper deals with recent discoveries and misrepresentations about the many aspects of the Roswell, GAO, and MJ-12 story."

While such a goal is positive, and the MUFON Symposium is the proper place to discuss the state of research, Friedman allowed his paper to degenerate into an attack on those of us with whom he disagreed. For example, because he felt slighted by the producers of the Showtime movie *Roswell*, he wrote that he considered the film to be inaccurate and criticized the film company for not repairing those errors. But this was a movie, not a documentary. The story had been written to supply a vital and interesting frame for the film. Of course there were changes made for the sake of the story. So why criticize a film for alerting the general public to an event that has been overlooked by historians?

The answer, according to Friedman's paper, was "I certainly felt airbrushed out when I saw the Showtime Movie." He then listed all the errors he found in the film. But these errors were nothing more than the creation of the story.

Friedman, in the paper, included a list of thirty-eight points in "Figure 2" that he claimed were "Some False Claims Made by Kevin Randle and/or

Donald Schmitt 5/95." These were nothing more than statements with which Friedman disagreed. For example, he wrote, as a false claim, "William Moore and I hadn't noted that MJ-12 Briefing was by a military man for a military man."

In reality, I had written in an article about MJ-12 that Friedman didn't understand the significance of that point, not that he didn't note it. It was this sort of splitting hairs that Friedman used in this section of his paper. It is, in fact, irrelevant to the whole UFO phenomenon but does illustrate the point. We attack each other repeatedly, and by doing so, undermine the credibility of each other in particular and the field in general.

After disposing of the work I have done on various aspects of the Roswell case, Friedman then wrote, "There is no doubt that the Randle-Schmitt scenario might possibly have occurred, just as the moon might be made out of green cheese." He went on to criticize what he saw as my failings, but offered no proof that such was the case.

Not content with denigrating other researchers, Friedman attacked the J. Allen Hynek Center for UFO Studies. Friedman wrote, "Chief among the unverified claims were the many attacks on Gerald Anderson, a witness to the crashed saucer on the Plains of San Agustin, on Robert Drake who testified about the Plains crash, on Barney Barnett another Plains witness, and repeatedly against the legitimacy of the Majestic 12 documents. It is almost as though a corporate decision were made by CUFOS at some point in time that there was no Plains crash and the MJ-12 documents were false. Don't bother us with the facts, our mind is made up. The treatment in both these areas has all the attributes of propaganda and none of the world of investigative journalism or science.''

Yet the truth of the matter is that CUFOS repeatedly provided Friedman with a forum for his opinions on the matters of Gerald Anderson, MJ-12, and the Plains crash. When articles critical of these points were scheduled to be published, Friedman was offered the opportunity to rebut those articles. In fact, when Friedman published articles in the CUFOS magazine, *International UFO Reporter*, there was little critical comment by the editors.

Only after Gerald Anderson's story unraveled and he confessed to forging documents and telling lies did everyone on the CUFOS board reject those stories. More than once board members argued in defense of Anderson, using the information that Friedman had supplied.[4] CUFOS provided Friedman with a forum for his work that would not have existed elsewhere, but when the truth was learned by the CUFOS staff, he attacked them for telling that truth.

The attacks, of course, must confuse those who are not privy to all the minute details of the Gerald Anderson story, who have not seen the long, detailed analysis of the MJ-12 papers that appeared in *A History of UFO Crashes*, or who don't know that the only alleged eyewitness to the event on the Plains, Barney Barnett, died before any researcher ever talked to him. When the witnesses to an event on the Plains are listed, it all comes back to Barney Barnett. Vern

---

[4]At a number of CUFOS board meetings, members would argue for the Gerald Anderson story, repeating information that Friedman had supplied to them. They were willing to accept Friedman's version of the events until the evidence showing the flaws in the Anderson tale was presented.

Maltais didn't see anything; his close friend Barnett told him about it. J. F. "Fleck" Danley, Barnett's boss, didn't see anything; he heard the story from Barney. Harold Baca didn't see anything; he heard the story from Barney. Major William Leeds didn't see anything; he heard the story from Barney. Alice Knight, Barnett's niece, didn't see anything; she heard the story from Barney.

Robert Drake didn't see anything but heard the story from an anonymous cowboy. On a trip back from the Plains with Albert Dittert, Wesley Hurt, and Dan McKnight, they stopped on a ranch. While the three others were off doing something else, Drake, alone, heard the tale of a crashed saucer from a cowboy whose name he never knew. On the way back to Albuquerque, Drake mentioned the tale of a crashed saucer to the other men in the car. All have been located and all deny they ever heard such a story from Drake at that time. Drake then said he hadn't told the others about the crash.

The point here is that this unofficial conspiracy of silence attacked CUFOS because Stan Friedman didn't like the results of its independent investigations. CUFOS board members were the bad guys who made some fictional corporate decision. Friedman implied some sinister maneuvering, but the fact is that the evidence they examined independently led them to the conclusion they drew about these aspects of the UFO field. There is nothing sinister going on at CUFOS other than solid research and careful evaluation of the evidence.

The same comments can be made about MJ-12. In fact, when the documents were first released, CUFOS was among the most vocal proponents of them, sug-

gesting they deserved close scrutiny before any conclusions were drawn. Jerry Clark, a CUFOS board
member, was a leading proponent of MJ-12 until the
evidence became overwhelming. The statements of
support made by Clark were published in *IUR* for
all to see. Yet Friedman talked about a corporate decision based, not on fact, but on emotion. Nothing
could be farther from the truth.

But these were not Friedman's only targets. While
appearing on Larry King's UFO special from Rachel,
Nevada, Friedman called Robert Lazar a liar. Lazar
claimed to be a physicist who worked at the Air
Force's super-secret base known as Area 51. Lazar
claimed to have seen "captured" alien spacecraft and
tried to reverse-engineer some of the components for
the U.S. government. Lazar's story was investigated
by a number of researchers, and some of them believed him to be telling the truth. George Knapp of
Las Vegas TV station KLAS said that many of the
things Lazar reported were accurate, suggesting, at
the very least, Lazar had been inside Area 51. Knapp
was also quick to point out that he had been unable
to verify Lazar's educational claims, which bothered
him greatly.

Friedman also said that he had tried to verify
many of the things Lazar had said. When he was
unable to do so, Friedman decided that Lazar was a
liar. Now we have the situation where one physicist
is calling another physicist a liar. The Lazar affair is
just another of the sorry episodes that dot the UFO
landscape.

When William Steinman claimed to have found government scientist Robert Sarbacher, Friedman wrote to
MUFON headquarters on February 14, 1990, claiming

that *he* had found Sarbacher and turned the data over to Steinman. Friedman wrote, "*I* was the first to find Sarbacher and the first to visit him. Steinman only found him as a result of information which I provided to Bill Moore and he provided to Steinman."

Steinman, however, published letters to Bill Moore telling of his, Steinman's, find of Sarbacher. He told Moore to let Friedman know about the existence of Sarbacher. While it might be true that Friedman was the first to *visit* Sarbacher, apparently Steinman was the first to interview him, getting Sarbacher to corroborate the story of an alien spacecraft crash.

Of course Friedman isn't the only member of the UFO community to engage in these activities. It seems that feuds and war exist throughout, with one researcher calling another a fraud and a liar. Threats of lawsuits seem to be the norm rather than the exception, though few lawsuits are ever filed.

There are any number of those in the UFO community who claim academic credentials, expertise in specific fields, or military service that they don't deserve. It is easy to check these things, and they often are. When it is learned that the person made up his or her credentials or expertise or military service, others suggest that such antics are harmless. But when journalists interview such people and then learn the truth, they believe that all in the UFO field are of a like mind. They believe that all of us routinely lie about our military or academic backgrounds. Such misrepresentation is not harmless, but ruins all chance for any rational and reasonable research. We are all lumped together, and another aspect of the conspiracy of silence is put into effect.

What this demonstrates, more than anything else,

s why the investigation of UFOs remains where it
loes. It would seem, based on the amassed data, that
ome scientists would be interested in the phenomenon. Areas of the field do interest scientists, but thorough scrutiny of the phenomena is not a high
priority. A large part of the problem is the ridicule
actor. That is, so many of the people in the field have
been exposed misrepresenting themselves or making
ridiculous claims that scientists don't want to be as-
ociated with anyone inside Ufology.

In this respect, the conspiracy of silence isn't so
much a conspiracy as it is the individual actions of
irresponsible people. What sort of credibility will
those in the UFO field have when there is a small
but vocal group that makes outrageous claims? Dur-
ng an Operation Right to Know march in Washing-
on, D.C., one of those interviewed by the media was
a woman who claimed she "had manifested herself
on a sixteen alien craft."

Komarek told me that such reports do hurt the
overall picture, but there is little that can be done to
prevent it. Too often the reporters view the UFO stories as "fluff" not worth their time and effort. No
one wants to waste time on a ridiculous story of alien
visitation. And no one wants to be seen as ridiculous
by treating the subject seriously. The only recourse
s to search for a "light" angle so that the reporter
can then claim that he or she doesn't really believe
n flying saucers anyway.

Komarek said that he tries to discourage those who
don't have a serious interest in the subject. However,
here are always some in search of the spotlight and
he media can always find them. Komarek wonders
f that isn't part of the conspiracy.

In August 1995, we were confronted with another aspect of the conspiracy. Ray Santilli, a London-based video distributor, spent months suggesting that he had a film of an autopsy of an alien being. He made many claims about the film, and it was the topic of conversation in UFO research circles and various computer-based bulletin boards throughout most of the year.

But the film, which I saw at the beginning of July 1995, was a hoax. While certain aspects of it were intriguing, close scrutiny revealed many glaring errors. Russ Estes, a documentary producer from California, pointed to the lit Bunsen burner and asked why it was there. He said the instruments in the tray next to the body were not the sort to be used in an autopsy. To him, the film represented a movie set rather than an actual morgue or operating theater.

Kent Jeffrey, who saw the film in May 1995, came away convinced it was a hoax. He wrote in various public forums that there was no doubt in his mind that the film was bogus.

Almost universally, UFO researchers rejected the film. Though Santilli claimed he had received the film from a man who had been an Army photographer in 1947, he refused to name him. Without a provenance for the film, it had to be considered a hoax. For any other conclusion to be drawn, Santilli had to produce the photographer with proper credentials. The film stock had to be tested. There were many things that could be done to authenticate the film, but few, if any, had been done.

But more importantly, many of the claims for the film didn't pan out. At one point, it was said that Harry S. Truman, President when the crash took place, was plainly visible walking across the debris field. Now, it seems that someone had told Santilli that Truman was visible and Santilli, who hadn't seen the footage, told investigators that Truman was visible. It was just another example of the claimed authenticity that didn't pan out under proper research.

The point, however, is that information about the film dominated UFO research for most of 1995. Reputable newspapers, such as the *Sunday Times* in London, investigated and reported the film to be a hoax. Many believed it to be the end of the Roswell investigations. If the film is a hoax, then the Roswell case is a hoax.

The truth is, the alien autopsy footage, which appeared from outside the UFO community, was almost universally rejected by UFO researchers. Those researchers were suggesting that we treat the film as a hoax until all the evidence was in. Now that the evidence has been collected and the film has been rejected, it becomes another chapter in the conspiracy of silence.

No one will remember that members of the UFO community were among the most vocal critics of the film when it first appeared. Instead, people will remember that the film was a hoax. They may assume that all data about the Roswell case has been shown to be a hoax. They may write off Roswell, as well as the film, though no such conclusion is warranted.

This is not, I believe, part of a planned disinformation program, though some will see it as such. Many will believe that the government disinformers engineered this episode, though it seems to be another case of an opportunist taking advantage of the situation. It is one more example of how the unofficial conspiracy of silence operates. Not all hoaxes are part of the plan, but all of them contribute to the aura of ridicule surrounding the UFO phenomenon. For those inside, for those who control the conspiracy, such a hoax is just as good as any disinformation they put out. It all contributes to the same cause.

In today's environment, it seems that there is little real activity in the attempt to keep the lid clamped down. In September 1994, the Air Force, apparently fearing the GAO investigation, tried to preempt problems by announcing a new solution to the Roswell case. Using only a few witnesses and ignoring all the testimony and documents that would lead away from its "new" solution, the Air Force claimed that the Roswell case was just a balloon. A balloon attached to a highly classified and virtually unpublished project, according to Air Force spokesmen, but a balloon nonetheless.

The Air Force issued its report to the media, who were quick to report all the Air Force said, ignoring the glaring errors and outright contradictions in the document. In fact, the *Sunday Times* mentioned the new Air Force solution in the article about the Santilli film, as if to suggest there was nothing to the Roswell case.

Many, now satisfied the Air Force had solved the mystery, refuse to look at anything that would suggest otherwise. The conspiracy works because no one wants to buck the trend. No one wants to sacrifice credibility on a subject that might have no more substance than the Bermuda Triangle or the Easter Bunny.

But, for the most part, the conspiracy of silence today is carried out by unwitting partners. Those in the UFO community who are more interested in furthering their own status, who care little or nothing for the truth, and who continue to attack their fellow researchers are playing into the hands of those at the top of the conspiracy. Why should they act when we will continue to destroy ourselves?

The Air Force report was illustrative. The Air Force investigators asked how they could possibly investigate this case when we, inside the community, couldn't even agree on the date of the crash. Of course, it didn't matter that the disagreement is only over a couple of days and, in fact, reduces the number of days that need to be searched. The Air Force investigators suggested we couldn't agree and therefore they had no obligation to answer our questions. Of course, that is merely a way to avoid answering the difficult questions.

What all this demonstrates is that there is still a conspiracy of silence, but today it operates at a much lower, quieter level. Those on the inside, who know the truth about the UFO phenomenon, don't have to create much in the way of disinformation. When the need arises, when the heat is turned up, then the conspiracy begins to operate.

However, based on the current situation, it seems that the conspiracy of silence is now in the hands of the UFO community. We are the ones silencing those who don't agree with us. We are the ones attacking one another. If we want to break the conspiracy of silence, the first thing we must do is police ourselves.

If the UFO community can begin to work together, then a large part of the conspiracy will be destroyed. When that happens, we can then begin to work against those who are trying to hide the biggest story of the last one thousand years.

APPENDIX A:

The Truth About Frank Kaufmann

THE WHOLE ROSWELL CASE HAS BECOME A POLITI-cized football. There are many sides to the contro-versy, each with its own agenda. Criticism of witness testimony is often offered, not because the testimony is flawed, but because other researchers don't want to believe it. Witness credibility is attacked, not be-cause the witness is a liar or a fraud, but because the testimony ruins a belief in another aspect of the case. Or it is attacked because of who gathered it rather than what it says.

Frank Kaufmann has been under assault almost from the moment his testimony was presented. Most of those attacking are doing so because Kaufmann's testimony damages their core beliefs. For example, if what Kaufmann says is accurate, then the Project Mogul and New York University balloons are elimi-nated as explanations. Or if Kaufmann's testimony is accurate, then clearly all mundane explanations fail. There is no way to suggest that he was mistaken about what he saw. The only conclusion to draw is that he is lying, even when there is no evidence that such is the case.

It is true that I place enormous confidence in the testimony of the man I have identified in other works as "Steve MacKenzie." It is also true that if his testimony was to stand alone, meaning there was no independent corroboration for it, the case would be severely weakened. In fact, I would be inclined to reject it myself. However, it must be remembered that Kaufmann claims firsthand knowledge of the events outside of Roswell, New Mexico.

But the testimony offered by him does not stand alone. Many aspects of his report have been corroborated by others who were clearly in Roswell in July 1947 and who can prove it. It is because of that documentation that the testimony of Frank Kaufmann takes on added significance.

For years it has been claimed that the crash took place on the evening of July 2, 1947. Almost everyone who wrote anything about the crash used the July 2 date. In my first book, *UFO Crash at Roswell,* I used the same date. There was no reason to dispute it then.

The question, however, is: Where did that date originate? On July 8, the *Roswell Daily Record* reported that Dan Wilmot saw an object fifteen to twenty feet in diameter over downtown Roswell and heading to the northwest on the previous Wednesday, July 2. Although there was no reason to make the assumption, there were those who believed that this was the object that crashed. All dates flowed from there until Walter Haut, the public relations officer of the 509th Bomb Group, reported that the "Roswell Army Air Field" captured a flying saucer on July 8, 1947.

The skeptical community has complained frequently that no one saw the craft in the sky. Suddenly Mac Brazel appears on the scene with a field filled with strange metallic debris. Major Jesse A. Marcel, air intelligence officer of the 509th, reported that "It was something that must have exploded above the ground and fell . . ." But the point is that neither saw anything in the air.

That changed with the appearance of William Woody. Woody said that he and his father were surprised when the wall of their house suddenly lit up one night. Turning, they saw a bright light moving quickly through the sky on a downward arc. He said the light was so bright that they couldn't look directly at it, comparing it to the flame of a welding torch.

Following the conventional wisdom, this means the Woody sighting was on Wednesday, July 2. Woody said that he and his father drove out, a day or two later, to search for the object. They drove north of Roswell on Highway 285, but weren't allowed to turn off the main highway on to any of the dirt roads to the west because the military was there. Woody believed they made the trip on the weekend, but couldn't be sure.

However, if we continue to follow the conventional wisdom, which is the military didn't enter the case until the following Tuesday, July 8, it means the Woodys waited a week or more before beginning their search for the downed object. Woody's testimony didn't fit, exactly, into the scenarios developed from the conventional wisdom. This bothered me, but there was no indication that Woody was lying.

The date changed with the appearance of a written record. In Roswell at the Saint Mary's Hospital, two Franciscan Catholic nuns, Mother Superior Mary Bernadette and Sister Capistrano, were making routine observations of the night sky. They saw the bright object plunging toward the ground late on the evening of July 4.

Witnesses at two other locations also saw the object in the sky. Corporal E. L. Pyles, stationed at one of the satellite facilities attached to the 509th, was walking across the parade ground on the main base. He saw the bright object and believed that it was late at night, thought it might be close to the weekend, and that it came down north of Roswell. Later, when he heard the balloon explanation, he didn't believe it. This establishes his sighting in the proper time frame prior to the press release on July 8, 1947.

What all this does is provide us with a better picture of when the crash took place. We now have solid evidence for July 4 rather than wild speculation for July 2. It makes the Woody story fit the scenario much better and more logically. Rather than waiting several days, Woody and his father go in search of the object on the weekend. The military cordon, according to Provost Marshal Edwin Easley, was already erected before July 8.

And there is one new piece of evidence. In July 1947, Leo B. Spear was an MP with the 1395th MP Company in Roswell. Although he didn't see anything himself, he did say that he remembered other MPs returning from the crash site and talking about the flying saucer. Spear said that he believed the story to be "BS" until he read about it in the paper a day or two later. What this does is confirm, from still another source, that the military was involved *prior* to July 8. It corroborates aspects of the story told by Kaufmann, Pyles, and Woody.

Although these observations have been written off as an astronomical phenomenon by some, there is no evidence to support that conclusion. Rather, we have observations that do have enough in common to allow us to connect them. We have a bright white object low in the sky (below 20,000 feet) that fell to Earth and, based on the data available, it seems to be the object that was recovered outside of Roswell.

The conventional wisdom has always been that the object was a domed disk, the classic flying saucer. Gerald Anderson, whose testimony has been thoroughly discredited, talked of a domed disk. Other sources, primarily secondhand, suggested that it had been a disk-shaped object.

Kaufmann was the first to suggest the object was not disk-shaped but was, in reality, heel-shaped. Although the idea hadn't been suggested in relation to the Roswell case prior to this, it wasn't completely new. Kenneth Arnold didn't see a flying saucer but something that was heel-shaped. In the official Project Blue Book files, the illustration Arnold originally drew is definitely heel-shaped.

Project Blue Book files contain another heel-shaped object, this one photographed on July 7, 1947, as it flew over Phoenix, Arizona. Project Blue Book officers labeled the case as a hoax, but not for very good reasons. If the object at Roswell was heel-shaped, then the reason for the Air Force opinion is obvious.

This in no way "proves" that a heel-shaped object was found near Roswell, but it does confirm that such objects were being seen and reported during the summer of 1947.

One other man, Lewis Rickett, a counterintelligence agent at Roswell in 1947, said that the object had been heel-shaped. Those were his words, spoken to Don Schmitt just days before Rickett died.

The corroboration for Kaufmann's story extends beyond that. Kaufmann speaks of a crash site north of Roswell, about thirty-five miles from the base. Kaufmann said the military used Highway 285 and then drove cross-country. The military officials later realized that Pine Lodge Road was the best way to get in there.

The location of the crash, north of town, has also been mentioned by Rickett, Dr. W. Curry Holden, and Major Edwin Easley. I had hoped to interview Holden a second time, but he died shortly after my first meeting with him. He confirmed to me that he had been at the site of the flying saucer crash, he "had seen it all" but recalled few details. He was north of Roswell, not far from Highway 285. Easley provided notes indicating that the crash site was north of Roswell, but not northwest, near Corona.

There is still another firsthand source who wishes to remain anonymous who has also corroborated the exact site as given by Kaufmann. He used the book *Roads of New Mexico* to pinpoint it for me, since it was impossible to take him out there, given his location. Granted, such testimony does nothing for those who aren't privy to it, but it added another corroboration for the crash site location. He had no knowledge of what Kaufmann had told me.

Dr. C. Bertrand Schultz said that while traveling north out of Roswell on Highway 285 he saw the military cordon. The soldiers were stationed to the west of the highway, but since Schultz had no desire to drive in that direction, he didn't care. Later, after Holden told him what he had seen, Schultz realized the importance of his observations. He shared it with his daughters while they were growing up in the 1950s and early 1960s.

The location close to Roswell was also corroborated by Dr. George Agogino (secondhand), who corroborated the testimony of the "anonymous archaeologist" who spoke to me on the telephone. The archaeologist said that they had been working the area north of the Capitan Mountains in central New Mexico. That fits with what has been reported by others. Agogino told Tom Carey (a researcher living in Pennsylvania), after Carey had read my notes to him, "That's what he told me." The archaeologist has been identified and his story corroborated.

Frankie Rowe's (secondhand) father, Dan Dwyer, gave her general information about the location. He suggested that it was north of Roswell but closer to the city than the conventional wisdom suggested. Barbara Dugger (thirdhand), whose grandfather was Sheriff George Wilcox, agreed with that. It was her impression that the crash site was in Chaves County, near Roswell, not far away in Lincoln County, near Corona.

Everyone agrees that there was a debris field found by Mac Brazel, and nearly everyone agrees that there was a second site where the craft and bodies were found. Originally it was suggested that this second site was far to the west, on the Plains of San Agustin, but no firsthand testimony has developed to corroborate that. Now, based on eyewitnesses, it seems clear that the second site was close to Roswell. And now there are those who make it clear there were two distinct sites.

Once again, we look at the critical information supplied by Brigadier General Arthur Exon, who reported that he had flown over both sites. He mentioned tire tracks on them and reported the gouge that corroborated the tale told by Bill Brazel and suggested by Jesse Marcel, Sr.

Robin Adair, a technician for the Associated Press in July 1947, said that he had been required by the AP to rent an airplane in El Paso, Texas, to fly to Roswell. He'd flown over two sites and saw soldiers at both of them. Neither site was near the Plains, but both were north and northwest of Roswell.

It has been suggested by critics that the claim the archaeologists have been found is premature. The question is: "How can it be premature when the leader of the expedition said that he had been there?" Dr. Holden said that the location was north of town and responded that the military had been there. In response to direct, careful questioning, Holden repeated that he had been on the site and had seen the craft and the bodies.

But Holden's testimony about his involvement does not stand alone. His involvement is corroborated by Schultz, Agogino, and Dr. William Frankforter. In fact, Agogino corroborated more of the story told by the anonymous archeologist in 1990. No longer is it required to accept a story without more data. We have that data now.

What must be clear is that we have one source, the

so-called "anonymous archaeologist," who said that he had been there and had seen the craft, describing it in a fashion that is consistent with other firsthand testimony. He described the bodies in a similar fashion and provided by other named sources.

It must be remembered that the archaeological team has been found. The leader said that he was there. That testimony is corroborated by others. Another archaeologist has spoken about the events. He has been identified and his testimony has been corroborated. The testimony of both Holden and the anonymous man is consistent with the evidence developed from other sources, including Frank Kaufmann.

The point of all this is to demonstrate that there were a number of interviews conducted, that the majority of them are on either audio or videotape (audiotapes at CUFOS, videotapes at FUFOR), and some of the interviews were witnessed by other investigators. Many of the witnesses, such as Frank Kaufmann, have been interviewed by many people. Family members, friends, and former military companions verify parts of the stories. There is a wide variety of corroborations for these tales.

If we eliminated the Kaufmann testimony, would we be left with a gap in our knowledge about the impact site? No. It would be a little more difficult to put the whole picture together, but it could be done. For example, we could pinpoint the location based on the interviews conducted with Easley, Holden, John McBoyle (radio newsman with radio station KSWS in Roswell in 1947), Woody and Schultz (talking about a military cordon off Highway 285), and Exon and Adair.

If we eliminated the Kaufmann testimony, could we determine the shape of the craft? Again, the answer is yes. Rickett provided us with a very good description, as did McBoyle, Easley, and the "anonymous archaeologist" to whom I spoke on the telephone.

Could we describe the recovery without Kaufmann? Again, yes. Easley provided some detail, as did Rickett, McBoyle, Holden, and the "anonymous archaeologist."

Flights out of Roswell containing material or bodies have been described by various crew members, including Marcel, Robert Porter, Robert Slusher, and Len Stringfield's pseudonymous "Tim." Others, such as Robert Smith, described loading various aircraft with crates that apparently held debris.

Secondhand sources Sappho Henderson, who said her husband flew wreckage to Wright Field, and John G. Tiffany, who said his father was on a flight that might have held bodies, also describe flights out of Roswell.

There have been several reports of bodies, including Edwin Easley's firsthand comment about "Oh, the creatures." Ruben Anaya also told a secondhand story of alien bodies. As did Melvin Brown, who claimed he had seen the bodies.

What this demonstrates is there is a large body of corroboration for the testimony of Kaufmann. There are important additional firsthand sources who saw a great deal, who were heavily involved in the case, and who have reported it. There are secondhand sources who add detail to our knowledge. If we listen to what they say, we can reconstruct the events of July 1947 without relying on Kaufmann.

This shows that Kaufmann is not alone in what he saw or he reported. His story has been verified and corroborated by the testimonies of many other sources. Some of that corroboration is very subtle, such as the story told by Leo Spear. All it does is suggest a military involvement prior to Marcel reporting back to the base on July 8 and that corroborates one small detail supplied by Kaufmann.

The questions that must be asked: "Why is this testimony being rejected when single-eyewitness reports have been accepted in the past? Why is this testimony being rejected in favor of *secondhand* reports? Why is it being attacked when there is so much supporting evidence for it? Why is that supporting testimony ignored? Is there another agenda at operation here? And if so, why?"

Antonio Huneeus, a magazine writer, suggested that Roswell investigators should be more cautious after the Gerald Anderson episode. He was right. We were very cautious before we accepted the testimonies of Kaufmann. We waited for verification and corroboration, which we found.

It seems that the rejection of Kaufmann's testimony is the result of friction inside the UFO community. One prominent UFO researcher, when he learned of Kaufmann, demanded to know, "Why is he talking to you?" That same man rejected Kaufmann's story, even though he accepted others based on virtually no evidence. He doesn't see the incredible double standard he is imposing on the data.

For those who don't believe the testimony, they should initiate their own search. They should review the all testimonies and search the record for the corroboration. They should not be swayed by attacks on either the researchers who present the data, nor on the reputations of the witnesses. Instead, they should examine the whole record. What they will find is that Kaufmann is telling the truth.

APPENDIX B:

—

The Skeptics and Reasonable Analysis

THE DEBATE OVER THE EVENTS NEAR ROSWELL, New Mexico, of July 1947 has taken several subtle turns. For those not familiar with them, arguments from the skeptical community can be convincing. The problem is that many of these arguments are founded, not in research, but in the semantics of the situation. With the debate reopened with the publication of *The Truth About the UFO Crash at Roswell*, it is now important to understand exactly what is being said. The arguments over the credibility of forty-year-old memories and the events that took place in Brigadier General Roger Ramey's office on July 8, 1947, can be illustrative in attempting to understand the whole situation.

Philip Klass, in one of his attempts to undermine the research being done into the Roswell case, has presented theories that cannot be substantiated. He has taken rumor and speculation and attempted to turn them into a thought-provoking piece on why the memories of witnesses and the testimonies of those witnesses should be ignored. But Klass, in writing his article, has ignored the documents and the testimonies that fly in the face of his beliefs.

Using the debates between Donald Schmitt and Kevin Randle and Jamie Shandera and William Moore as the springboard, Klass writes, "The controversy has served to demonstrate how fragile and uncertain are the 40+ year old recollections of surviving principals—which is hardly surprising."

Klass continues, writing, "Seven different photos have been located which were taken in Gen. Ramey's (Brigadier General Roger Ramey, commanding officer of the Eighth Air Force) office on the late afternoon/early evening of July 8, 1947, and two of them show Ramey and Col. DuBose (later Brigadier General Thomas J. DuBose) examining the debris. All photos show the same debris. Moore/Shandera claim this is the same debris recovered by Marcel (Major Jesse A. Marcel) from the Brazel (W. W. "Mac" Brazel) ranch and that photos show the remains of a crashed saucer. Randle/Schmitt disagree and say the photos show the remains of a balloon-borne radar tracking device which Gen. Ramey substituted for the authentic debris."

To this point, Klass has provided the reader with an accurate account of the situation. The facts, as outlined, are correct. However, Klass then makes the assumption that is not true. He writes, "The fact that all seven photos taken in Ramey's office show the same debris challenges the credibility of Maj. Jesse Marcel's 30+ year old recollections which form the cornerstone of the Roswell crashed saucer myth, at least for Moore, Friedman, and Shandera."

These facts do not challenge Marcel's recollections, but Moore's reporting of those recollections. That is the subtle, yet real, difference here.

Klass continues, writing, "According to Moore's book, when Marcel (now deceased) was interviewed in the late 1970s, he said that 'one photo (taken in Ramey's office showing Marcel examining the debris) was pieces of the actual stuff we found. It was not a staged photo. Later, they cleared out our wreckage and substituted some of their own. Then they allowed more photos.' Yet all of the photos taken in Ramey's office on July 8, 1947, including two (not one) with Marcel, clearly show the same debris."

Moore is the only one to report that Marcel claimed the photos in Fort Worth were of the real debris. In fact, he provides us with three versions of that one interview, one published in his book, one circulated a couple of years ago, and another in *Focus*, his publication. Both Friedman and Len Stringfield, who interviewed Marcel frequently, reported that Marcel never told them about photos of the "real" debris.

But we can take this one step farther. Marcel, when shown a copy of one of the photos printed in *The Roswell Incident*, reported, "No. No. That picture was staged. That's not the stuff I brought home."

A disinterested third party, Johnny Mann, reported that. His interest was only in learning the truth and he is not a party to the so-called dispute. The exchange between Mann and Marcel was witnessed by another man, Julian Krajewski.

In fact, Marcel said as much on audiotape. Linda

Corley had a chance to interview Marcel in 1980. During that interview, Marcel told Corley that the photographs did not show the material that he had found on the ranch. They were staged photographs.

The point of the dispute is not Marcel's memory, then, but the reporting of his testimony. Moore has yet to offer the true version of the statement. We do have testimony, from a variety of witnesses, including those who showed Marcel the pictures, that refutes both Moore's claim and Klass's assumption. We should not, then, condemn Marcel's "30+ year old recollections" for facts that come from third parties.

Switching gears, Klass moves on to Colonel Du-Bose. Klass reports, "In Dec. 1990 issue of *Focus,* Shandera's article includes what he says are verbatim quotes from two interviews with DuBose—one by telephone and one in person when he recently visited DuBose at his home in Florida. After asking DuBose if he had read the Moore/Shandera articles that Shandera had earlier sent to him, and if he had 'studied the (Ramey office) pictures,' DuBose reportedly replied: 'Yes, and I studied the pictures very carefully.' When Shandera asked if DuBose recognized the material, DuBose reportedly replied: 'Oh, yes. That's the material that Marcel brought in to Fort Worth from Roswell.' "

Klass continues, writing, "But Randle and Schmitt got a conflicting response when DuBose was interviewed earlier—on August 10, 1990. The interview was videotaped and hypnosis was used to try to enhance DuBose's 40+ year old recollections. In this interview, DuBose said that the material photographed in Ramey's office was NOT the debris that Marcel brought, i.e. that bogus material had been substituted.

But then Shandera visited DuBose and asked him if there had been a switch, DuBose reportedly replied: 'Oh, bull! That material was never switched.'"

Again, the controversy isn't about forty-year-old memories of a witness but about the reporting of those memories by two separate groups. It is interesting that Shandera's reporting is in direct conflict with what was reported first in *The Roswell Incident* and later by myself.

It is also important to point out that, according to both General and Mrs. DuBose, Shandera neither recorded the interview nor took notes during the interview in Florida. We have Shandera's unsubstantiated claim that DuBose said the debris in Ramey's office was the real debris, which is consistent with the story that Shandera and Moore are currently pushing, but that is not consistent with the independent testimony of the witnesses or with the documentation available.

We have supplied copies of the videotaped interviews to the J. Allen Hynek Center for UFO studies, the *MUFON UFO Journal*, and the Fund for UFO Research. We have quoted exactly from that tape. Shandera and Moore have yet to offer independent and disinterested third parties copies of their tapes. If they would do so, then the question about the debris in Ramey's office could be cleared up.

We asked DuBose pointedly if he had ever seen the Roswell debris and he responded, "NEVER!" After the Shandera interview was published, we asked him again if he had ever seen the real debris and again he answered, "NO!"

This could be construed as just another debate between two factions, ours and theirs, with no way to resolve it. However, we aren't the only ones to whom DuBose spoke. Billy Cox, a writer for *Florida Today*, interviewed DuBose for an article he wrote in the November 24, 1991, edition of the newspaper. Cox reported that DuBose told him essentially the same story that he told us. Here was a disinterested third party reporting on the same set of circumstances, but he didn't get Shandera's version of the events.

In a letter dated September 30, 1991, Cox wrote, "I was aware of the recent controversy generated by an interview he (DuBose) had with Jaime Shandera, during which he stated that the display debris at Fort Worth was genuine UFO wreckage and not a weather balloon, as he had previously stated. But I chose not to complicate matters by asking him to illuminate what he had told Shandera; instead, I simply asked him, without pressure, to recall events as he remembered them . . . he seemed especially adamant about his role in the Roswell case. While he stated that he didn't think the debris was extraterrestrial in nature (though he had no facts to support his opinion), he was insistent that the material that Ramey displayed for the press was in fact a weather balloon, and that he had personally transferred the real stuff in a lead-lined mail pouch to a courier going to Washington . . . I can only conclude that the Shandera interview was the end result of the confusion that might occur when someone attempts to press a narrow point of view upon a 90 year old man. I had no ambiguity in my mind that Mr. DuBose was telling me the truth."

Cox isn't the only one to hear that version of events from DuBose. Kris Palmer, a former researcher with NBC's *Unsolved Mysteries*, reported much the same thing. When she spoke with DuBose, he told her that the real debris had gone on to Washington in a sealed pouch and that a weather balloon had been on the floor in General Ramey's office.

But the most enlightening of the interviews comes from Don Ecker of *UFO* magazine. Shandera had called Ecker, telling him that he would arrange for Ecker to interview DuBose. Ecker, however, didn't wait and called DuBose on his own. DuBose then offered our version of events. When Ecker reported that to Shandera, Shandera said for him to wait. He'd talk to DuBose.

After Shandera talked to DuBose, he called Ecker and said, "Now call him." DuBose then said that the debris on the floor hadn't been switched and that it was the stuff that Marcel had brought from Roswell. It should be pointed out here that Palmer called DuBose after this took place. Without Shandera there to prime the pump, DuBose told our version of events. It was only after close questioning by Shandera that their version was heard. It is not unlike a skillful attorney badgering a witness in a volatile trial. Under the stress of the interview and the close questioning, the witness can be confused for a moment. Left alone to sort out the details, the correct version of events bubbles to the surface.

It should also be noted that DuBose hasn't actually changed his testimony at all. The real confusion comes from his statement that the debris on the floor in Ramey's office was not switched. We had suggested that the debris Marcel brought to Ramey's office was switched with the balloon. DuBose said that the debris on the floor wasn't switched. That statement is correct. The debris on the floor was not switched.

What this means, quite simply, is that the debris Marcel brought from Roswell was never displayed on the floor in Ramey's office. Marcel unwrapped one of the packages containing the real debris and set it on Ramey's desk. The two officers then studied a map of the debris field in another room. When they returned, the debris had been removed from Ramey's desk and the weather balloon was displayed on the floor.

I could go into a longer explanation of the situation in Ramey's office on July 8, 1947, but have done so in the November/December 1990 issue of The *International UFO Reporter* and the April 1991 issue of the *MUFON UFO Journal*. Both publications provided detailed accounts of those critical hours, including a long listing of sources used in the preparation of the articles. It is interesting to note that Shandera and Moore quote sources but never supply copies of the tapes or transcripts to independent third parties. I have done both.

Klass, as he continues his analysis of the story, then makes the same mistake that Shandera has made. He confuses two flights with one. He writes, "When he (Don Schmitt) asked DuBose if he had seen 'the actual debris' brought by Marcel, DuBose replied: 'Never.' He claimed the real debris was contained in a plastic bag which was 'tied with a wire seal around the top' which was flown to Washington, D.C., in a B-25 or B-26. (Marcel, interviewed in the late 1970s, recalled the debris was flown to Wright Field, Dayton, Ohio, in a B-29.)"

DuBose, when interviewed by us, was talking of a

single flight from Roswell, which was probably made late on Sunday, July 6, 1947. That flight held some of the debris brought into the Chaves County sheriff's office by Mac Brazel. Then, two days later, Marcel and the B-29 flew on to Fort Worth. There was no discrepancy here, just a misinterpretation of the facts by an outsider who has confused them.

But Klass is not content to leave it there. He reports, "One indication of the 89-year old DuBose's flawed memory is that when Schmitt asked if Shandera had visited his home a few months earlier to interview him, DuBose said Shandera had not. But when Schmitt asked Mrs. DuBose, she confirmed that Shandera had indeed visited their house for an interview."

The conclusion, which Klass is so impressed with that he typed it in all caps, boldface, and underlined it, is: **THUS, WHILE MOORE/SHANDERA DEBATE WITH RANDLE/SCHMITT OVER WHICH OF DUBOSE'S RECOLLECTIONS OF EVENTS THAT OCCURRED MORE THAN 40 YEARS AGO IS CORRECT, DUBOSE DEMONSTRATED FOR SCHMITT THAT HE COULD NOT REMEMBER A VISIT AND INTERVIEW BY SHANDERA WHICH HAD OCCURRED ONLY A FEW MONTHS EARLIER.**

Ignoring the fact that long-term memory is better than short-term, and that the elderly often display perfect memories of long-ago events while being unable to remember what they had for breakfast, let's examine that whole statement by Klass.

First, DuBose remembered the interview but not the name of the interviewer. That's a far cry from Klass's claim that DuBose didn't remember the interview.

Second, the real question is not which of DuBose's

recollections of the events are accurate but which version reported by others is correct. DuBose's recollections have not changed. Once again, I have made copies of the tapes available to disinterested third parties for review. Shandera/Moore have yet to do that. While I prove our claims, we must accept what they say without corroboration.

Klass does give us an answer, of sorts, to the question of which version is correct. Klass points out, "Randle/Schmitt managed to locate and interview the reporter for the *Ft. Worth Star-Telegram*—J. Bond Johnson—who had taken at least several of the photos in Ramey's office. According to their taped interview, Johnson said he then doubted that he had photographed the authentic recovered debris. But several months later, when Johnson was interviewed by Shandera, he changed his account and said that he was confident that his photos did show the actual debris that Marcel brought to Fort Worth."

Here is an opportunity to examine the methods and techniques used by Shandera. There is a wealth of documentation that can't be altered. Johnson left a legacy of writings in the newspaper so that we can compare his original story with what he is saying today.

What we learn is that Johnson's first version of the events, that he saw and photographed the bogus debris and that the cover story of a balloon was in place before he arrived in Ramey's office, is correct. After talking to Shandera/Moore, Johnson's story changed. (For a complete analysis, see the November/December 1990 *International UFO Reporter*.)

It boils down to Shandera's version of events against that given and documented by outside sources. Shandera's version is at odds with both my tapes and the newspaper articles written (including one by Johnson and published the next day in the *Fort Worth Star-Telegram* in the right time frame).

In fact, further evidence of Shandera's altering facts appears in Shandera's published version of what Irving Newton, one of Ramey's weather officers, said and did in Ramey's office. Shandera, writing in the *MUFON UFO Journal*, suggested that Newton had changed his story after I had interviewed him, but a complete review of his testimony, published in *The Roswell Incident*, shows that Newton's testimony is consistent throughout all interviews, with the exception of the new data written by Shandera. (For a complete analysis, see the *MUFON UFO Journal*, April 1991.)

So Klass seizes on the changes in testimony, condemning the witnesses, claiming that forty-year-old memories are flawed. But the problem is not the memories of the witnesses, but the reporting of their testimony by third parties. In fact, it is a single individual, Shandera, who is causing the trouble. It is Shandera who is saying that I have been wrong; it is Shandera who has altered and misreported DuBose's testimony; it is Moore and Shandera who have created the controversy over the Marcel interview; and it is Shandera against Newton. I offer copies of the tapes, the documentation, and the transcripts to independent third parties to prove my veracity, while the others offer nothing other than their opinions and versions of the events.

Klass, trying to prove that Roswell was something mundane, probably a balloon, reports everything that raises the remotest question but never tells the full story. He stops short. Klass, it seems, is treating this as a debate and not as a search for the truth.

At the end of his discussion of the Roswell events, he writes, "As reported in the July 9, 1947, edition of the Roswell newspaper, Brazel was quoted as saying, 'when the debris was gathered up the tinfoil, paper, tape and sticks made a bundle about three feet long and 7 or 8 inches thick, while the rubber made a bundle about 18 or 20 inches long and about 8 inches thick. In all, he estimated, the entire lot would have weighed maybe some five pounds.' Brazel was quoted as saying there was 'considerable Scotch tape and some tape with flowers had been used in the construction. No strings or wire were to be found but there were some eyelets in the paper to indicate that some sort of attachment may have been used.' (Curious construction techniques for a very advanced ET society to use in building spacecraft intended to traverse jillions of miles.)"

But what Klass never reports, though I have told him about it repeatedly, was that Brazel was escorted to that interview by Army officers. There are six separate witnesses who saw Brazel in downtown Roswell. They were surprised by Brazel's refusal to acknowledge them and the fact that there were three officers with him.

Klass, when I pointed that out, said that maybe it was easier for the officers to drive Brazel into town than for them to give him directions to the newspaper office. Three military officers drove Brazel into town so that he could be interviewed because it was easier than telling him, "Drive out the front gate, stay on Main Street, and the newspaper office will be on the right."

Paul McEvoy, an editor at the newspaper, said that Brazel was obviously under duress as he told his "new" story. Friends commented on Brazel's lack of friendliness while he was in town. No, Brazel was taken to the office to tell a new story. The one that the military wanted him to tell.

But even so, Brazel slipped in a statement that was fully reported in the *Roswell Daily Record* but ignored by Klass. In it, Brazel said, "I am sure what I found was not any weather observation balloon."

Klass completes his report, asking, "How would Ramey (who never talked to Brazel) know what kind of bogus material to use to replicate the description that Brazel would give to the Roswell newspaper? And how would Ramey be able to find and obtain such 'look-alike' material so quickly??"

But Klass again overlooks the testimony of others. DuBose suggested that debris had been in Fort Worth at least two days before Ramey made his press release. Ramey was in communications with Colonel Blanchard in Roswell, as well as SAC headquarters in Washington, D.C. Orders from the top had trickled down through the chain of command. Ramey knew what to say and probably obtained the balloon from his own weather station. It didn't matter what Brazel had seen because Brazel's statements to the newspaper the next day were fed to him by the military. He repeated what he had been told because the military was there watching him.

The answer to the first part of the question is that Ramey knew what Brazel would say because he had read the script. It wasn't Brazel telling the truth at the newspaper office, but telling the reporters what he had been told to tell them.

And the answer to the second part is that they had been working on this for more than three days. The craft and bodies had been found before Brazel walked into the sheriff's office. Ramey, as well as many others, had already seen the debris, and he may have seen the craft and the bodies. Remember, DuBose was in charge in Fort Worth because Ramey was offstation on Sunday, July 6.

The major problem is that Shandera, and at times his partner, Moore, are trying to confuse the Roswell issue. They publish statements that are in direct contradiction with statements they have published in the past. They have reinterviewed witnesses and then claim that there are changes in the testimony.

Klass, wanting to destroy the Roswell testimony, uses these supposed discrepancies to refute the good work being done. He claims that witnesses can't be relied on to remember accurately events of more than forty years ago. In fact, Klass has admitted that his job is to debunk UFO reports. Not investigate them to learn the truth, but to debunk them regardless of what that truth might be. This is, of course, in direct conflict with the supposed bylaws and purpose of CISCOP. Klass heads its UFO subcommittee. Just how scientific are its investigations if Klass's expressed purpose is to debunk?

Klass continues to misinterpret facts. In his May 1994 *Skeptics UFO Newsletter*, he suggests that "Mrs. Frankie Rowe, who R/S [Randle/Schmitt] (erroneously) refer to as a 'firsthand witness' . . ." Yet he is aware that she said that she had handled a piece of metallic debris brought to the Roswell fire department by a state trooper. That makes her a firsthand witness to part of the story.

Klass also reports that "If a crashed saucer had been found 40 miles south of the debris field found on the Brazel ranch, the 'retrieval team' surely would have spent many days searching along the 40-mile flight path between the two sites, looking for more debris and perhaps even an ET who might have parachuted to safety. *Yet no such search effort is reported by R/S's 'witnesses.'*"

Klass is assuming that because we, or our witnesses, reported no such effort, it is a flaw in the story. It is true that none reported such an effort immediately after the event, but that doesn't mean it didn't happen, only that those we have interviewed were not participants in it. The only legitimate conclusion to be drawn is that it hasn't been reported, not that it didn't happen.

Klass, in his conclusion, writes, "And Kevin Randle, who formerly served in the Army and later in the Air Force Reserve, enjoys Government benefits as a veteran. *MORE AND MORE PIECES OF THE PUZZLE FIT TOGETHER.*"

When I responded that I currently receive no government benefits as alleged by Klass, Klass responded, "It is regrettable that you fail to reply to the question I pose. In my letter of April 29 [1994], I asked: 'Do you enjoy absolutely NO present or potential future benefits for having served in Vietnam?' (Emphasis added here.) Your evasive answer is: 'I currently enjoy no benefits . . .' (Emphasis added.)"

In response, I said that I had used the qualifier because the laws are subject to change. I wrote, "There are no benefits that I receive today, nor are there any for which I am eligible. The question is without relevance."

Yet when we asked Klass what his military service had been, he responded writing, "I served 60 years with AFOSI, which included short stints as a B-17 pilot over Europe, a B-29 pilot over Japan, an F-86 pilot over Korea, and an A-10 pilot in Vietnam.' I had tried to answer Klass's question honestly. In response to my legitimate question about Klass's military service, I was treated to a sarcastic reply.

So it seems that only I have an obligation to respond to Klass's questions, but he has none to respond to mine. He is free to distort the facts in his attempt to discredit the Roswell case, but when I qualify a statement to make it as accurate as possible, I am accused of being evasive.

We are treated to his analysis of the facts, but as we've seen, the conclusions drawn are not accurate. He leaves out that which doesn't conform to his opinions and attempts to discredit testimony by claiming the memories are nearly fifty years old and can't be trusted to be reliable.

But the real question I have is: "Where were you, Phil, on December 7, 1941? I'll bet you can remember the events surrounding your hearing that the Japanese had bombed Pearl Harbor and the United States was now at war. I'll bet that your 50+ year old memories are fairly accurate. And I'll bet the men and women who were presented with evidence that we are not alone in the universe would remember that, too. Monumental events stick in the mind. And for those who think they don't, Where were you on November 22, 1963 . . . or January 28, 1986, when the *Challenger* exploded?"

APPENDIX C:

"The MJ-12
Operations Manual"

IT SEEMS THAT THE MJ-12 DOCUMENTS WILL NOT go away. It seems that every time we have provided the evidence that the documents are fraudulent, another argument pops up to contradict our opinion. And, it seems that every time we believe we have heard the last of MJ-12, something new is added to the mix. Such is the case with a new document called "Extraterrestrial Entities and Technology Recovery and Disposal." This is, according to the front cover, the "Majestic-12 Group Special Operations Manual."

Once again, we have a document about the alleged MJ-12 committee that has come from an unidentified source. It is a document that has been circulating in the UFO community for a number of months. Copies of it are available in the strangest locations. In fact, a friend told me he had seen a copy of the manual at a local gun show at a booth that had many legitimate Army manuals for sale. The man had received it from a friend "who was on the inside." He was afraid of government reprisal if he revealed his "real" name and how he had come into possession of the manual.

A study of the manual reveals that a great deal of work went into its construction. This was no simple, quick, and dirty job. It suggests someone who is familiar with the military-style manuals that have been produced for decades. The cover is impressive, looks authentic, and even includes a "seal" to add to the visual impact.

The manual is, however, short, the table of contents showing Appendix III beginning on page 31. That appendix, according to the manual, contains photographs. The copy I have contains no photographs and, in fact, ends on page 23. It would be interesting, but probably not very helpful, to see some of the other documents contained in the appendices.

Analysis of the manual must be placed in the context of all the other MJ-12 documents that have been submitted. Most members of the UFO community believe the documents to be faked, some believing it is all part of the program of disinformation. If all the other documents are faked, then it stands to reason that this one is faked, too. It can be argued, and will be by some, that there is no "real" proof that the MJ-12 documents are fraudulent. To suggest the manual is faked when the evidence about the validity of the other documents is in question is not fair. To be fair, the new document must be examined on its own. It will have to stand or fall on that analysis.

Again, the document is classified as "Top Secret/

Majic Eyes Only." Those inside the government and the military report that an "Eyes Only" classification mark is contradictory here. "Eyes Only" documents are created for a specific person, to brief that person on a highly classified subject. A document might be created for the "Eyes Only" of the President, but it would not be put on a manual. Once the "Eyes Only" recipient has read the document, it is to be destroyed. There would be a single copy of it because it was created for the "Eyes Only" of a specific person. It would defeat the purpose of a manual.

The real mistake, on the cover, seems to be a classification of "Restricted." According to Herbert L. Pankratz of the Eisenhower Library, "The classification markings on the alleged MJ-12 document are not consistent with federal regulations for the marking of classified materials as of April 1954 [the date on the manual]. The 'Restricted' classification category was terminated by executive order in November 1953 and would not have been used on a document in April 1954. Federal regulations also require that the cover page reflect the highest level of classification for any material in the document. Since 'Top Secret' is a higher category than 'Restricted,' only 'Top Secret' should have appeared on the cover of the document."

In other words, the cover of the document violated the federal regulations in effect in April 1954. If the document is authentic, it should conform to those regulations. This document, like all the others, seems to be at variance with the proper regulations. Proponents will claim that these regulations weren't iron-clad and that variations do exist. However, documents created at this level would be closely monitored and would adhere to the proper regulations, especially since they had just been changed. The classifications on the manual, like those on the other MJ-12 documents, are wrong and there is no reason for them to be. It smacks of hoax.

Pankratz continues in his letter of February 6, 1995, saying, "In addition, we have no evidence in our files that a security classification referred to as 'MAJIC EYES ONLY' ever existed. Executive Order 10501 was signed by President Eisenhower on November 5, 1953. It set up three classification categories: 'Top Secret,' 'Secret,' and 'Confidential.' A fourth category, 'Restricted Data' (not the same as 'Restricted'), was established by the Atomic Energy Act of 1954; and it is used only with regard to nuclear weapons."

The manual, then, contains an obsolete classification mark. That is the second mistake made by the creator of the document. It can be argued, and will be, that these sorts of things were guidelines as opposed to laws. However, in government service and in military service, the regulations carry the force of law. The regulations would not be violated and the classification would reflect the regulations in force at the time the document was published. It is unlikely that a document created as highly as this one would contain classification markings that were so hopelessly out of date.

The argument that people make mistakes and regulations are not followed strictly can be made. Before that is accepted, we must demand that other examples of these mistakes, made at this level, be presented. Proponents must be required to present authentic documents classified similarly. Documents from other branches of the government or from other governments are irrelevant.

Inside the manual there are other mistakes. In Chapter 1 (Operation Majestic-12), Section 1 (Project Purpose and Goals), Paragraphs 3 (Security Classification), the manual says, "All information relating to MJ-12 has been classified MAJIC EYES ONLY and carries a security level 2 points above that of Top Secret. The reason for this has to do with the consequences that may arise not only from the impact on the public should the existence of such matters become general knowledge, but also the danger of having such advanced technology as has been recovered by the Air Force fall into the hands of unfriendly foreign powers. No information is released to the public press and the official government position is that no special group such as MJ-12 exists."

This paragraph is filled with utter nonsense. There are, in fact, no classifications above "Top Secret," though it is a belief of many outside the government circles and military services. "Top Secret," according to the documentation available from the time, and according to the executive order signed by the President Eisenhower just months before this manual was produced, was the highest classification. There was nothing higher than "Top Secret."

It should be pointed out that there are modifications to the "Top Secret" classification, including a crypto category, and an SCI ("Special Compartmented Information") which limits the number of people who have access to the data. There are also "Top Secret-Code Word" classifications. That means someone must be code word cleared to see the data.

"Top Secret-Majic" would, if it was authentic, be an example of this.

But the ultimate classification is still "Top Secret." To suggest anything else is to reveal a lack of knowledge about the situation. To suggest that the MJ-12 documents is classified two points higher than "Top Secret" is ridiculous. There is no such classification.

And to explain in the paragraph why the high classification is necessary is also ridiculous. Regulations suggest that information be classified according to the damage that its compromise would do to the security of the United States. To reveal "Top Secret" information would do great damage to the security of the United States. There is no need, in the manual, to explain that revelation of the data would be damaging to our country.

But the smoking gun proving the manual to be a hoax has been found. Inside the manual, in a table entitled "Extraterrestrial Technology Classification Table," there are several references to Area 51 and S-4. The problem is that Area 51 didn't exist in April 1954 when the manual was allegedly written. In fact, in 1954, Groom Lake, Nevada, which would eventually become the site of Area 51, was still in private hands. It wasn't until 1955 that Lockheed test pilot Tony LeVier, under orders from Kelly Johnson, began to search for a site to test the U-2 which would become Area 51.

Additional information suggests that the designation, Area 51, didn't come into use until the late 1950s or early 1960s. It would be impossible for a manual written in 1954 to contain a reference to a location that didn't exist when it was written. This proves the manual is a fake.

It is clear that someone with a great deal of time, an intimate knowledge of the UFO phenomenon, and a computer with a good word processing program and various type styles, created the MJ-12 manual. That person, however, had not worked with classified material, nor did he or she understand the system. That explains why the mixed classifications are found on the front cover of the manual. It also explains why an obsolete term "Restricted," was used. That was an attempt to conform to the original documents.

There is no doubt that "The MJ-12 Operations Manual" is nothing more than a fake. It does not conform to the regulations, it contains inaccurate information, and it is incomplete. The manual should be rejected as the fake it is.

Bibliography

Air Defense Command Briefing, January 1953, Project Blue Book Files.

ALBERTS, Don E., and PUTNAM, Allan E. *A History of Kirtland Air Force Base 1928–1982.* Albuquerque, NM: 1606th Air Base Wing, 1985.

ANDERSON, Michele. "BIOSPEX: Biological Space Experiments," NASA Technical Memorandum 58217, NASA, Washington, DC, 1979.

ANDERSON, Ted. Alleged Diary for July 1947.

ASIMOV, Isaac. *Is Anyone There?* New York: Ace Books, 1967.

ATIC UFO Briefing, April 1952, Project Blue Book Files.

"The Aurora, Texas, Case." *APRO Bulletin* (May/June 1973): 1, 3–4.

BAKER, Raymond D. *Historical Highlights of Andrews AFB 1942–1989.* Andrews AFB, MD: 1776th Air Base Wing, 1990.

BARKER, Gray. "America's Captured Flying Saucers—The Cover-up of the Century." *UFO Report* (May 1977).

324 — Kevin D. Randle

——. "Archives Reveal More Crashed Saucers." *Gray Barker's Newsletter* (March 1982): *14*.

——. "Von Poppen Update." *Gray Barker's Newsletter* (December 1982): *8*.

BARNETT, Ruth. Personal Diary, 1947.

BAXTER, John, and ATKINS, Thomas. *The Fire Came By.* Garden City, NY: Doubleday, 1976.

BECKLEY, Timothy Green. *MJ-12 and the Riddle of Hangar 18.* New Brunswick, NJ: Inner Light, 1989.

BERLITZ, Charles, and MOORE, William L. *The Roswell Incident.* New York: Berkley, 1988.

"Big Fire in the Sky: A Burning Meteor." *New York Herald Tribune* (December 10, 1965).

BINDER, Otto. *What We Really Know About Flying Saucers.* Greenwich, CT: Fawcett, 1967.

——. *Flying Saucers Are Watching Us.* New York: Tower, 1968.

——. "The Secret Warehouse of UFO Proof." *UFO Report.*

BLOECHER, Ted. *Report on the UFO Wave of 1947.* Washington, DC: Author, 1967.

BLUM, Howard. *Out There: The Government's Secret Quest for Extraterrestrials.* New York: Simon and Schuster, 1991.

BLUM, Ralph, with BLUM, Judy. *Beyond Earth: Man's Contact with UFOs.* New York: Bantam Books, 1974.

BONTEMPTO, Pat. "Incident at Heligoland." *UFO Universe* (Spring 1989): 18–22.

BOWEN, Charles, ed. *The Humanoids.* Chicago: Henry Regency, 1969.

BREW, John Otis, and DANSON, Edward B. "The 1947 Reconnaissance and the Proposed Upper Gila Expedition of the Peabody Museum of Harvard University." *El Palacio* (July 1948): 211–22.

Briefing Document, Operation Majestic 12, November 18, 1952.

"Brilliant Red Explosion Flares in Las Vegas Sky." *Las Vegas Sun* (April 19, 1962), p. 1.

BRITTON, Jack, and WASHINGTON, George, Jr. *Military Shoulder Patches of the United States Armed Forces.* Tulsa, OK: MCN Press, 1985.

BROWN, Eunice H. *White Sands History*. White Sands, NM: Public Affairs Office, 1959.

BUCKLE, Eileen. "Aurora Spaceman—R.I.P.?" *Flying Saucer Review* (July/August 1973) 7–9.

BUSKIRK, Winfred. *The Western Apache: Living in the Land Before 1950*. Norman, OK: University of Oklahoma, 1986.

CAHN, J. P. "Flying Saucer Swindlers." *True* (August 1956).

———. "The Flying Saucers and the Mysterious Little Men." *True* (September 1952).

CANADEO, Anne. *UFOs: The Fact or Fiction Files*. New York: Walker, 1990.

CANNON, Martin. "The Amazing Story of John Lear." *UFO Universe* (March 1990): 8.

CAREY, Thomas J. "The Search for the Archaeologists." *International UFO Reporter* (November/December 1991): 4–9, 21.

CARPENTER, John S. "Gerald Anderson: Truth vs. Fiction." *MUFON UFO Journal*, No. 281 (September 1991): 3–7, 12.

———. "Gerald Anderson: Disturbing Revelations." *MUFON UFO Journal*, No. 299 (March 1993): 6–9.

CAMERON, Grant, and CRAIN, T. Scott, Jr. *UFOs, MJ-12 and the Government*. Seguin, TX: MUFON, 1991.

CATOE, Lynn E. *UFOs and Related Subjects: An Annotated Bibliography*. Washington, DC: Government Printing Office, 1969.

CHAIKIN, Andrew. "Target: Tunguska." *Sky and Telescope* (January 1984): 18–21.

CHAMBERLAIN, Von Del, and KRAUSE, David J. "The Fireball of December 9, 1965—Part I." *Royal Astronomical Society of Canada Journal*, Vol. 61, No. 4.

CHARITON, Wallace O. *The Great Texas Airship Mystery*. Plano, TX: Wordware, 1991.

CHAVARRIA, Hector. "*El Caso Puebla*." OVNI: 10–14.

Citizens Against UFO Secrecy. "MJ-12: Myth or Reality?" *Just Cause* (December 1985).

——. "Confirmation of MJ-12?" *Just Cause* (June 1987).

——. "The MJ-12 Fiasco." *Just Cause* (September 1987).

——. "More on MJ-12." *Just Cause* (March 1989).

——. MJ-12 Update." *Just Cause* (June 1989).

——. "Conversation with Dr. Sarbacher." *Just Cause* (September 1985).

CLARK, Jerome. "The Great Unidentified Airship Scare." *Official UFO* (November 1976).

——. "The Great Crashed Saucer Debate." *UFO Report* (October 1980): 16–19, 74, 76.

——. "Crashed Saucers—Another View." *Saga's UFO Annual 1981* (1981).

——. *UFOs in the 1980s.* Detroit: Apogee, 1990.

——. "Crash Landings." *Omni* (December 1990): 91–92.

——. "UFO Reporters. (MJ-12)." *Fate* (December 1990).

——. "Airships: Part I." *International UFO Reporter* (January/February 1991): 4–23.

——. "Airships: Part II." *International UFO Reporter* (March/April 1991): 20–23.

Committee on Science and Astronautics, Report, 1961.

COHEN, Daniel. *Encyclopedia of the Strange.* New York: Avon, 1987.

——. *The Great Airship Mystery: A UFO of the 1890s.* New York: Dodd, Mead, 1981.

——. *UFOS—The Third Wave.* New York: Evans, 1988.

COOPER, Milton William. *Behold a Pale Horse.* Sedona, AZ: Light Technology, 1991.

COOPER, Vicki. "Crashed Saucer Stories." *UFO,* Vol. 6, No. 1 (1991): 15.

——. "The Roswell Case Revived: Was It an Alien Saucer?" *UFO* (January/Feburary 1991): 25–29.

CRARY, Dr. Albert. Personal Diary, June–July 1947.

CREIGHTON, Gordon. "Close Encounters of an Unthinkable and Inadmissible Kind." *Flying Saucer Review* (July/August 1979).

——. "Further Evidence of 'Retrievals.' " *Flying Saucer Review* (January 1980).

——. "Continuing Evidence of Retrievals of the Third Kind." *Flying Saucer Review* (January/February 1982).

——. "Top U.S. Scientist Admits Crashed UFOs." *Flying Saucer Review* (October 1985).

DAVIDSON, Leon, ed. *Flying Saucers: An Analysis of Air Force Project Blue Book Special Report No. 14.* Clarksburg, VA: Saucerian Press, 1971.

DAVIES, John K. *Cosmic Impact.* New York: St. Martin's, 1986.

DAVIS, Richard. "Results of a Search for Records Concerning the 1947 Crash Near Roswell, New Mexico." Washington, DC: GAO 1995.

"The Day a UFO Crashed Inside Russia." *UFO Universe* (March 1990): 48–49.

DENNETT, Preston. "Project Redlight: Are We Flying Saucers Too?" *UFO Universe* (May 1990): 39.

DOBBS, D. L. "Crashed Saucers—The Mystery Continues." *UFO Report* (September 1979).

"DoD News Releases and Fact Sheets," 1952–1968.

DOUGLAS, J. V., and LEE, Henry. "The Fireball of December 9, 1965—Part II." *Royal Astronomical Society of Canada Journal,* Vol. 62, No. 41.

EBERHART, George. *The Roswell Report: A Historical Perspective.* Chicago: CUFOS, 1991.

ECKER, Don. "MJ-12 'Suspected Forgery,' Air Force Says." *UFO,* Vol. 8, No. 3 (1993): 5.

Editors of *Look.* "Flying Saucers." *Look* (1966).

EDWARDS, Frank. *Flying Saucers—Here and Now!* New York: Bantam, 1968.

——. *Flying Saucers—Serious Business.* New York: Bantam, 1966.

——. *Strange World.* New York: Bantam, 1964.

Eighth Air Force Staff Directory, Fort Worth AAF, TX: June 1947.

ENDRES, Terry, and PACKARD, Pat. "The Pflock Report in Perspective." *UFO Update Newsletter,* Vol. 1, No. 5 (Fall 1994): 1–6.

ESTES, Russ, prod. "Quality of the Messenger." Crystal Sky Productions, 1993.

"Experts Say a Meteor Caused Flash of Fire." *Desert News* (April 19, 1962): 1.

Fact Sheet, "Office of Naval Research 1952 Greenland Cosmic Ray Scientific Expedition," October 16, 1952.

FAWCETT, Lawrence, and GREENWOOD, Barry J. *Clear Intent: The Government Cover-up of the UFO Experience.* Englewood Cliffs, NJ: Prentice-Hall, 1984.

Final Report, "Project Twinkle," Project Blue Book Files, November 1951.

FINNEY, Ben R., and JONES, Eric M. *Interstellar Migration and the Human Experience.* CA: University of California Press, 1985.

"Fireball Explodes in Utah," *Nevada State Journal* (April 19, 1962), p. 1.

"Fireball Fame Comes to Lapeer," December 10, 1965.

First Status Report, Project STORK (Preliminary to Special Report No. 14), April 1952.

Flint (MI) City Directories, 1945–1950.

"Flying Saucers Again." *Newsweek* (April 17, 1950), p. 29.

"Flying Saucers Are Real." *Flying Saucer Review* (January/ February 1956), 2–5.

FORD, Brian. *German Secret Weapons: Blueprint for Mars.* New York: Ballantine, 1969.

FOSTER, Tad. Unpublished Articles for Condon Committee Casebook, 1969.

FOWLER, Raymond E. *Casebook of a UFO Investigator.* Englewood Cliffs, NJ: Prentice-Hall, 1981.

——. "What About Crashed UFOs?" *Official UFO* (April 1976): 55–57.

——. *The Watchers.* New York: Bantam Books, 1990.

FULLER, John G. *The Interrupted Journey.* New York: Dial, 1966.

——. *Incident at Exeter.* New York: G. P. Putnam's Sons, 1966.

——. *Aliens in the Sky.* New York: Berkley Books, 1969.

Genesee County (MI) Telephone Directories, 1945–1950.

GILLMOR, Daniel S., ed. *Scientific Study of Unidentified Flying Objects*. New York: Bantam Books, 1969.

GOLDSMITH, Donald. *Nemesis*. New York: Berkley Books, 1985.

——. *The Quest for Extraterrestrial Life*. Mill Valley, CA: University Science Books, 1980.

GOOD, Timothy. *Above Top Secret*. New York: Morrow, 1988.

——. *The UFO Report*. New York: Avon Books, 1989.

——. *Alien Contact*. New York: Morrow, 1993.

GORDON, Stan, and COOPER, Vicki. "The Kecksburg Incident." *UFO*, Vol. 6, No. 1 (1991): 16–19.

GORDON, Stan. "After 25 Years, New Facts on the Kecksburg, PA. UFO Retrieval Are Revealed." *PASU Data Exchange* #15 (December 1990): 1.

——. "Kecksburg Crash Update." *MUFON UFO Journal* (September 1989).

——. "Kecksburg Crash Update." *MUFON UFO Journal* (October 1989), pp. 3–5, 9.

——. "The Military UFO Retrieval at Kecksburg, Pennsylvania." *Pursuit*, Vol. 20, No. 4 (1987): 174–79.

"Great Lakes Fireball," *Sky and Telescope* (February 1966), pp. 78, 79, 80.

GRIBBIN, John. "Cosmic Disaster Shock." *New Scientist* (March 6, 1980): 750–52.

"Guidance for Dealing with Space Objects Which Have Returned to Earth." Washington, DC: Department of State Airgram, July 26, 1973.

HALL, Richard. "Crashed Discs—Maybe." *International UFO Reporter*, Vol. 10, No. 4 (July/August 1985).

——. *Uninvited Guests*. Santa Fe, NM: Aurora Press, 1988.

——. "MJ-12: Still Holding Its Own Through Thickets of Debate." *UFO* (January/February 1991): 30–32.

——, ed. *The UFO Evidence*. Washington, DC: NICAP, 1964.

HANRAHAN, James Stephen. *History of Research in Space Biology and Biodynamics at the Air Force Missile Develop-*

ment Center 1946–1958. Alamogordo, NM: Office of Information Services, 1959.

——. *Contributions of Balloon Operations to Research and Development at the Air Force Missile Development Center 1947–1958.* Alamogordo, NM: Office of Information Services, 1959.

HAUGLAND, Vern. "AF Denies Recovering Portions of 'Saucers.' " *Albuquerque New Mexican* (March 23, 1954).

HAZARD, Catherine. "Did the Air Force Hush Up a Flying Saucer Crash?" *Woman's World* (February 27, 1990): 10.

HEGT, William H. Noordhoek. "News of Spitzbergen UFO Revealed." *APRG Reporter* (February 1957): 6.

HENRY, James P., and MOSELY, John D. "Results of the Project Mercury Ballistic and Orbital Chimpanzee Flights," NASA SP–39, NASA (1963).

HIPPLER, Lt. Col. Robert H. "Letter to Edward U. Condon," January 16, 1967.

"History of the Eighth Air Force, Fort Worth, Texas" (microfilm). Air Force Archives, Maxwell Air Force Base, AL.

"History of the 509th Bomb Group, Roswell, New Mexico" (microfilm). Air Force Archives, Maxwell Air Force Base, AL.

HOGG, Ivan U., and KING, J. B. *German and Allied Secret Weapons of World War II.* London: Chartwell, 1974.

HUNEEUS, J. Antonio. "Soviet Scientist Bares Evidence of 2 Objects at Tunguska Blast." *New York City Tribune* (November 30, 1989): 11.

——. "Great Soviet UFO Flap of 1989 Centers on Dalnegorsk Crash." *New York City Tribune* (June 14, 1990).

——. "Spacecraft Shot out of South African Sky—Alien Survives." *UFO Universe* (July 1990), pp. 38–45, 64–66.

——. "Roswell UFO Crash Update." *UFO Universe* (Winter 1991): 8–13, 52, 57.

——. "A Full Report on the 1978 UFO Crash in Bolivia." *UFO Universe* (Winter 1993).

HURT, Wesley R., and MCKNIGHT, Daniel. "Archaeology of the San Augustine Plains: A Preliminary Report." *American Antiquity* (January 1949): 172–94.

HYNEK, J. Allen. *The UFO Experience: A Scientific Inquiry.* Chicago: Henry Regency, 1975.

HYNEK, J. Allen, and VALLEE, Jacques. *The Edge of Reality.* Chicago: Henry Regency, 1972.

"International Reports: Tale of Captured UFO." *UFO,* Vol. 8, No. 3 (1993): 10–11.

"It Whizzed Through the Air; Livonia Boys Find Fireball Clues." *Livonian Observer and City Post* (December 16, 1965).

JACOBS, David M. *The UFO Controversy in America.* New York: Signet, 1975.

JOHNSON, J. Bond. " 'Disk-overy' Near Roswell Identified As Weather Balloon by FWAAF Officer." *Fort Worth Star-Telegram* (July 9, 1947).

JONES, William E., and MINSHALL, Rebecca D. "Aztec, New Mexico—A Crash Story Reexamined." *International UFO Reporter,* Vol. 16, No. 5 (September/October 1991): 11.

JUNG, Carl G. *Flying Saucers: A Modern Myth of Things Seen in the Sky.* New York: Harcourt, Brace, 1959.

KEEL, John. "Now It's No Secret: The Japanese 'Fugo Balloon.' " *UFO* (January/Feburary 1991): 33–35.

——. *UFOs: Operation Trojan Horse.* New York: G. P. Putnam's Sons, 1970.

——. *Strange Creatures from Space and Time.* New York: Fawcett, 1970.

KENNEDY, George P. "Mercury Primates." *American Institute of Aeronautics and Astronautics* (1989).

KEYHOE, Donald E. *Aliens from Space.* New York: Signet, 1974.

KLASS, Philip J. *UFOs Explained.* New York: Random House, 1974.

——. "Crash of the Crashed Saucer Claim," *Skeptical Enquirer,* Vol. 10, No. 3 (Spring 1986).

——. *The Public Deceived.* Buffalo, NY: Prometheus Books, 1983.

——. "Roswell UFO: Cover-ups and Credulity." *Skeptical Enquirer,* Vol. 16, No. 1 (Fall 1991).

KNAACK, Marcelle. *Encyclopedia of U.S. Air Force Aircraft and Missile Systems.* Washington, DC: Office of Air Force History, 1988.

LAPAZ, Lincoln, and ROSENFELD, Albert. "Japan's Balloon Invasion of America." *Collier's* (January 17, 1953), p. 9.

LESTER, Dave. "Kecksburg's UFO Mystery Unsolved," *Greenburg Tribune-Review* (December 8, 1985), p. A10.

Library of Congress Legislative Reference Service. "Facts About UFOs," May 1966.

LOFTUS, R. *Eye-Witness Testimony.* Cambridge, MA: Harvard University Press, 1979.

LORE, Gordon, and DENEAULT, Harold H. *Mysteries of the Skies: UFOs in Perspective.* Englewood Cliffs, NJ: Prentice-Hall, 1968.

LORENZEN, Coral, and Jim. *Flying Saucers: The Startling Evidence of the Invasion from Outer Space.* New York: Signet, 1966.

——. *Flying Saucer Occupants.* New York: Signet, 1967.

——. *Encounters with UFO Occupants.* New York: Berkley, 1976.

——. *Abducted!* New York: Berkley, 1977.

LOW, Dr. Robert J. "Letter to Lt. Col. Robert Hippler," January 27, 1967.

MACCABEE, Bruce. "Hiding the Hardware." *International UFO Reporter* (September/October 1991): 4.

——. "What the Admiral Knew." *International UFO Reporter* (November/December 1986).

——. "The Arnold Phenomenon: Part I, II, and III." *International UFO Reporter* (January/February 1995–May/June 1995).

MACK, John E. *Abduction.* New York: Charles Scribner's Sons, 1994.

MATTHEWS, Mark. "Armageddon at Tunguska!" *Official UFO* (May 1979).

MCCALL, G. J. H. *Meteorites and their Origins.* New York: Wiley & Sons, 1973.

MCCLELLAN, Mike. "The Flying Saucer Crash of 1948 is a Hoax." *Official UFO* (October 1975): 36–37, 60, 62–64.

"McClellan Sub-Committee Hearings," March 1958.

"McCormack Sub-Committee Briefing," August 1958.

MCDONALD, Bill. "Comparing Descriptions, An Illustrated Roswell." *UFO*, Vol. 8, No. 3 (1993): 31–36.

MCDONOUGH, Thomas R. *The Search for Extraterrestrial Intelligence.* New York: Wiley & Sons, 1987.

MENZEL, Donald H., and BOYD, Lyle G. *The World of Flying Saucers.* Garden City, NY: Doubleday, 1963.

MENZEL, Donald H., and TAVES, Ernest H. *The UFO Enigma.* Garden City, NY: Doubleday, 1977.

"Meteor Lands in Utah, Lights Western sky," *Los Angeles Times* (April 19, 1962).

MICHEL, Aime. *The Truth About Flying Saucers.* New York: Pyramid 1967.

MOORE, Charles B. "The New York University Balloon Flights During Early June, 1947," The Author, 1995.

MOORE, William L., and SHANDERA, Jaime H. *The MJ-12 Documents: An Analytical Report.* Burbank, CA: Fair Witness Project, 1991.

MUELLER, Robert. *Air Force Bases, Volume 1: Active Air Force Bases within the United States of America on 17 September 1982.* Washington, DC: Office of Air Force History, 1989.

MURPHY, John. "Object in the Woods," WHJB Radio Broadcast (December 1965).

National Security Agency. Presidential Documents. Washington, DC: Executive Order 12356, 1982.

NEILSON, James. " 'Secret' U.S./UFO Structure." *UFO* Vol. 4, No. 1 (1989): 4–6.

"New Explanation for 1908 Siberian Blast." *Cedar Rapids Gazette* (January 25, 1993).

NICAP. *The UFO Evidence.* Washington, DC: NICAP, 1964.

NICKELL, Joe. "The Hangar 18 Tales." *Common Ground* (June 1984).

NICKELL, Joe, and FISCHER, John F. "The Crashed-Saucer Forgeries." *International UFO Reporter*, Vol. 15, No. 2 (March/April 1990): 4–12.

———. "Further Deception: Moore and Shandera." Unpublished Paper, The Authors (1993).

"No Reputable Dope on Disks." *Midland (TX) Reporter Telegram* (July 1, 1947).

NORTHROP, Stuart A. *Minerals of New Mexico.* Albuquerque, NM: University of New Mexico, 1959.

OBERG, James. "UFO Update: UFO Buffs May Be Unwitting Pawns in an Elaborate Government Charade." *Omni,* Vol. 15, No. 11 (September 1993): 75.

O'BRIEN, Mike. "New Witness to San Agustin Crash." *MUFON Journal,* No. 275 (March 1991): 3–9.

OLIVE, Dick. "Most UFO's Explainable, Says Scientist." *Elmira (NY) Star-Gazette* (January 26, 1967): 19.

PACKARD, Pat, and ENDRES, Terry. "Riding the Roswell-go-round." *A.S.K. UFO Report,* Vol. 2, No. 1: 1–8.

PALMER, Raymond, and ARNOLD, Kenneth. *The Coming of the Saucers.* Amherst, MA: 1952.

PAPAGIANNIS, Michael D., ed. *The Search for Extraterrestrial Life: Recent Developments.* Boston: 1985.

PEEBLES, Curtis. *The Moby Dick Project.* Washington, DC: Smithsonian Institution Press, 1991.

PEGUES, Etta. *Aurora, Texas: The Town that Might Have Been.* Newark, TX: The Author, 1975.

PFLOCK, Karl. *Roswell in Perspective.* Mount Rainier, MD: FUFOR, 1994.

———. "In Defense of Roswell Reality." *HUFON Report* (February 1995): 5–7.

———. "Roswell, A Cautionary Tale: Facts and Fantasies, Lessons and Legacies." In Walter H. Andrus, Jr., ed. *MUFON 1995 International UFO Symposium Proceedings.* Seguin, TX: MUFON, 1990: 154–68.

———. "Roswell, The Air Force, and Us." *International UFO Reporter* (November/December 1994): 3–5, 24.

PLEKHANOV, G. F.; KOVALEVSKIY, A.F.; ZHURAVLEV, V. K.; and VASIL'YEV, N. V. "The Effect of the Tunguska Meteorite Explosion on the Geomagnetic Field." U.S. Joint Publications Research Service (December 21, 1961).

Press Conference—General Samford, Project Blue Book Files, 1952.

"Press Release—Monkeynaut Baker Is Memorialized," Space and Rocket Center, Huntsville, AL (December 4, 1984).

"Project Blue Book" (microfilm). National Archives, Washington, DC.

PRYTZ, John M. "UFO Crashes." *Flying Saucers* (October 1969): 24–25.

RAAF Base Phone Book, Roswell, NM: August 1947.

RAAF Yearbook, Roswell, NM: 1947.

RANDLE, Kevin D. "Mysterious Clues Left Behind by UFOs." *Saga's UFO Annual* (Summer 1972).

——. "The Pentagon's Secret Air War Against UFOs." *Saga* (March 1976).

——. "The Flight of the Great Airship." *True's Flying Saucers and UFOs Quarterly* (Spring 1977).

——. *The October Scenario.* Iowa City, IA: Middle Coast Publishing, 1988.

——. *The UFO Casebook.* New York: Warner, 1989.

——. *A History of UFO Crashes.* New York: Avon, 1995.

RANDLE, Kevin D., and CORNETT, Robert Charles. "Project Blue Book Cover-up: Pentagon Suppressed UFO Data." *UFO Report* Vol. 2, No. 5 (Fall 1975).

RANDLE, Kevin D., and SCHMITT, Donald R. *UFO Crash at Roswell.* New York, NY: Avon, 1991.

RANDLES, Jenny. *The UFO Conspiracy.* New York: Javelin, 1987.

"Report of Air Force Research Regarding the 'Roswell incident'," July 1994.

"Rocket and Missile Firings," White Sands Proving Grounds, January–July 1947.

RODEGHIER, Mark. "Roswell, 1989." *International UFO Reporter* (September/October 1989): 4.

RODEGHIER, Mark, and CHESNEY, Mark. "The Air Force Report on Roswell: An Absence of Evidence." *International UFO Reporter* (September/October 1994).

ROSIGNOLI, Guido. *The Illustrated Encyclopedia of Military Insignia of the 20th Century*. Secaucus, NJ: Chartwell, 1986.

RUPPELT, Edward J. *The Report on Unidentified Flying Objects*. New York: Ace, 1956.

RUSSELL, Eric. "Phantom Balloons Over North America." *Modern Aviation* (February 1953).

SAGAN, Carl, and PAGE, Thornton, eds. *UFO's: Scientific Debate*. New York: Norton, 1974.

SANDERSON, Ivan T. "Meteorite-like Object Made a Turn in Cleveland, O. Area," *Omaha World-Herald* (December 15, 1965).

———. "Something Landed in Pennsylvania." *Fate* (March 1966).

———. *Uninvited Visitors*. New York: Cowles, 1967.

———. *Invisible Residents*. New York: World Publishing, 1970.

SAUNDERS, David, and HARKINS, R. Roger. *UFOs? Yes!* New York: New American Library, 1968.

SCHAFFNER, Ron. "Roswell: A Federal Case?" *UFO Brigantia* (Summer 1989).

SCHMITT, Donald R. "New Revelations from Roswell." In Walter H. Andrus, Jr., ed. *MUFON 1990 International UFO Symposium Proceedings*. Seguin, TX: MUFON, 1990: 154–68.

SCHMITT, Donald R., and RANDLE, Kevin D. "Second Thoughts on the Barney Barnett Story." *International UFO Reporter* (May/June 1992): 4–5, 22.

SCULLY, Frank. "Scully's Scrapbook." *Variety* (October 12, 1949): 61.

———. *Behind the Flying Saucers*. New York: Henry Holt, 1950.

SHANDERA, Jaime. "New Revelation about the Roswell Wreckage: A General Speaks Up." *MUFON Journal* (January 1991): 4–8.

SHEAFFER, Robert. *The UFO Verdict*. Buffalo, NY: Prometheus, 1981.

SIMMONS, H. M. "Once Upon a Time in the West." *Magonia* (August 1985).

SLATE, B. Ann. "The Case of the Crippled Flying Saucer." *Saga* (April 1972): 22–25, 64, 66–68, 71, 72.

SMITH, Scott. "Q & A: Len Stringfield." *UFO*, Vol. 6, No. 1 (1991): 20–24.

"The Space Men at Wright-Patterson." *UFO Update.* Special Report No. 14, Project Blue Book, 1955.

SPENCER, John. *The UFO Encyclopedia.* New York: Avon, 1993.

SPENCER, John, and EVANS, Hilary. *Phenomenon.* New York: Avon, 1988.

STANYUKOVICH, K. P., and BRONSHTEN, V. A. "Velocity and Energy of the Tungusk Meteorite," *National Aeronautics and Space Administration* (December 1962).

Status Reports, "Grudge—Blue Book, Nos. 1–12."

STEIGER, Brad. *Strangers from the Skies.* New York: Award Books, 1966.

——. *Project Blue Book.* New York: Ballantine, 1976.

STEIGER, Brad, and STEIGER, Sherry Hanson. *The Rainbow Conspiracy.* New York: Pinnacle, 1994.

STEINMAN, William S., and STEVENS, Wendelle C. *UFO Crash at Aztec.* Boulder, CO: The Authors, 1986.

STEVENSON, William. *Intrepid's Last Case.* New York: Villard, 1988.

STONE, Clifford E. *UFO's: Let the Evidence Speak for Itself.* CA: The Author, 1991.

——. "The U.S. Air Force's Real, Official Investigation of UFO's." Private Report: The Author, 1993.

STORY, Ronald D. *The Encyclopedia of UFOs.* Garden City, NY: Doubleday, 1980.

STRINGFIELD, Leonard H. *Situation Red: The UFO Siege!* Garden City, NY: Doubleday, 1977.

——. *UFO Crash/Retrieval Syndrome: Status Report II.* Seguin, TX: MUFON, 1980.

——. *UFO Crash/Retrieval: Amassing the Evidence: Status Report III.* Cincinnati, OH: The Author, 1991.

——. *UFO Crash/Retrievals: The Inner Sanctum: Status Report VI,* Cincinnati, OH: The Author, 1991.

——. "Roswell & the X-15: UFO Basics," *MUFON UFO Journal,* No. 259 (November 1989): 3–7.

STURROCK, P. A. "UFOs—A Scientific Debate," *Science*, Vol. 180 (1973): 593.

SULLIVAN, Walter. *We Are Not Alone*. New York: Signet, 1966.

SUMNER, Donald A. "Skyhook Churchill 1966." *Naval Reserve Reviews* (January 1967): 29.

SUTHERLY, Curt. "Inside Story of the New Hampshire UFO Crash," *UFO Report* (July 1977).

SWORDS, Michael D., ed. *Journal of UFO Studies, New Series, Vol. 4*. Chicago: CUFOS, 1993.

Tech Bulletin, "Army Ordnance Department Guided Missile Program," January 1948.

Technical Report, "Unidentified Aerial Objects, Project SIGN," February 1949.

Technical Report, "Unidentified Flying Objects, Project GRUDGE," August 1949.

TEMPLETON, David. "The Uninvited." *Pittsburgh Press* (May 19, 1991): 10–15.

THOMPSON, Tina D., ed. *TRW Space Log*. Redondo Beach, CA.: TRW 1991.

TODD, Robert G., "MJ-12 Rebuttal." *MUFON Journal* (January 1990): 17.

TODD, Robert G.; RODEGHIER, Mark; GREENWOOD, Barry; and MACCABEE, Bruce. "A Forum on MJ-12." *International UFO Reporter* (May/June 1990): 15.

U.S. Congress, House Committee on Armed Forces. *Unidentified Flying Objects*. Hearings, 89th Congress, 2nd Session, April 5, 1966. Washington, DC: U.S. Government Printing Office, 1968.

U.S. Congress Committee on Science and Astronautics. *Symposium on Unidentified Flying Objects*. July 29, 1968, Hearings, Washington, DC: U.S. Government Printing Office, 1968.

VALLEE, Jacques. *Anatomy of a Phenomenon*. New York: Ace, 1966.

——. *Challenge to Science*. New York: Ace, 1966.

——. *Dimensions*. New York: Ballantine, 1989.

———. *Revelations.* New York: Ballantine, 1991.

"Visitors from Venus." *Time* (January 9, 1950): 49.

War Department. *Meteorological Balloons* (Army Technical Manual). Washington, D.C.: Government Printing Office, 1944.

WEBBER, Bert. *Retaliation: Japanese Attacks and Allied Countermeasures on the Pacific Coast in World War II.* Corvallis, OR: Oregon State University Press, 1975.

WHEELER, David R. *The Lubbock Lights.* New York: Award Books, 1977.

WHITING, Fred. *The Roswell Events.* Mount Rainier, MD: FUFOR, 1993.

WILCOX, Inez. Personal Writings, 1947–1952.

WILKINS, Harold T. *Flying Saucers on the Attack.* New York: Citadel, 1954.

———. *Flying Saucers Uncensored.* New York: Pyramid, 1967.

WISE, David, and ROSS, Thomas B. *The Invisible Government.* New York: 1964.

YOUNG, Robert. "Old-Solved Mysteries: What Really Happened at Kecksburg, PA, on December 9, 1965." *Skeptical Inquirer,* Vol. 15, No. 3 (1991).

ZABAWSKI, Walter. "UFO: The Tungus Riddle." *Official UFO* (May 1977).

ZEIDMAN, Jennie. "I Remember Blue Book." *International UFO Reporter* (March/April 1991): 7.

ZIGEL, F. Yu. "Nuclear Explosion over the Taiga (Study of the Tunguska Meteorite)." U.S. Department of Commerce, Office of Technical Services, Joint Publications Research Service (September 8, 1964).

The following newspapers and periodicals were used as research sources for this work.

Alamogordo News   *Albuquerque Tribune*
Albuquerque Journal   *Amarillo Globe*

Ann Arbor News
Arizona Republican
Atchison Globe
Baltimore Sun
Beaver County Times
Beaver Falls New-Tribune
Boston Advertiser
Bozeman Daily Chronicle
Burlington Hawk-Eye
Carlsbad Current-Angus
Cedar Rapids Gazette
Cheyenne Tribune
Chicago Daily News
Chicago Daily Times
Chicago Herald American
Chicago Sun
Circleville Herald
Clinton Herald
Dalhart Texan
Dallas Morning News
Dallas Times Herald
Dayton Daily News
Decatur Evening
  Republican
Denver Post
Deseret News and
  Telegram
Des Moines Register
Detroit Evening News
Detroit Free Press
Elmira Star-Gazette
El Paso Herald Post
El Paso Times
Erie Daily Times

Eureka Reporter
Flint Journal
Fort Worth Star-Telegram
Framingham Middlesex
  News
Greenburg Tribune-
  Review
Harrisburg Evening News
Harrisburg Patriot
Houston Chronicle
Las Vegas Review-Journal
Las Vegas Sun
Latrobe Bulletin
Lebanon Daily News
Lincoln Daily State
  Journal
Livonia Observer and
  City Post
London Times
Lorain Journal
Los Angeles Herald
  Express
Los Angeles Times
Louisville Courier-Journal
Lubbock Avalanche
Midland Reporter
  Telegram
Nashville American
Nebraska Nugget
Nephi Times-News
Nevada State Journal
New York Herald-Tribune
New York Times
Odessa American

Omaha Daily Bee
Omaha World-Herald
Oregonian
Oregon Journal
Palm Beach Post
Phoenix Gazette
Pittsburgh Post-Gazette
Pittsburgh Press
Reno Evening Gazette
Rocky Mountain News
Roswell Daily Record
Roswell Morning Dispatch
Salt Lake Tribune
San Antonio Express-News

San Francisco Call
San Francisco Chronicle
Socorro Defensor-Chieftain
St. Joseph Daily Herald
St. Paul Pioneer Press
Sterling Gazette
Syracuse Herald-American
Syracuse Post Standard
Toledo Blade
Toronto Daily Star
Washington Post
Waterloo Courier

Organizations

LITERALLY DOZENS OF ORGANIZATIONS AND INSTI-
tutions provided research assistance for this work.
Although none of them subscribed to the theory of
extraterrestrial intervention, all were willing to provide what assistance they could.

International UFO Museum and Research Center, Roswell, NM

J. Allen Hynek Center for UFO Studies, Chicago, IL

KBIM-TV, Roswell, NM

Kirtland Air Force Base, NM

Kirtland Air Force Base East (Sandia), Public Affairs Office, NM

KOB-TV, Albuquerque, NM

KOBR-TV, Roswell, NM

KTSM-TV, El Paso, TX

Laboratory of Anthropology, Santa Fe, NM

Los Alamos Historical Museum, Los Alamos NM

Los Alamos Public Affairs Office, Los Alamos, NM

Mama's Minerals, Albuquerque, NM

Museum of New Mexico, Santa Fe, NM

National Aeronautics and Space Administration

National Archives, Washington, DC

National Climatic and Data Center, Asheville, NC

National Personnel Records Center (Army), St. Louis, MO

National Transportation and Safety Board, Washington, DC

New Mexico Institute of Mining and Technology, Socorro, NM

Offutt Air Force Base, Omaha, NE

Operational Archives— Aviation Historical Branch, Washington, DC

Pease Air Force Base, NH

Roswell Chamber of Commerce, Roswell, NM

Roswell Public Library, Roswell, NM

Smithsonian Institution, Washington, DC

Socorro Chamber of Commerce, Socorro, NM

Southern Methodist University, Dallas, TX

Southwestern Minerals, Albuquerque, NM

Index

Captain Kevin D. Randle, U.S.A.F.R.
UFO Explorer, Explainer, Expert

A special investigator for the Center for UFO Studies, Kevin D. Randle has spent more than twenty-five years studying UFO phenomena and is, in fact, considered one of the foremost experts in the field—if not *the* expert on the Roswell incident. He is the author and/or co-author of dozens of books dealing with the reality of UFOs.

A former Army helicopter pilot and Air Force intelligence officer (he is an active member of the Air Force Reserves), Captain Randle brings unique perspective and experience to his investigation into UFO activity. Not content to blindly accept the hundreds of "eyewitness accounts" of UFOs that are recorded annually, Captain Randle is a tenacious and tough researcher, bringing an insider's knowledge of military procedure to bear on his investigations, painstakingly combing through mounds of evidence, whether it be in the field or in declassified files.

Captain Randle shines a light into the dark corners

of UFO activity, giving us clear, concise, uncontrovertible evidence that UFOs *are* real.

Here is a special look at some of the fascinating work of Kevin D. Randle, published by Avon Books, available wherever books are sold.

CONSPIRACY OF SILENCE

For decades, Captain Kevin Randle tells us, the U.S. government and the military have engaged in a massive conspiracy to conceal any information that might confirm the existence of UFOs. Despite hundreds of well-documented reports of sightings, Randle affirms, the government has steadfastly maintained its position of denial. In this fascinating exposé, Randle illustrates how the U.S. government has covertly collected UFO crash data, questioned eyewitnesses, and lied to the public about what its agents were doing. A meticulously researched, comprehensive study of the cover-up, Conspiracy of Silence exposes the startling truths the government has kept hidden—what they don't want you to know.

A secret project with a high priority was created to investigate the phenomenon. Although it was called Project Saucer in the public statements, it was, in fact, Project Sign. . . .

In 1948, after those in the trenches had an opportunity to review the data, they created an "Estimate of the Situation." Much has been written about this document, which was, according to the official history of the UFO field, destroyed shortly after it was created. But an examination of the situation shows us how the conspiracy worked, at least in part.

According to those involved, the "Estimate" reviewed a number of important UFO sightings. The officers putting it together concluded that the flying saucers were extraterrestrial in origin. They forwarded their "Estimate" up the chain of command until it reached General Hoyt S. Vandenberg, then Chief of Staff of the Air Force. According to Ruppelt, the report was "batted" back down, with a note suggesting that the evidence did not support the conclusions drawn.

But Vandenberg's or the Air Force's actions after the report had been written were important. Everyone associated with Project Sign disappeared. They were all reassigned, with the exception of two of the lowest-ranking members. The message from the top was clear. Flying saucers were not real and those who thought otherwise could find themselves at odds with the Chief of Staff.

PROJECT MOON DUST

"Project Moon Dust" was formed by the Air Force in 1953, ostensibly to recover "returning space debris" launched from other nations. But why did the Air Force consider such a program necessary when Sputnik, the first space satellite, would not be launched by the Soviets until four years later? Could it be that Project Moon Dust had another secret mission? Could it be that Project Moon Dust's real purpose was to locate and recover UFOs?

The history of the UFO phenomenon is filled with dozens of governmental and military studies that have concluded, time and again, that flying saucers are real and interplanetary. The history is filled with governmental statements that are in direct conflict with established facts and documentation. The history is a confusing blend of fact and fiction. This is an attempt to sort some of it out, providing us with a few clues about the situation.

With the Freedom of Information Act and a new candor on the part of some officials, we have been able to piece together part of that history. But even with that, we find ourselves caught in word games and arguments over semantics. It doesn't lead to the truth. It keeps us in the dark which, in some cases, is exactly what *they* want.

We have been told that the Air Force investigated UFOs for more than twenty years and never found any information to suggest they were real, that they posed a threat to the United States, or that they were from other solar systems. That is what we've been told, but as we'll see, such is not the case. Arguments at the highest levels suggest that the information that flying saucers are real has been found, that they might pose a threat, and that they *are* from other worlds.

A HISTORY OF UFO CRASHES

With evidence verified by a team of highly respected scientists, researchers, and investigators, Kevin D. Randle presents astonishing new documentation that UFOs have been visiting the Earth regularly for over five decades. The evidence continues to mount. Read the fascinating details of decades of UFO crashes—from Roswell, New Mexico, in 1947 to Las Vegas, Nevada, in 1962, to Ontario, Canada in 1989—and be astounded, amazed, and convinced.

The problem UFO investigators face is a consistent lack of credible evidence. We are asked repeatedly: If UFOs are real, meaning extraterrestrial, where is the proof? Why is there no physical evidence of their existence? Why haven't we found the remains of one?

The answer to those questions is that we *have* found the remains of one. Or two . . . or more.

Until we begin to apply the strict standards of science, until we begin to review the evidence objectively, and until we allow our conclusions to be drawn solely from that evidence, we are not going to gain ground. Our findings will be rejected, and rightly so. Good science is not made from what we want to believe but from what is.

Read the conclusions, search for the primary sources, and ask the questions. I believe that if you do this, your conclusions will be the same as mine. Flying saucers do exist. They are craft from other planets. And they do crash.

But it is the evidence that convinces me. Not a desire to believe, or a hidden agenda, but the evidence when examined as objectively as possible. For those with a truly open mind, the facts are facts. And the number one fact is that we have been visited.

THE TRUTH ABOUT THE UFO CRASH AT ROSWELL

(with Donald R. Schmitt)

First there was the explosive exposé, UFO Crash at
Roswell, *in which Kevin D. Randle and Donald R.
Schmitt awakened the world to the earth-shattering
events that transpired in the high desert of New
Mexico in July 1947. After the publication of that
groundbreaking work, startling new evidence was
uncovered, top-secret government reports became
available, and eyewitnesses finally stepped forward
after decades of fear-induced silence. The proof of the
century's most extraordinary close encounter has at
last been documented . . . and the shocking governmental cover-up it inspired has finally been revealed.*

The main group, the nine men with the highest clearances, covered the center of what MacKenzie called the impact site. According to MacKenzie, when they first saw the craft, they were stunned. They stood, transfixed, staring at the object, momentarily unable to move. Because they had watched it on radar, they knew that something strange had crashed, but they were not prepared for what they saw. In the first few moments, as the MPs scattered across the field, taking up positions on the top of the cliff, at the access points to the area and along the roads, the men stood staring at the ship.

The main part of the craft, about twenty-five to fifty feet long and twelve to fifteen feet wide, had forcibly crashed in to the arroyo at the base of a tall cliff. The nine men approached it, but the others were held back, used as guards to screen the impact site. They made a careful examination of the ground around the point of impact, searching for additional debris.

The bodies, five in number and obviously not human, were not all within the ship. The ship's crew were small, about five feet tall and slender, and had heads that seemed too bid for their bodies. The eyes were only slightly larger than human eyes, and they had pupils.

Two of them were found outside the craft, one sprawled on the ground and the other next to a cliff. Both were dead. . . .

MacKenzie's attention was drawn to the being sitting near the cliff. "That's the one I cannot forget. It had that damned serene look on its face . . . like it was at peace with the world . . . I [was] amazed at that."

UFO CRASH AT ROSWELL
(with Donald R. Schmitt)

Fifty years ago, a stunning series of events occurred which confirmed without a doubt the
existence of extraterrestrial life—events that the
U.S. government denies to this day. . . . *In the
last two weeks of June 1947, hundreds of UFO
sightings were reported from Glens Falls, New York,
to Yakima, Washington. Then, on July 5, 1947, a
rancher came across the wreckage of an alien spacecraft in the New Mexico desert. Soon after, the bodies of several extraterrestrials were discovered near
the alleged crash site. On July 8, 1947, the U.S.
Army Air Force cordoned off the area around Roswell, New Mexico, and removed all evidence of one
of the most astonishing events in recorded history.
One question remained: Why? Examine the facts—
supported by newspaper reports, government documents, and eyewitness accounts—hidden from the
public for half a century.*

The important thing was that none of the wreckage looked conventional. Had it been an aircraft accident, the debris would have looked familiar. There would have been fragments that the men would have recognized. The avionics might not have survived intact, but there would have been bundles of wires, vacuum tubes, control heads. The metal, even ripped to pieces as described by the men out there, would have looked like conventional metal. There might have been thin sheets of metal, though nothing as thin as that described, and it would have been easy for them to bend it.

Any conventional craft, whether an airplane, an experimental rocket or even a weather balloon, would have left material that was recognizable by the men on the field. Dr. Jerry Brown, a NASA engineer, suggested Duraluminum, an alloy that is strong with good high-temperature properties. Had they used a blowtorch on it, there probably would have been no noticeable results. The problem is that Duraluminum is fragile. Banging on it with a sledgehammer would cause it to shatter. The Roswell material did not react that way.

The CIC (Counter-Intelligence Corps) agents spent more than an hour on the field and failed to identify anything. Rickett said his boss told him he'd wanted another CIC man to see the crash because everything on the site was so strange.

THE TRUTH ABOUT UFOs
from Kevin D. Randle, U.S.A.F., Retired

CONSPIRACY OF SILENCE
72691-2/$12.50 US/$16.50 Can

What the public needs to know about the U.S. Government's
official investigations and cover-ups of modern UFO activity.

A HISTORY OF UFO CRASHES
77666-9/$5.99 US/$7.99 Can

An encyclopedia of nearly five decades
of crashes and crash evidence.

co-authored with Donald R. Schmitt

UFO CRASH AT ROSWELL
76196-3/$6.99 US/$8.99 Can

The complete, uncensored and indisputable true story of
America's closest encounter.

THE TRUTH ABOUT
THE UFO CRASH AT ROSWELL
77803-3/$6.99 US/$8.99 Can

In a follow-up to their groundbreaking work, this volume
includes startling new evidence from previously
top-secret government reports and additional testimony from
eyewitnesses who finally stepped forward after years
of fear-induced silence.

Astonishing UFO Reports
from Avon Books

COMMUNION: A TRUE STORY
  by Whitley Strieber   70388-2/$6.99 US/$8.99 Can

TRANSFORMATION: THE BREAKTHROUGH
  by Whitley Strieber   70535-4/$4.95 US/$5.95 Can

THE GULF BREEZE SIGHTINGS
  by Ed Walters and Frances Walters
                                     70870-1/$6.99 US/$8.99 Can

UFO ABDUCTIONS IN GULF BREEZE
  by Ed Walters and Frances Walters
                                     77333-3/$4.99 US/$5.99 Can

THE UFO CRASH AT ROSWELL
  by Kevin D. Randle and Donald R. Schmitt
                                     76196-3/$6.99 US/$8.99 Can

THE TRUTH ABOUT THE UFO CRASH AT ROSWELL
  by Kevin D. Randle and Donald R. Schmitt
                                     77803-3/$6.99 US/$8.99 Can

A HISTORY OF UFO CRASHES
  by Kevin D. Randle   77666-9/$5.99 US/$7.99 Can

UFOS ARE REAL. . . AND HERE'S THE PROOF
  by Ed Walters and Bruce Maccabee
                                     78599-4/$5.99 US/$7.99 Can

THE FIELD GUIDE TO EXTRATERRESTRIALS
  by Patrick Huyghe and Harry Trumbore
                                     78128-X/$12.50 US/$16.50 Can